Frances Gerard

Some celebrated Irish beauties of the last century

Frances Gerard

Some celebrated Irish beauties of the last century

ISBN/EAN: 9783337125028

Printed in Europe, USA, Canada, Australia, Japan

Cover: Foto ©Suzi / pixelio.de

More available books at **www.hansebooks.com**

ELIZABETH, DUCHESS OF HAMILTON AND BRANDON.

[Frontispiece.

SOME CELEBRATED

IRISH BEAUTIES

OF THE

LAST CENTURY

BY

FRANCES GERARD

AUTHOR OF "ANGELICA KAUFFMANN: A BIOGRAPHY"

WITH NUMEROUS PORTRAITS AND ILLUSTRATIONS

LONDON

WARD AND DOWNEY

Limited

12 YORK BUILDINGS, ADELPHI, W.C.

1895

CONTENTS.

LIST OF ILLUSTRATIONS.

I HAVE to acknowledge my indebtedness for much valuable help to Mr. Algernon Graves, Mr. Colnaghi, and the Hon. Gerald Ponsonby, and to the owners of the various Portraits, who have been most courteous in giving every information.

FRANCES GERARD.

April, 1895.

INTRODUCTION.

Thus often shall memory, in dreams sublime,
  Catch a glimpse of the days that are over;
Thus sighing, look through the waves of time,
  For the long-faded glories they cover.
                                    MOORE.

LOOKING back across the gulf of years which divides us from
the last century, we are struck by the total change that has
passed over society generally. No men like those giants in
intellect, Chatham, Fox, Swift, Johnson, now fill the canvas;
no fine gentlemen, who, as Thackeray says, were in themselves a product of the past. And the women!—those
wondrously fair creatures, whose faces have been handed
down to us by Reynolds, Romney, Gainsborough, and who
smile at us from their gilt frames! What witchery in the
almond-shaped eyes, long and languishing; what pouting lips;
what arched and lovely necks; what queenly dignity in their
gait and carriage!

To this last the fashion of dress then prevailing contributed
not a little. The loose flowing robes and floating draperies
give an air of indescribable grace; while the choice of
colours, the soft blues and browns, charm the eye. Setting
this aside, however, there can be no question that the women
of the last century possessed more of actual beauty than
is to be found amongst the belles of our day. There is
no lack of pretty faces, but beauty of the highest order is
rare; so too is the lady of high degree with her brocaded
skirt, her courtly grace, and her grand air. She belongs to
the past, like the fine gentleman.

Many of these "goddesses" were Irishwomen—not pure
Celts, but of a mixed race, born of the industrious planting
of English settlers upon Irish soil.

In dealing with social life in Ireland during the last century we are confronted with many difficulties. Its brighter aspects are so inextricably mixed up with the graver and sadder past that it is impossible to touch upon one portion without introducing subjects which might seem out of place in a book of such slight pretensions as this purports to be. Still, if we wish to gather a faithful picture of Irish society as it was constituted more than a hundred and fifty years ago, we must examine, be it ever so slightly, into the conditions of the country before we shall be able to understand certain national characteristics.

We have to recall, in the first place, that for many centuries Ireland was the battle-field of four different races, each of whom left its trace upon the conquered people and country. Henry the Second, the most successful of these invaders, made no attempt at either civilizing or subjugating the country he had annexed. Neither did his immediate descendants,[1] who contented themselves with maintaining an army of occupation to keep the native tribes in order. The English law was confined to a level district round the capital containing the small shires or counties of Louth, Meath, Kildare and Dublin. To these was limited the jurisdiction of the viceroy or deputy ; all beyond was supposed, in law, not to exist. In court language, says the author of the Church in Ireland : " The land of Ireland was synonymous with the Pale. Outside this Pale ran an ample stripe (comprehending a third, and sometimes the half of each county) of borderland in which a mixed code of English, Brehon and martial law prevailed."

Outside the Pale, and occasionally within it, general chaos prevailed. The country was held by chieftains, who made war one upon another, and upon the descendants of Henry's army of occupation ; these last were distinguished from the native chiefs by nothing but superior skill in the arts of predatory

---

[1] Richard III. was the first to make the experiment of an English plantation. In his reign two from every family in England were transplanted to Ireland at the king's charges. No Irishman was to leave the country without a licence, and killing a mere Irishman was punishable only by Brehon law.

warfare. Some of them had, in the course of years, renounced the laws, the language, and the usages of their own country. In the space of fifty years, eight Palatinates had been formed; within each the lord or chief possessed absolute rights. They spent their time making forays upon their own country-men of a better class, who were possessed of richer meadows and finer cattle than the natives, and from them they carried away corn and oxen.

James the First was the first to upset this state of anarchy. Elizabeth[1] had attempted the task, but had limited her efforts to destroying, or trying to destroy, the power of the nobles. James went to work thoroughly, and, with excellent in-tentions, he visited the country, and made himself master of the situation. Unfortunately he began at the wrong end. It is true he abolished the Pale, and extinguished the Brehon law; but his transplanting bodily an English settlement, and his forcing an English constitution all at once upon a half savage people, was an experiment fraught with too much risk to be prudently tried; the result was shown in the great rebellions, the bloody retribution of the Cromwellian army, followed by a new Cromwellian settlement, and the final and disastrous struggle between James the Second and William.

When the din of war had ceased, and politicians and thinking people gathered their senses so as to look round them at what remained after the general upheaval, a strange and wonderful change met their gaze. The face of the country was entirely altered; clans and chieftains had disappeared; the old oligarchy was extinct; the surface of society was entirely re-arranged upon a new and English method; the whole proprietary of the island had become British and Protestant; the original owners had, with few exceptions, descended to the middle class or peasant life, and the new race of landlords, English and Scotch, were mostly soldiers of fortune, adventurers, or younger sons of English noblemen.[2]

---

[1] Elizabeth made an English plantation in Munster.
[2] James I. abolished the old feudal customs of Thanistry and

xii *Introduction.*

The minds of these men were filled with one idea. They were, says a writer on the history of the Church in Ireland,[1] "imbued with the new doctrine of liberty, that undefined quantity which is so easily stretched into total freedom from all responsibility; it was only natural that these men, flushed with victory, new to power, and anxious to build up a fortune for their families, should stretch the word to its most licentious signification. Liberty meant to them liberty taken with the rights of others, and a close observance and respect for their own rights, together with an impatience of all authority, and a decided appetite for power. They had nothing to restrain them in pursuing the object of their desires; the Viceroy was not a resident official, and the length of the Parliament, which lasted without a break through the life of

Gavelkind. By the law of Thanistry every man of noble blood was eligible to be chief of his tribe: the law of Gavelkind was equally liberal; it gave to every vassal a fair share of the land. For this James substituted the English law of entail. Lord Chesterfield considered that it was unfair to exclude the Papists from the Gavel act: "it was," he said, "the only honest means of governing the country." Ulster was planted by James. The word "undertaker," which will appear often in this volume, dated from this plantation. Large estates were assigned to the Scotch or English planters, and their heirs, and in return, those of 2000 acres were to hold of the king in Capite; those of 1500 acres by knights service; those of 1000 in common socage The first named were to build a castle and strong courtyard, or bawn within four years. The second named were to finish a house and bawn within two years—the third class to enclose a bawn The first were to plant upon their land, within three years, forty-eight able men of English or Scotch birth, to be reduced to twenty families, to keep a demesne of 600 acres in their own hands; to have four fee farmers on 120 acres each, six leaseholders, each on 100 acres, and or. the remainder, eight families of husbandmen, artificers, and cottagers. James was ill-advised in breaking up the spirit of clanship which was similar to that which prevailed (and still prevails in a modified degree) in Scotland; the principle of subordination was eradicated and no adequate system substituted. Sir John Davies condemns the system of transplanting people of a different nation, or even province, to another, and lays the fault of all the troubles in Ireland upon "the pride, covetousness, and ill counsel of the English planted there; idleness and fear," he adds, in his quaint manner, "made the Irish the most *inquisitive* people after news in the world (a failing they possess to this day), and because such miscarriers did, by their false intelligence, many times raise troubles and rebellions, the statute of Kilkenny doth punish *newstellers* by the name of 'Skelaghes' with fine and ransom."

[1] Phelan's *History of the Church of Rome.*

the Sovereign, offered no chance of redress to those whose politics or religion placed them in a minority."

It was not surprising that this condition of things should have brought on the result that usually follows upon a dominant party pressing upon the weaker with the iron heel of despotism; hatred was engendered between class and creed, and showed itself in secret societies, assassinations, rebellions. The story has been set forth by many historians, by none with more clearness and intelligence than by Mr. Lecky, in his admirable review of the eighteenth century. Mr. Lecky puts before us, with all the fidelity of a photograph, the true picture of the social and political condition of Ireland as it was before the Union, as well as the causes of the failure of all attempts to govern it. He writes without the strong religious feeling which biassed Macaulay, or the prejudice which influenced Froude; his story, calmly told, impresses the reader with its sincerity.

Socially, as well as politically, the Ireland of two hundred years ago differed in all particulars from Ireland of to-day. Up to the date of the union between the countries it was, to all intents and purposes, a separate kingdom. In all official documents it is spoken of as "this kingdom." The sea that rolls between the two countries, and which is now designated a fishpond, was then an effectual barrier to English legislation, as it took days instead of minutes, to know what was occurring, especially in the provinces. The journey from London to Dublin was supposed to occupy four days, but this was in case there were no accidents either on sea or by land, and as accidents were the rule, delays spread out the journey to a week or more. For this reason, as well as for the more important one that the country to which they were bound had the worst of reputations as to safety in regard to life and limb, it was customary for strangers going to Ireland to make their wills before undertaking the journey. Once arrived, however, there was enough of enjoyment to make them forget their fears. There were certain elements of importance about Dublin that raised it above provincial towns such as York, Bristol or Edinburgh, especially the fact of there being a Parliament with two Houses, the Lords having one hundred members, the Commons three hundred, with all necessary functionaries ; a Prime Minister, a handsome revenue, a Chancellor of the Exchequer,[1] and a set of brilliant debaters, whose fame for wit and eloquence became almost European. Add to this the standing army of Irish-raised troops, paid by the Irish revenue, with a Commander-in-Chief and a brilliant staff ; and again the Viceregal Court, provided with all officials necessary for the importance of the mimic sovereign, chamberlains, secretaries, aides-de-camp, and " beef-eaters." The whole thing partook, perhaps, more or less, of the Gilbert and Sullivan kingdoms, but with a certain character and distinction of its own.

All the important offices just named were held in deputy, that is to say, the ostensible holders mostly resided in London, visiting the country from which they drew large salaries only once in two years, the duties being fulfilled by paid deputies. Even the Viceroyalty was no exception to this system of government, which was carried on all over the kingdom, with the result that the people were overtaxed, ground down, rack-rented, hunted, and ill-used by a set of hirelings, whose only interest was to build up fortunes for themselves. Lord Chesterfield, who during his short period

---

[1] The Parliament House, as it was called (now the Bank of Ireland), was built by Sir Arthur Chichester, one of the governors or deputies, for his own dwelling house; it was then of mean pretensions; in the 25th year of Charles II.'s reign it was bought by Government for the sittings of the Parliament of Ireland; it was rebuilt in 1728 from designs originally made by Castle, and supposed to have been either stolen or appropriated by Major Pearce. The first session was opened by the Duke of Dorset, 1731. The Irish Parliament was highly insubordinate. Lord Chesterfield thus describes it : " The House of Lords is an hospital for incurables, but the Commons can hardly be described. Session after session presents one unvaried waste of provincial imbecility." This may have been true to a certain extent, in the days when the elegant Stanhope ruled, but later on the character of the House stood very high in the estimation of even foreign powers for the cleverness and eloquence of its members. Such men as Anthony Malone, Flood, Grattan, Laugrishe, Ponsonby, and Hely Hutchinson could not have been stigmatized as " imbeciles." The debating was of the first order. Unfortunately, there was a good deal of froth in this effervescence of rhetoric, which disappeared, in some instances, on the first application of *silver.*

of Viceroyalty studied the conditions of Irish life, left it as his opinion that the poor people were used worse than negroes by their lords and masters and "deputies of *deputies* of *deputies.*" Arthur Young, who made an exhaustive study of the peasantry during his tour through Ireland, adds that this system "formed an insolent, reckless, unprincipled type of character." Drunkenness and extravagance went hand in hand amongst the gentry (especially the lower gentry), who treated the unfortunate peasants as slaves, allowing them no rights; the Irish landlord was in fact an absolute despot; his tenants were *serfs*. So far as they were concerned, he yielded obedience to no law.

The passion for horse-racing and gambling was so great, that in 1739 Parliament framed some laws to check the day labourers from taking part in these idling amusements; but these had little effect; the whole nation being given up to a passion for sporting, drinking, cock-fighting, and dancing. Young adds, "a strong preference of brilliancy, reckless daring and generosity to public spirit, high principle, order, sobriety or economy."

In the early part of the eighteenth century, Dublin, as it now is, did not exist. It was a straggling, ill-built, ill-smelling place, the streets as narrow as lanes, the houses tall and in some parts near the quays almost touching those on the opposite side of the street, so narrow was the pathway between. A cynic of the day wrote some halting lines which give us an idea of the city :

> Mass-houses, churches, mixed together,
> Streets unpleasant in all weather,
> The church, the Four Courts and hell [1] contiguous,

----

[1] Hell, a name given to a passage close to the Four Courts. Over the entrance there was a black image of the devil. This is alluded to in Burns' story of Death and the Horn-book where he says :

> "But this that I am gaun to tell,
> Which lately on a night befell,
> Is just as true as the Deil's in Hell,
>   In Dublin City."

The presence of his Satanic Majesty in the neighbourhood is thus accounted for : Near to where the Law Court stood there had been a church dedicated to St. Michael Le Poule or Le Paule. Over the archway or entrance, two statues were placed, one of St. Michael, the other

Castle, College-green, and Custom-house gibbous ;
Few things here are to tempt ye,
Tawdry outsides, pockets empty.
Five theatres, little trade, and jobbing arts,
Brandy and Snuff-shops, post-chaises and carts ;
Warrants, bailiffs, bills unpaid,
Masters of their servants afraid ;
Rogues that daily rob and cut men,
Patriots, gamesters, and footmen ;
Women lazy, drunken, loose,
Men in labour slow, of wit profuse,
Many a scheme that the public must rue it,
This is Dublin, if ye knew it.

At this time only a portion of Stephen's Green was finished.
Nassau Street and its surroundings. including Merrion Square,
were not begun until 1728, and up to this period the tide of
fashion flowed in a totally different quarter, the nobility and
wealthy citizens living for the most part in what was then
called the Liberties (this name indicating that there was a
royal immunity from all taxation).   In this now obsolete part
of the town beyond St. Patrick's Cathedral, there are remains
of some fine houses once belonging to the great nobility.
Here lived the Earls of Kildare in what was called the Carbric,
one of the Cage houses, which was only taken down when the
family removed to Leinster House.   In Lord Meath's liberty
there was also a family mansion, and the Bishop's liberty included the Cathedral with that strange rookery of streets and
small alleys which surrounded it.   These were inhabited
by men of property and position, for, writes Arthur
Young, "the nobility and gentlemen of Ireland live in a
manner that a man of £700 a year in England would disdain."   Mrs. Pendarves (better known as Mrs. Delany), who
visited Mrs. Clayton, the Bishop of Killaloe's wife, in 1731,
gives a graphic picture of Dublin city as it then was.   The
streets are narrow and the houses dirty looking, but she adds

of his adversary, the Devil. Cromwell's troopers, in their zeal for the
destruction of images, threw the effigy of the saint into the Liffey, but
left undisturbed his adversary, who remained over the archway until the
Law Courts were removed to the quays in 1786. A gentleman living
in Dublin remembered seeing in 1837, the figure thrown into a corner
of the old archway—the boys of the neighbourhood amusing themselves
by making an Aunt Sally of it. Subsequently it was moved to the
museum in Trinity College.—Gilbert's " History of Dublin."

there are some good ones scattered about. " One of these is Bishop Clayton's, on the south side of Stephen's Green, with a frontage like Devonshire House and a flight of steps leading up. There is a good hall; a room eighteen feet square wainscoted with oak panels carved; doors and chimney finished with very fine high carving, ceiling stucco, window curtains, chairs, yellow gemma velvet; portraits and landscapes well done round the room. Marble tables, looking-glasses,—the busts and pictures the bishop brought from Italy. The living too is good—six dishes of meat for dinner, and the same for supper. The generality of people are anything but solicitous to have good houses or good furniture more than is necessary, hardly so much, but they make it up in eating and drinking."

The immense consumption of wine in Ireland was a national calamity, nine gentlemen in ten, writes Chesterfield, are impoverished by the great quantity of claret which from mistaken notions of hospitality and dignity they think it necessary should be drunk in their houses. If the upper classes were badly housed and consumed hogsheads [1] of claret, the poor were lodged worse, and spent all the small wages they earned in whisky. This vice, together with the overcrowding in the miserable alleys where they were huddled, and the general filth in which they lived, generated the most terrible epidemics from which Dublin was rarely free, and which decimated the half-starved and drunken population of the narrow lanes near the Liffey.

In spite of all these drawbacks, Dublin was a pleasant little city, with its mimic Court, its theatres, and its concerts, for the Irish have always been a music-loving people. Early in the eighteenth century a musical club society was formed in Dublin called the Bull's Head Society; it was principally for catch singing; in 1741, this Society erected by means of sub-

[1] The claret was generally imported in hogsheads, and in most country houses in Ireland at the time of which I am writing there was a cellar underneath the dining-room. By means of a trap-door, the host could descend and bring up bottle after bottle of wine. Lord Chesterfield wittily said, that except in providing that their claret should be three or four years old, the Irish gentry thought less of three years hence than any people under the sun.

scriptions, in Fishamble Street, a large hall, for the performance of their concerts.   Shortly after it was opened the great
Maestro Handel came on the invitation of the then Viceroy,
the Duke of Devonshire, to Dublin; he remained nine months
and produced several of his great works.   The "Messiah" [1] was
performed for the first time at Fishamble Street, on April 15th,
to an audience of 600 people; the ladies were induced to come
without hoops, the gentlemen without swords.   Signora Avolio,
Mrs. Cibber, Mrs. Church, and Ralph Roseingrave were the
soloists.   Jennens, the librettist, was not satisfied with the
music : "It was not near so good as it might and ought to have
been.   I have with great difficulty made him correct some of
the grossest faults, but he retained his overture obstinately,
in which there are passages far unworthy of Handel, but much
more unworthy of the 'Messiah.'" [2]   It was felt to be an honour
to Dublin that such a work should have been produced there,
and the inhabitants showed their appreciation by doing all
honour to the great master.   "I cannot sufficiently express,"
he writes to his friends, "the kind treatment I receive here;
but the politeness of this generous nation cannot be unknown
to you.   So I let you judge of the satisfaction I receive, passing my time with honour, profit and pleasure." [3]

The *Dublin Evening Post* in its notice of the performance
says :—

"On Tuesday last Mr. Handel's oratorio of the 'Messiah'
was performed in the new Musical Hall, Fishamble Street; the
best judges allowed it to be the most finished piece of music.
It is but justice to Mr. Handel that the world should know
that he generously gave the money from this great work to be
equally shared by the Charitable Infirmary, Mercer's Hospital
and the relief of prisoners.   There were over 700 persons
present and £700 was collected."

---

[1] The "Messiah" *was* performed for the *first* time in Dublin. Mainwar-
ing, Handel's biographer, speaks of a performance at Covent Garden,
but there is no evidence to support this statement.   Later on, in 1742,
" Judas Maccabeus " was given for the first time.—*Nat. Bio.*

[2] National Biography, vol. 24, page 217.

[3] Letter to Lord Howe.

This calculation would lead one to suppose the tickets were £1 a piece, but this is not possible.

The Hospital authorities gave in 1887 a commemoration of Handel's visit. The performance took place in St. Werburgh's Church, close to Christ Church. St. Werburgh's was chosen for the reason that the great master used to play the organ there, to the delight of the crowded congregation, the church being a fashionable temple where the beaux and belles came to see one another and listen to the music. The organ upon which he played is still to be seen. It is an instrument of extraordinary beauty—the carving on the panel over the keyboard being in fine relievo, but the tone is nothing wonderful.

St. Werburgh's was a small, elegant-looking church; its steeple stood 160 feet high and the roof was a masterpiece, but in 1810 both were found to be in a dangerous condition and had to be removed. Now it is little known and rarely visited—strangers sometimes come to see it for the sake of the organ and because in the vaults below the unfortunate Lord Edward FitzGerald is interred. On the wall is an epitaph to one John Edwin, an actor at Crowe Street Theatre, who died of a broken heart from the criticisms passed upon him. The player of our time is much tougher in the cardiac region.

On the Dublin boards, however, many celebrated actors made their *début*—Macklin, Mossop, Ryan, the handsome and elegant Barry, and a host of others. There were theatres in Fishamble Street and Crowe Street, and Smoke or Smock Alley. In truth a pleasant book could be written anent the drama in Dublin; the amateurs took their share, some of them being good performers. A taste for amateur theatricals has always prevailed in Ireland. "It is impossible," says a writer on the subject, "to peep into any social corner of Irish life without getting a glimpse of the amateur stage with lamps lit and noble ladies and noble gentlemen in rich dresses playing their parts. Every old faded newspaper is full of complimentary notices. Nor must we pass by a picturesque reference to music which is not so regarded in our time. St. Cecilia, the patroness of music, had her day kept with all honour. At

the Castle was maintained a full state band generally under
the command of some musician of eminence. Dubourg, who
played with Handel (and was much commended by him), filled
this office for many years. On St. Cecilia's Day all the Court
and persons of quality repaired in great pomp to St. Patrick's
Cathedral, where the Reverend Doctor Swift no doubt objected
to such 'tweedledum and tweedledee'; a fine orchestra was
erected, and Mr. Dubourg and his men fiddled away at Corelli,
Dr. Blow and Purcell. The performance lasted from ten till
three o'clock, and there was not standing room. Another
custom prevailed, that of keeping the King's birthday with
great state and solemnity; there was a court in the morning
with a ball at night, and Sheridan, Mrs. Brooke, Captain
Jephson, or some Irish laureate wrote an ode, usually full of
fulsome compliments, which was 'set' by Mr. Dubourg and
sung and fiddled by a large choir and orchestra. "A Castle
'festival' a hundred and seventy years ago took place in the
Beef-eaters' Hall, the ladies were all seated in tiers, the topmost
row touching the ceiling.'

Sir Bernard Burke (Ulster), who lived all the days of his life
under the shadow of Dublin Castle, has left us a curious record
of the forms in use at the Mimic Court in the days of the first
Georges; the strict etiquette enforced as to the social position
of those who were presented. No solicitors' nor doctors' wives
were admitted—only those who had undoubted claims, either
of birth or position, were allowed to enter within the charmed
circle of the cross-benches. Peeresses sat in dignified seclusion
on the red benches. No lady was allowed to dance before the
vice King and Queen except those whose station allowed them
seats on the cross-benches, and no young lady was allowed to
be taken out if she came to the ball without lappets.

By ten o'clock (sometimes earlier) the minuets were over,
and the Viceroy and his lady adjourned to the basset table in
another room. The supper room, however, was the great
attraction; on the table was a holly tree lit up with a hundred
wax tapers, much after the fashion of a modern Christmas tree;
it was, however, the eatables that were sought for. The guests,
whose manners were not on a par with their pretensions, would
often sweep everything off the tables and a lady who was at

one of these festivities, gives an amusing account of a disorderly scene at which she was present, when Lady Santry's head-dress was torn off her head.

What was wanting in refinement was made up in that *gaieté du cœur* in which the Irish have, or at least had, a strong resemblance to the French, and which gave a peculiar charm to society. There was a give and take of wit, a daring spirit of fun and frolic, blended with a singular charm of manner and much real cleverness.[1] The distance from the English capital kept men of talent more in their own country than in our days of quick locomotion, when a man of genius may truly be said to belong to the world at large. Round Dublin, in the early part of the last century, there was gathered quite a scintillation of talent. "We have cleverer men here in a nutshell than can be produced in the whole circle of London," wrote Chesterfield. The gigantic genius of the great Dean of St. Patrick's towered over the lesser lights such as Sterne, Berkeley, Delany.

Nor were the women behindhand. In intellectual matters it may be claimed for Irishwomen that they were in the advance-guard of female philosophers, and took the initiative as blue-stockings. Mrs. Pilkington,[2] Mrs. Sycon (Psyche),[3] Mrs. Grierson,[4] Mrs. Vesey, Mrs. Brooke,[5] make

[1] "They are the most cordial people in the world," writes a lady who visited Dublin, "with a heartiness that reminds me of Cornwall. Now and then an oddity breaks out, but none so extraordinary but that I can match it in England."

[2] Letitia Pilkington, daughter to Dr. Vanlevin, a physician. Dean Swift was of great service to her husband, who was a clergyman. He turned out ungrateful and profligate. Mrs. Pilkington did not behave much better.

[3] Mrs. Sycon, one of the wits. Swift transformed her name into Psyche, and addressed some verses to her.

[4] Constantia Grierson, a native of Kilkenny. She was brought to Dr. Vanlevin when eighteen to be instructed in obstetric science. She was mistress of Hebrew, Latin, Greek, and French; understood mathematics as well as most men. She wrote elegantly in prose and verse, and, Mrs. Pilkington declared, conversed delightfully. She was one of the most extraordinary women that any age has ever produced. She died in 1731, at the early age of twenty-seven. Lord Carteret, when he was Viceroy, obtained a patent for her husband to be the King's printer, and to show his appreciation of the wife's talents, had her life inserted in it.

[5] An authoress of repute, although now her books would not repay reading. She translated some letters from Lady Catesby to Mrs.

a group of clever women who, as it were, sat at the feet of
the great Dean. Some of these " chaste wits " were affiliated
to their sister literati in London. Mrs. Vesey belonged to
Mrs. Montagu's coterie, where Miss Burney used to meet
her; and Lady Lucan, who was also blue, was of Irish
descent. It was a brilliant society. We shall follow in
these pages its gay doings : go to the mimic court, play
quadrille and basset, mix with the unruly crowd jostling one
another at the supper tables, visit Ranelagh, and see the
beauties walk in the beaux walk, where come "the fair bare-
bosomed maidens of Dublin," [1] hear the rather coarse jests
listened to with smiling approval, or get a glimpse at Lucas's
coffee-house, where the gentlemen went to drink claret, sit in
the bar window and make bets, or talk scandal.

Lucas's was a haunt for "the Bucks," another word for a
fine gentleman. Some were called Pink Dandies from the
pastime they indulged in of pinking their victims with the
blade of the sword; others were Mohawks and Bullies, like
Tiger Roche and Fighting Fitz-Gerald. These last were a
veritable scourge swarming all over the town and ranging the
city in search of excitement; pinking, sweating, chalking, and
picking quarrels which ended in duels. The most eminent
statesmen, the most successful lawyers, even the fellows of
university whose business was the training of the young,
were experienced duellists. The great centre of duelling was
Daly's Club, which stood next to the old Parliament House;
and here the members would come and excite their political
animosities with copious draughts of wine, then hot with rage,
rush off to the Phœnix [2] to satisfy their honour by making

Hamilton with "a sad distress" in the story; and wrote a novel
called "Julia." She was a lovely woman.—Ballard's "Lives of Eminent
Women."

[1] *The Spy* discourses at length upon the extreme indelicacy of the
mode of dress worn in the public streets and places of amusement.
Arthur Young says Irishwomen walked very seldom in the streets, so
those remarks probably applied to another class of women. Not so with
their conversation, which was singularly coarse, even for the time in
which they lived.

[2] The Phœnix Park took its name from the chalybeate spring
near the Viceregal lodge; the Irish word Fiomnioge has been cor-
rupted into *Phœnix*. Lord Chesterfield erected the column with the

targets of one another.   Every imaginable and trivial cause was made the subject of a duel.   The Buck or Bully would walk up and down before Lucas's coffee-house, trailing his cloak on the pavement, and if anyone trod upon it by accident, he at once drew his sword.   Another device was to jostle the chairman.[1]   It was a rotten, corrupt society this of little Dublin city; the immorality prevailing amongst the upper classes being second to no capital in Europe; the doings of the Hell Fire Club rivalled those of the Medenham brothers; the extravagance of men and women amounted to a species of madness; those with no money spent as freely as those who had thousands, while these last were not content with spending what was theirs rightfully, but laid burdens on the family property, which could only be wiped out by the Encumbered Estates Court.

We come now to the chapter of Irish beauty which has ever been a full one; since the days when Strongbow fell a victim to the charms of the lovely Eva, and Surrey sang the praises of the fair Geraldine,[2] there have been celebrated Irish

---

figure of the fabulous bird upon it. "The park is large in extent," says Mrs. Delany, in 1731, "fine turf, agreeable prospects, and a delightful wood, in the midst of which there is a ring where the beaux and belles resort in fine weather; it is far beyond Hyde Park."

[1] The jostling of a chairman was the ostensible immediate cause of one of the most bloody duels between a certain Mr. Mathews of Thomastown Castle, and Major Pack, an Englishman, who, with his friend Creed, came over from London in quest of adventure. These two forced a quarrel upon Mathews, who was supported by his friend Macnamara, who challenged Creed. The four men locked themselves into a room at a tavern, and fought with such ferocity that the walls, tables, floor, were in a sea of blood. Nobody thought of interfering in this sanguinary encounter, which lasted until the two Englishmen were stretched senseless on the floor.

[2] The Fair Geraldine, or Lady Elizabeth FitzGerald, second daughter to the tenth Earl of Kildare.

> Her sire an Earl, her dame of Prince's blood,
>   From tender years in Britain she doth rest,
> With Kinges child where she tastes costly food.
>   Hunsden did first present her to mine eine.
> Bright is her hue and Geraldine she hight,
>   Hampton me taught to wish her first for mine,
> And Windsor (las) doth chase her from my sight.
> Her beauty of kind, her virtues from above,
> Happy is he that can obtain her love.
>
> *Surrey's Poems.*

beauties. When people talk of Irish beauty they generally instance " the Gunnings ; " it comes trippingly off the tongue. But beautiful as were those typical examples, there were many others quite as deserving of notice whose names have fallen into oblivion. We are about to review some of these fair magicians, and tell the story of their lives. Short stories are nowadays the rage ; they are the favourite bantlings of the popular author, and on the principle of *multum in parvum* a short story is generally acceptable. The short stories here presented have at all events the flavour of actuality. They come to us from that far-away and picturesque past, which holds an interest the present can never possess ; and therefore it is that an old letter, yellow with age, and tied with a faded ribbon, a withered flower lying in a secret drawer, or a few pages from the diary of some unhappy lady which comes to light now and again, touches the true chord of romance which lies in every heart. The story of human life never wearies, for the reason that it is made up of the same hopes, fears, trials, troubles, and struggles that beset our own every-day existence.

Some of the stories relating to the celebrated Irish beauties have been told before—a few are, I think, new—and even in the oft-told tale of the Gunnings there is fresh material, and a good deal, that to the ordinary reader may have the interest of novelty. The record of Irish beauty being so extensive, I have had to leave out many who have every claim to admission. It would be, however, an endless task to chronicle all, therefore I have chosen 1731 as the starting point, that being the time when social life in Ireland began again to form itself after the disastrous consequences of the civil war of 1680. . . To my regret, 1 am therefore forced to exclude the Comtesse de Gramont . . . together with Stella and Vanessa. I must add that the interesting memoir of Lady Barrymore, *née* Coghlan, is from the pen of Miss Currey, who has likewise contributed the sketch of Ardo.

SOME CELEBRATED IRISH BEAUTIES
OF THE LAST CENTURY.

— ✦ —

MARY MOLESWORTH, COUNTESS OF BELVEDERE.
1731.

In Lodge's Peerage—the record of the faded glories of the Irish nobility—we learn that the Molesworths of Pencarrow in Cornwall sent, as was then the custom, a superfluous younger son to make his fortune by assisting the English garrison to subdue the troublesome Celt. This custom, which had originated in the reign of Elizabeth, had been utilized by James the First, to whom was due the large settlement called the "Ulster Plantation." These settlers were rewarded by grants of land, from which the original owners had been driven, and these lands having to be defended against the constant raids made by the exasperated natives, a strong English garrison was formed, whose business it was to support the Government, and lend its aid in subduing any attempt at rebellion.

Robert Molesworth of Pencarrow, having done good service in this manner, was rewarded by a grant of 2500 acres of excellent arable land situated in the fertile plains of Meath. This he held valiantly against all invaders, and in more peaceful times turned his attention to increasing his fortune by other means. Later on, we find he entered into a contract to supply the government with men to serve in the Spanish war, and likewise to defend the coast from invaders. He charged the modest sum of forty-five shillings per man. For these useful services he was well rewarded; he became a very wealthy man, and built for himself a fine house called Moles-

worth Court,[1] at the corner of Fishamble Street.   There his
son, Robert Molesworth, was born in 1656.

Robert was more distinguished than his father had been.
He was an Ambassador to the Court of Denmark, an advocate
for civil and religious liberty, the friend and associate of
Locke, Shaftesbury, and Molyneux.   He wrote a book on the
political situation of Denmark, which, according to Horace
Walpole, overturned the constitution of that country ; and he
was before his death raised to the rank of Viscount.   Coming
nearer to our own time we get acquainted (again through
Lodge) with Richard, the second son of the Ambassador, who
ultimately succeeded to the family honours as third viscount.
Richard   followed   the   fortunes   of   Churchill,   Duke   of
Marlborough,   and   was   his   aide-de-camp   at   the   battle   of
Ramilies, where he, with great gallantry, saved the general's
life at the risk of his own.   For this and his good military
service, he received rapid promotion ; passed from one command to another, being Master of Ordnance, Field-Marshal,
and   Commander-in-Chief   of   the   army   in   Ireland—a post he
held up to the time of his death.   He married twice, his first
wife being a Miss Lucas, and by this lady, who died 1739, he
had a family of eight children, five sons, and three daughters.
Of these last, Mary was the eldest and the handsomest.   She
made her *début* in Dublin society when she was only sixteen,
and was at once acknowledged to be one of " the belles."

Considering its size and mean pretensions, the Irish capital
could boast in the season of having as good Society as was to
be found in the larger metropolis across the water.   There
was, at that time, a resident nobility in Ireland ; and although
even then complaints of absenteeism were frequent, the distance

---

[1] Mr. Gilbert, in his history of Dublin, states that Robet Molesworth's office was confined to victualling ships for the Government ;
which was a great convenience, ships having to go to Liverpool or
Chester for the purpose.   The fortune amassed by Robert Molesworth
was considerable, a great portion of the Mynchens Fields, which later
on became the best building sites in Dublin, being his, Molesworth
Street, called after the family, St. Patrick's Well Lane, which now
includes Leinster Street, Nassau Street (formerly Coote Street) and
Grafton Street,   Merrion   Square   West,   including   where   Leinster
House stands, and Merrion Street.—*The Irish Builder*, June, 1st, 189..

from the larger capital, and the difficulties involved in getting there, left a number of persons amply sufficient to form an attractive Society in the capital of their own country. In like manner, Edinburgh and the larger English towns had then their set "seasons," and furnished the adjoining neighbourhood with social amusements. Without entering upon the vexed and tangled skein of Irish politics, I, with much humility, would venture to draw the attention of the Reader to one important fact . . . the expectation that with the return of the old system of government, would come renewal of the golden days of Dublin's prosperity, is fallacious. That prosperity, which was only on the surface, and was more social than commercial, was *not* destroyed by the Union, but by the force of the same events which has driven trade from the shores of Waterford and Cork. In other words, centralization has crushed with its iron heel the life out of Edinburgh, Dublin, Cork, York, Worcester, and all large towns.

It is the story of Humpty Dumpty over again. Having once fallen, no power of Home Rule, no House of Lords, nor Assembly of Commons can ever put him sitting on his wall again. In 1731, he had a very secure seat. It was a hundred years before Stephenson's puffing, snorting engines had been thought of; Squire Jones and family travelled in large, commodious coaches, and Madam Jones and her daughters were content with what gaiety could be got out of York or Bristol; and what contented Mrs. Jones in England, satisfied Mrs. Murphy, or Mrs. O'Grady in Ireland. Dublin had a winter season when Parliament was sitting, and there was a round of gaiety, dinners, balls, and suppers every night in the week, besides two good theatres, Ranelagh Gardens, and assemblies at Fishamble Street on the plan of London. Mrs. Pendarves,[1] whose letters to her sister, Mrs. Anne Granville, give the best account of Dublin society, says, "We go out every evening, except when we stay at home to receive company, when we have two tables, one for quadrille for the elders, and the other over which I preside for commerce." There was also plenty of dancing, "for the men are excellent

[1] Mary Granville married first Mr. Pendarves; secondly, Dean Delany.

dancers," and the rooms never too crowded; not more than twenty-four couples at private balls; the crush was greater at the court balls, which were given in the Beefeaters' Hall. Here the ladies were all placed in rows one above the other, so raised that the last touched the ceiling; "the gentlemen told us that we looked very handsome, and compared us to Cupid's Paradise in the puppet show." It must, however, have been hard for those seated on the highest bench. . . The English visitor is enthusiastic over the beauty of the Irish women. . . "Lady Ross is the top beauty, but I never saw so many pretty faces collected. Last night I held a commerce table of absolute beauties. Miss Kelly,[1] who is a perfect beauty, sweet Letty Bushe,[2] Miss Usher,[3] Miss Wesley,[4] Miss Ormsby." That Mrs. Pendarves does not name Miss Molesworth, was probably owing to the fact that the young lady

---

[1] In 1731 Swift was just recovering from the death of Stella. Those who have read the terrible picture of his mental condition after her death may feel surprised that he should be once more playing his old game of platonic flirtation with all the pretty girls gathered round Mrs. Clayton's commerce table. He went from bud to bud, as our American cousins would say, and poor Mrs. Delany, who was more of a full-blown rose, records rather piteously that Miss Kelly's beauty gained him, although he admired Miss Usher amazingly. "As for me, I come in only as a little by-the-bye." No doubt, had Miss Kelly lived (she died in 1733) she would have formed a pendant to Stella and Vanessa. The saturnine Dean had marked her for his plaything, and we all know the fate that awaited his toys. Miss Kelly was the daughter of Captain Denis Kelly; she was a wit and a beauty. The Dean superintended her education, and guided her conduct—he would sit by her bedside when she was ill.

[2] Bushe is a well known and respected name in Ireland. Miss Letty is constantly mentioned in Mrs. Delany's correspondence. "A prettier creature than Letitia Bushe I never saw before that malicious distemper seized upon her (the distemper was the small-pox). Good-humoured and innocent, without the least conceit of her beauty—she paints delightfully. All the men," she goes on, "were dying for her whilst she was in danger, but, notwithstanding their admiration, not one of them will be generous enough to marry her while a certain lawsuit is pending, and now indeed their adoration will cease. They will not acknowledge her for a divinity since she is divested of those charms that occasioned their devotion." Miss Bushe, however, recovered her beauty. She remained Miss Bushe to the end of the chapter.

[3] Mary Usher, daughter to the Archdeacon of Clonfert. She was the second wife of Richard, third Viscount Molesworth, and met a disastrous fate. See page 10.

[4] Miss Wesley, a charming girl, daughter to Garret Wesley, Earl of Mornington.

was still in the schoolroom when Mrs. Pendarves paid her visit to Mrs. Clayton.

We hear of her, however, a few months later, when, in January, 1732, she took part in Lord Mountjoy's private theatricals. The play was "The Distressed Mother," a stock piece at the theatres, for which reason one would have supposed that amateurs would have avoided it, but we all know the stale saying as to fools and angels.

In any case, the natural temerity of the amateur was, in Ireland, intensified by the appreciation the natives are said to have of themselves, this opinion being justified to a certain extent by the success of their histrionic performance. The native is, in fact, always acting; at all times, and in every social corner of Irish life, we find amateur stages set up, lamps lit, and ladies and gentlemen busy with some sort of public performance. History repeats itself, and when we turn from the old faded newspaper that chronicles Lord Mountjoy's theatricals to the *Irish Times* of to-day, there is the same complimentary notice to be found of private theatricals at Coolmore or Ardee, Belfast or Kilkenny. The caste of "The Distressed Mother" was as follows :—

Hermione.—Miss Molesworth.

Andromache.—Miss Parker.

Pyrrhus.—Lord Mountjoy.

Orestes.—Honourable Mr. Barnewall (brother to Lord Kingsland).

N.B. Every performer had twelve tickets to give away.

It could hardly be expected that so young a girl as Miss Molesworth could have given effect, comparatively, to a part such as Hermione, in which Mrs. Woffington and Baddeley could melt their audience to tears. Mary was, however, singularly thoughtful for her age, and much given to reading and study; moreover, her beauty and youth naturally appealed to her audience, who were ready to excuse short-comings in a girl so graceful and beautiful. On one of the spectators she made a lasting impression.

Her admirer was Colonel Rochfort, afterwards created the Earl of Belvedere. He was a man of fashion, and although he had recently married Miss Tenison, he made no secret of his admiration for the lovely Hermione. That his admiration was sincere was proved later, for his wife dying of small-pox the year after their marriage, he, after a decent interval, declared himself to be Miss Molesworth's devoted suitor, and it wasn't likely that his suit would be rejected. The Rochforts, or de Rupe-forti, were of old descent and highly considered; Rochfort sat in the Irish House of Commons as member for Westmeath, where he had large property. He was twenty-eight, handsome, more elegant in his manners than Irish country gentlemen were at that period, as he had spent much of his time about the Court, and was a favourite with George the Second, who bestowed upon him many proofs of favour. It seems strange that such a man should have selected as a wife a mere girl like Mary Molesworth, uneducated in the ways of the world where he shone. One would have supposed that, like his prototype, Chesterfield, he would have sought to please his royal master by marrying one of the numerous royal offshoots. He was, however, given to sudden impulses, and determined to trample upon any obstacle that might stand in the way of his sudden passion; it was very unlikely that any obstacle would present itself, Colonel Rochfort being a suitor most pleasing in the eyes of the parents of his choice, who considered his fortune and position a sufficient reason for accepting him as their daughter's husband.

In the last century there was no " revolt of the daughters." Women, indeed, were of little account, and parents were absolute disposers of their destiny. The times were rough, and those who refused to obey the parental decree were soon brought into subjection by stringent measures, and submitted, as best they could, to the fate that lay before them; so it was with Mary. Her objections were overruled; her nervous dread of and evident dislike to her handsome lover were put aside as ridiculous; the preparations for the wedding were made, and on August 1st, 1736, she was married to Colonel Rochfort by Dean Delany—the second husband of Rochfort's mother-in-law, Mrs. Tenison.

From the first the marriage was not a happy one. Rochfort soon made the discovery that his wife did not reciprocate his affection, and that no tenderness on his part could conquer the shrinking fear she seemed to have of him. Spoiled as he had been by the adulation of flatterers and the easy conquest of women of fashion, his imperious temper could not brook the coldness of Mary's nature. He gave way to bursts of passion which terrified her so much that on one occasion she fled to her father's house, to be sent back next morning under the charge of a trusty servant.

The year after the marriage Colonel Rochfort was raised to the peerage, with the title of Baron Belfield (later on he was made Earl of Belvedere). This honour, which gave him great satisfaction, increased his desire to have an heir to his new dignity. When the first child was born, and proved to be a daughter, his rage and disappointment were vented upon Mary, whose timid nature was terrified at his violence. Fortunately, the next year a son was born. This event was made the occasion of magnificent rejoicings; the country, far and near, was blazing with bonfires; oxen were roasted and barrels of whisky drank; the king was godfather, and the boy was christened after him, George Augustus.

The gratification of his wishes revived all Rochfort's love for his young wife, and had she known how to adapt herself to circumstances, or, in other words, had she been taught any idea of her duty to the man to whom she had sworn to be faithful, her painful story would not have been made the subject of different romances. Romances they may truly be called, for although there is some truth in the story first given to the world in *Chambers' Journal*, and copied by later writers, a close examination goes to prove there is much exaggeration and distortion of the actual facts.

No two people could have been less suited to one another than the tempestuous, irascible Rochfort, and his timid, cold, unloving wife, whose heart was entirely given to another—and that other her husband's brother, Arthur Rochfort,[1]

[1] Arthur Rochfort married Sarah, daughter to the Reverend Rowland Singleton of Drogheda.

already for many years married, the father of a large family, and of exemplary character, until, as Walpole says, "he looked upon this woman and thought her fair."

The Arthur Rochforts lived at Rochfort House, close to Gaulstown, Lord Belvedere's seat in Westmeath, and here the intimacy between the guilty pair began, a constant intercourse being kept up between the two families without exciting any comment. Lord Belvedere suspected nothing, he lived a great deal away, for not having much happiness at home he returned to the society of his gay friends in London, and it was said neglected his wife. It was in 1742 that his suspicions were for the first time aroused. A packet of letters[1] was brought to him by a woman with whom he had been intimate before his marriage, and who was supposed to owe Mary a grudge. The letters were however genuine, they were written under feigned names, and were passionate love letters. Lord Belvedere accused his wife, who found some means of informing her paramour, who fled precipitately and without making any defence. Lord Belvedere followed him to London. Mrs. Delany, who was connected with the Rochforts, saw him on March 10th, 1743, and writes to her sister of his unfortunate story, and that he had come to London to search for his brother and to kill him, wherever he might meet him. "But I hope," she adds, "his resentment will cool, and not provoke him to so desperate an action; and he does not appear to have any rash design, but is more cheerful and composed than one could expect him to be. He is very well bred and very well in his person and manners. His wife is extremely handsome, and he is miserable enough to love her even still. She has many personal accomplishments."

Lord Belvedere returned to Ireland without having found his brother, who had taken refuge abroad, where his wife and

---

[1] "And what names, think you . . they chose?" writes Walpole, who considered there was a strong circumstance of *Iriscism* over the whole fracas. "Silvia and Philander, the very same that Lord Grey and his sister-in-law took upon a parallel occasion, and which are printed in their letters." (This was Forde, the infamous Lord Grey of Werke and his sister-in-law, Lady Henrietta Berkeley). One would like to know where Walpole detected the circumstance of Iriscism.

family joined him, and where he resided for fifteen years. This circumstance perhaps precluded the possibility of getting a divorce. Lady Belvedere remained in the hands of her outraged husband, and her father, justly indignant at her frailty, made no effort to interfere. Although Lord Belvedere has been stigmatized as a cruel tyrant, it does not appear that the punishment he inflicted on his erring wife was too severe, when we take into account the provocation he had received,

LADY BELVEDERE.

together with the stricter views then prevailing as to the treatment of a wife's infidelity.

At the time of the discovery, he had just completed building a new and handsome mansion, which was to supersede Gaulstown as the family seat. This is still known by his name, although it has passed into other hands. "Belvedere"[1] being a favourite spot with all lovers of the picturesque.

[1] "Belvedere, now the property of Charles Brinsley Marlay, Esquire, is

Here Lord Belvedere fixed his own residence and that of his children and household; in the old and gloomy mansion of Gaulstown he kept his wife shut up, deprived of all intercourse with the outer world, and carefully watched by a staff of trusty retainers. In all other respects she had everything fitted to her station; a carriage was kept for her use, but never allowed to pass the boundaries of the Park; she was amply supplied with a good table and wardrobe, and allowed to correspond with her own family, and occasionally her children were sent to visit her.

The unfortunate lady was barely six-and-twenty when she was thus cut off from all the enjoyments of life, and as month followed month and year followed year with no break in the dull monotony of existence we may imagine how dreary must have been her lot. She was never visited by any of her own family, who appear all through to have been convinced of her guilt and sided with the injured husband. Her mother had died without knowing the disgrace that had fallen upon her daughter, and any association between Lady Belvedere and her unmarried sisters would have been considered injurious to their making suitable marriages. Two years after his wife's death Lord Molesworth married again a lady young enough to be his daughter;[1] she made him, however, an admirable wife, and Horace Walpole bears testimony to her engaging behaviour;

---

situated near Mullingar, and between it and Rochfort House there is still to be seen the artificial ruin of an old Abbey. The tradition that this ruin had arisen out of a family feud is generally known, and that it was built by one brother to exclude from his sight the residence of the other. Few are aware that the design originated with Lord Belvedere, who went to enormous expense in its erection, bringing over an Italian artist named Barrodotte to superintend the building." The fact would not be worth mentioning only that it shows how deep was the feeling in Lord Belvedere's mind as to the injury that had been done to him.—(From the *Irish Builder* of April, 1893.)

[1] Mary Jenny Usher, daughter to the Archdeacon of Clonfert. She is mentioned frequently in Mrs. Delany's autobiography, and was one of the commerce table of absolute beauties. After Lord Molesworth's death she resided in London, where, in 1763, she met a tragic death. Her house in Brook Street taking fire, she and nine of her household perished in the flames. This lamentable event caused a considerable sensation, and is mentioned in all the papers and letters of the day. Lady Molesworth was seen at one of the windows, trying to help her daughters to escape. The horrified spectators saw the heroic lady fall back into the burning

she was also very handsome. In accordance with her husband's wish, she kept aloof from her unfortunate step-daughter, who was wearing her heart out in the monotonous seclusion of Gaulstown.

Some tragic incidents are told which heighten the interest of her story. The one desire of the unfortunate lady's heart was to see her husband; she imagined a personal interview might revive the love he undoubtedly once felt for her. . . Lord Belvedere, fearing his own weakness, was careful to avoid a meeting which must be fraught with deep pain. One day, however, when he was overlooking some alterations in the park at Gaulstown, she forced herself into his presence, and, falling at his feet, implored not so much pity as justice. Lord Belvedere was softened, he hesitated, he was affected, and would probably have yielded, only for the presence of a third person who was decidedly adverse to Lady Belvedere. This marplot cried in a voice of warning, "My Lord, remember your honour," and dragged him away.

Another romantic incident was Lady Belvedere's escape from her prison to her father's house in Dublin. Under any circumstances it would have been doubtful whether Lord Molesworth would have received her, but it happened that her flight had been discovered sooner than she had calculated, and Lord Belvedere, losing no time, arrived in Dublin before her, and so worked upon Lord Molesworth's feelings, that when the wretched woman reached her father's house she was refused admission, and, as she turned away was seized, forced into a post-chaise that stood waiting, and ignominiously brought back to Gaulstown.

Lady Belvedere did not improve her lot by this attempt to obtain her freedom. Her attendants were changed and she was treated with more severity, no longer being allowed to see

mass; her eldest daughter also perished, as did her brother, Captain Usher The three remaining daughters, who had jumped from the windows with the help of their mother, were terribly injured. One was caught on the railings and tore her thigh so terribly that the limb had to be cut off; the other broke her leg. Horace Walpole is full of pity for these young creatures. "Lady Grosvenor has taken them into her house. The one whose leg is cut off has been kept for days intoxicated with landanum; she knows nothing of what has happened to her."

her children. The narrator of her story, says this incident occurred twelve years after her imprisonment, but a considera- tion of the case would lead one to think that it must have taken place later, and was consequent upon the trial of Mr. Rochfort. This gentleman, who had remained abroad sixteen years, returned to Ireland in 1757, imagining that time would have cooled his brother's anger, and that he would be content to let, as the saying goes, sleeping dogs lie. In any case he was so weary of his exile, that he preferred to take the chance of a trial, and refused Lord Belvedere's proposal that he should return abroad, in which case the matter should drop. The trial came on on May 12th, Dean Delany was one of the witnesses. The facts proved beyond all doubt the guilt of the pair, and the damages were assessed at twenty thousand pounds, which Mr. Rochfort not being able to pay, he was imprisoned in the debtors' prison; a "fate he well deserves," says Mrs. Delany.

On a man of Lord Belvedere's haughty nature this public exposure of his wrongs had the worst effect. It revived his jealousy, roused his fury against his wife, and as she was in his power, he, in an ungenerous manner, wreaked his vengeance upon her. What advantage could be expected in retaining his prisoner after the trial is not plain. For thirteen long years the miserable woman had to endure her punishment, for it was not until 1772 that the death of Lord Belvedere gave her her release. During these years her father had died without seeing her; her son had married, she herself had become a wreck, her features haggard, her hair white; her face wore a wild, scared look, and her voice had sunk almost to a whisper. She was dressed in the fashion of the day at the time she quitted the world thirty years before.

No sooner was Lord Belvedere's funeral over than her sons hastened to Gaulstown, where a most affecting interview took place. She hardly recognized them. For the rest of her life the unhappy lady was surrounded with care and affection. Her children (especially her daughter, who had married the Earl of Lanesborough [1]) showed her every atten-

[1] Lady Lanesborough had not the best reputation. She lived mostly abroad, with her second husband, Mr. King.

tion. They could not, however, minister to a mind diseased ; Lady Belvedere had lived too long in solitude to be able now, in her old age, to take up again the threads of life which had been so rudely broken. Her strange story was always before her. It was the Nemesis of her existence—pursuing her. She dreaded publicity and shrank from notice ; while to her dying hour she declared her innocence. She, however, appeared to be always oppressed with remorse.

The latter portion of her life was spent at Belvedere House,[1] the magnificent mansion built by her son, the second Earl of Belvedere.

---

[1] Belvedere House was sold in 1843 to the Rev. Patrick Meagher, S.J., who converted it into a college. It is now a junior college for youth under the care of the learned Society of Jesus. The following account of the sale may be interesting :—

"Belvedere House was sold for a sum under 1800*l*.—which included an organ built in Germany, valued at 400 guineas, and a set of valuable mahogany bookcases, the entire length of one of the principal rooms, value about 200*l*., with other less important matters—subject to a head rent of about 35*l*. per annum ; the purchase-money of the house may therefore be taken at about 1200*l*. at most.

"The house was magnificently designed. The three principal rooms on the drawing-room floor being dedicated to Venus, Diana, and Apollo, the ornamental architecture of each room is elaborately descriptive of the supposed attributes of each of the deities ; and the entire suite communicate by folding-doors—thus throwing the three splendid apartments into one. The grand staircase is also tastefully designed ; the carving on either side, together with the stucco-work, being in keeping with the rich ornamental work of the apartments just described.

In the story of Eleanor Ambrose we come face to face with one of those phases of society alluded to in the introduction, with which English readers are only superficially acquainted. I do not mean to say they are ignorant of the religious strife that existed between the Protestant minority and the Catholic majority, but that the results produced by this internecine warfare are understood by outsiders may fairly be doubted; or that any one, save the Irish themselves, comprehends the real significance of the two designations *Orange* and *Papist*.

The evils of the long-continued civil war, and the oppression which had followed upon James the Second's disastrous campaign, had left traces all over the country. The so-called Orange party, although not so rampant as in the first moment of victory, still trampled upon the rights of the Papists. The statue of the great champion of Protestantism stood in College Green, the principal thoroughfare of Dublin.[1] Here high festival was kept on the anniversary of the Battle of the Boyne, the Viceroy and magistrates of the city parading round the effigy in procession and a salute being fired in its honour.[2]

[1] Where raised on high equestrian William shows
In warlike majesty his Roman nose.

[2] This custom was continued far into this century. Thackeray could have gladly seen our generations of royal Georges in effigy abolished, but would have spared William III. in College Green. He was right, for a portion of the history and life of Dublin has gathered around his leaden majesty. Each year, from 1701 onward for more than a century, on the anniversary of William's birthday, the Lord Lieutenant, the Lord Mayor and aldermen, the Lord Chancellor and judges, the provost of Trinity College and other notabilities paraded thrice around the statue,

Woe betide any unfortunate Roman Catholic who was re-calcitrant enough not to take off his hat in passing the bronze presentment of the great and glorious William of immortal memory—he had to pay for his contumacy by seven days of bread and water in a very dirty cell in Newgate. The penal laws, although not always acted upon, were still in force, the existence of which, Mr. Lecky says, "rendered absolutely impossible in Ireland the formation of that habit of instructive and unreasoning reverence for law which is one of the most essential conditions of English civiliza-tion, and which," he adds, " by alienating the people from the Government, made the ecclesiastical organization to which they belonged the real centre of their affections and enthusiasm." [1]

trying to look grave, so to do honour to the "pious, glorious, and im-mortal memory." Many of the college lads were Jacobites, and some-times the gray of morning would discover two figures astride of the leaden horse—one the hero of the Boyne, dressed up with hay, the other a man of straw, leaning limp against the hero's shoulders. The volunteers would muster and bang off their cannons and blaze their *feu de joie* around the statue. King William survived the insults and defied the assaults of his enemies until a fatal night of April, 1836. A mysterious light was observed that night in his neighbourhood and presently there followed a deafening explosion; the king flew high in the air as if through some violent apotheosis, then fell, a shattered bulk of royalty, and lay flat, ignominiously indifferent to popery, pre-lacy, brass money, and wooden shoes. In the morning they carted the body to a police office, and held an inquest; physicians discovered an envious puncture between hip and saddle-skirt. Irish criminals have been restored to life after their execution by judicious blood-letting from the jugular vein. The grand monarch by this or some other device was revivified. His mangled limbs were made straight, his Roman nose was set, and when Thackeray pleaded in his behalf, my Lord Mayor, Daniel O'Connell, had the king under a canvas and was painting him of a bright green picked out with yellow—his lordship's own livery.—(From Mr. Dowden's " Dublin City," published in *Scribner's Magazine*, December, 1884.)

[1] The ill-feeling was cultivated assiduously by the advance guard of both parties. The toasts at a social or public dinner were of such a character that no Catholic could, with any respect for himself, be present. " To H—— with the Pope !" " Down with the Papist curs !" " No sur-render !" were favourites at most convivial meetings, while Libellero or the Protestant boys evoked a storm of applause. On the other side was equal intolerance, and a secret and deadly hatred to the Orange faction. This last, however, was not regularly organized until 1795, and the Orange lodges had their rise in the following lamentable incident :—
In these excited times skirmishes were constant between what was called the Defenders (i.e., the Protestants) and the Peep-o'-day boys

In 1744 the traces of civil war, says Mr. Lecky, still lingered. The statue of William the Fourth adorned the principal thoroughfare; the toast of the glorious, pious, and immortal memory was given at every public banquet; the walls of the House of Lords displayed the pictures of the Battle of the Boyne, and Roman Catholics were still rigidly proscribed. They could hold no land either by purchase or right of succession, unless, as was often the case, some member of the family conformed,[1] as it was called, to the Established Church. Neither could a Papist take a long or valuable lease, nor was he eligible for any office of dignity or emolument—he could not practise any of the professions, except medicine, and he was not allowed to enter Parliament —this restriction going so far as to prohibit his having a seat in the gallery as a spectator of the proceedings. No career of any dignity or importance was therefore open to the sons of a Catholic gentleman, unless they either went abroad and took service in the French or Spanish army or entered into business; but there the choice was limited, and became more so as time went on. Meantime, in the country parts, the condition of affairs was still worse. Swift's account of the Irish gentry, " that every squire almost to a man is an oppressor and racker, a jobber of publick works, very proud and generally illiterate," seems to have been a fair picture

(Catholics mostly). Some lives being lost in an encounter near Armagh a truce was agreed upon, but in twenty-four hours it was broken by the Catholics who fired upon a Protestant gentleman who was a surety, and after this 700 of the boys entered and sacked the lonely village of "the Diamond." The tocsin was at once sounded and the Protestant contingent flocked in from all quarters. A pitched battle ensued on September 21st, 1795. The troops from Armagh were sent to dispense the combatants, and so the matter ended. Out of this affair arose the organization of the Orange lodges, the first being instituted either on the field or immediately after. These lodges played a great part in the subsequent disastrous history of Ireland. They still exist, but in a most modified degree.

[1] The practice of " some member of a Catholic family conforming," in order to obtain possession of the family property, was general enough. A story is told of two brothers, of whom the elder offered to conform, but was too late, his brother having done so the *previous day*. In many instances property was preserved to the Catholic families by their Protestant neighbours, who held it in trust until better times came, when they loyally surrendered the estate.

of the men of his day who spent their time hunting, shooting and drinking hard, having no sense of duty to the unfortunate peasantry, who lived in a state of abject poverty unparalleled in Europe.

Such was the state of Ireland when, in 1744, Lord Chesterfield was sent over to try, by means of his "silver tongue" and urbane manners, to reconcile the different parties who were tearing one another to pieces in the little island. Philip Dormer Stanhope, fourth Earl of Chesterfield, filled a larger place in the time in which he lived than almost any of his contemporaries. He was a statesman, a diplomatist, and an author; besides these distinctions, his talent for conversation and powers of repartee gave him singular attractions in society. At one period he was the most admired and run-after man in London, and despite that he was "unlovely in his person" he found the greatest favour with women. The reverse of the picture is that he was in all respects more showy than solid—he was a gambler, a bad husband, a scoffer at all religion, profligate in his habits, heartless and unfeeling, and a very doubtful politician.[1] The character of Chesterfield is generally judged by his letters to his illegitimate son, which furnish the most extraordinary instance on record of a man displaying to the world his own want of moral principle. He was, in fact, the production of the time in which he lived. He was the representative of those men of the world who made manners serve for morals, and it may be said of him that he never affronted any code of society; his desire to excel others was the strongest passion he possessed. According to his own confession he wished to stand first amongst men of pleasure. "I always hated hard drinking," he says: "and yet I have drunk, with disgust, only because I considered drinking a necessity for a fine gentleman." With all his faults his vice-

---

[1] He married, in 1733, Melusina Schulenburg, Countess of Walsingham, the daughter of George I. and the Duchess of Kendal. Melusina had been in her girlhood a dark beauty; she was however not in her first youth when Chesterfield married her. She was one of the King's favourite children, and he left her a large fortune, of which, however, George II. would only pay twenty thousand pounds, and that only on the threat of the royal will being produced.

C

royalty in Ireland was eminently successful. He displayed much earnestness in dealing with the country, and studied the conditions of Irish life with more than ordinary care, doing his utmost to improve and civilize all classes. He has left upon record his opinion that the peasants only needed kind usage and the Gavel Act to be the most contented peasantry. In Dublin, where he resided constantly, he gathered round him all the wealth and talent of the country, and the elegance of his tastes, the refinement of his manners, soon had their effect upon the nobility and gentry who, up to the time of his coming amongst them, had cared little for the more refined luxuries to which their position entitled them. They lived anywhere, anyhow.

The English visitors and tourists give a lamentable account of the want of refinement amongst persons even of the highest position, and of the rough manner in which they lived. Arthur Young, whose tour through Ireland is a faithful transcript of the manners and customs of the day, tells us that in winter, when the Parliament season was going on, there was an amount of gaiety in Dublin that exceeded London. Balls, dinners, concerts almost every night; there was, however, he says, a total lack of decency in the way of living, even in families of the highest position.[1] "The tables indeed groaned with abundance, but there was neither order nor good taste in the establishments; dinner was at an early hour, and the claret[2] and whisky flowed till all hours of the morning. Furious quarrels, ending in duels, were frequent, and were sometimes

---

[1] It is amusing to take a peep into an etiquette book of the period— or, as it is called, "Hints to introduce Decorum at City Feasts and Sunday Ordinaries in Dublin." From this useful little work we learn that our grandfathers committed many a solecism against our present code of manners; but then, good Lord! they were twice the men we are, look at the appetites they had. Fancy being told "not to heap *more* than two pounds of victuals on your plate at *starting!* Not to be too eager to have the first cut. Not to drag the leg of a fowl through your teeth in order to secure your property in it, and then lay it by to *pick* at your leisure. To remember also that although fingers were made before forks, the latter were substituted for the sake of cleanliness. Not to throw the scraps off your plate into the dish."

[2] There was more Burgundy drunk in Dublin in a week than in London in a month.

inflamed by religious or political animosity when in a mixed company some drunken Squire, laying his pistol cocked upon the table, gave the toast of the glorious, pious, and immortal memory which would be the signal for a general riot.

Chesterfield's genial influence did much to soften some of this religious animosity. Unfortunately, the period of his Viceroyalty was too short to be of any permanent use. During his term of office, however, the condition of Catholics all over the country was infinitely improved, and so marked was the change that, during the stormy days of the Pretender, when both England and Scotland were almost in open rebellion, Ireland remained perfectly tranquil. When Chesterfield went over to London, he told the King and his ministers that it was poverty and not Popery that the country had to fear, adding that for his part he had only found one dangerous Papist.

" Who ? What ? Where is he ? " asked the inquisitive Monarch.

" She is a beautiful young lady," returned Chesterfield ; " the brightness of her eyes and the charms of her conversation are indeed perilous."

In this wise did Eleanor Ambrose (for it was of her Lord Chesterfield spoke) gain the *sobriquet* which will always make her fame live in story. She was the daughter of Mr. Michael Ambrose, who came of an old Catholic family, and who, being a second son, and having no career open to him, had gone into business as a brewer and was making a large fortune. The disabilities under which the proscribed religion suffered was felt even in social life, and Catholics were not on the same footing in society as their Protestant neighbours. Even those whose rank and position should have entitled them to attend the Court, held aloof, either from a feeling that their social status was not recognized, or because their finances were so crippled by the burden of heavy taxes that they could ill afford the necessary expenses. That Miss Ambrose should be singled out as the belle, *par excellence*, of the Viceregal Court, and be made the object of the Viceroy's particular attentions, was a species of triumph to the Catholic party, and it is highly probable (taking into consideration the character of Chesterfield) that his attentions were prompted quite as much by motives of policy as from admiration of the young lady's singular beauty. Eleanor, on her side, may have been put forward to obtain for her friends some exemption from the grinding rule of the existing laws. In this way we can account for an act which, at first sight, looks somewhat like a surrender of the principles hitherto advocated by herself and her family. I allude to her appearance at the ball given by Chesterfield in commemoration of the Battle of the Boyne, an anniversary which was kept by her co-religionists in sackcloth and ashes.[1] Not only did she lend her presence to the general rejoicing, but came wearing the colours of the dominant party, the bodice of her dress, according to the fashion adopted by the Court ladies, being ornamented with a profusion of orange lilies.

Chesterfield, whose acute and dangerous habit of reading the motives of others, not all his good manners could keep in check, addressed the fair traitress[2] in lines which showed he was not deceived by this apparent loyalty :—

> Tell me, Ambrose, where's the jest
> Of wearing Orange on thy breast,
> When underneath that bosom shows
> The whiteness of the rebel rose?[3]

The young beauty must have felt rather disconcerted at this sarcastic reminder that her wearing false colours did not impose upon her admirer, who, for the rest, was as much

---

[1] The anniversary was kept with great honour. Early in the day the Boyne Society, "according to their laudable and annual custom, would march in decent and regular order to St. Catherine's Church, stopping at the Mayoralty house to salute the Lord Mayor, who would join the procession in his grand coach ; then they would stop at King William's statue to give it the usual honours. In the evening the Lord Mayor and citizens of eminence dined in state at the Tholsel, and the city was brilliantly illuminated with large wax candles. Besides these manifestations, meetings were held all over the country to celebrate the day, and express thankfulness and remembrance of the wonderful deliverance."

[2] Some versions differ as to "lovely traitress" and "pretty Tory."

[3] These lines are quoted by Murphy in his life of Garrick as having been addressed to Mrs. Madden, the wife of Doctor Madden. This lady who, like Miss Ambrose, was a Catholic, was one of the beauties and a celebrated toast.

attracted by the brightness of her intellect as by her acknowledged beauty.

Eleanor's conversation was distinguished by much real cleverness, lighted up by witty sayings and quick repartee, a gift which fascinated the fastidious Chesterfield. Stanhope, "whose pencil never writ a dull line," was more likely to be captivated by intellectual than by mere personal charms. The union of both was sufficiently rare to be perilously attractive. Miss Ambrose seems to have been constantly in the company of the Viceroy, and to have attended at all State ceremonials such as the Government nights at the theatre, which were brilliant displays. The performances then began at five o'clock, and the Lord Mayor in his robes of office came from dining at the Tholsel, accompanied by his marshal bearing the sword of state, and the aldermen in their robes. The boxes on this occasion were altogether filled by ladies of rank, the pit being reserved for the gentlemen. The condition of the stage was, however, at a very low ebb, and it was a custom for the bucks and bloods of the town to climb over the spikes that separated the pit from the performers, and to get on the stage, where they mixed with the actors in such a manner as scarce to be distinguished from them. Sheridan, who was manager of Smock Alley, had imported from the London theatres more decency of behaviour, but his efforts to enforce decorum were unavailing until an accident happened which brought about a reform. This happened on a Government night, when Lord Chesterfield was present. A young buck from Connaught who had been long plaguing the pretty actress, George Ann Bellamy (later of notorious fame) with his attentions, was on this particular evening quite tipsy, and was so rude to the young lady as she went to her dressing-room that neither she nor the other actresses would return to the stage. A riot ensued, and this disturbance had the happy effect of banishing all intruders from coming on to the stage. It is probable that Miss Ambrose was present on the evening in question, as she was most certainly on other occasions, where her beauty would receive the compliment of three cheers and a "round of heels" from the gallery, a form of notoriety very usual and pleasing to the popular favourite. An amusing story, which shows the Viceroy in a different light, is told of the well-known occasion when a deputation from Drogheda waited on Chesterfield to offer him the freedom of that town. Miss Ambrose, who was *seated* beside the Viceroy, took a fancy to the gold casket in which the address was contained, and playfully asked her admirer to give it to her.

"Madam," replied the wily courtier, laying his jewelled fingers on his heart, "you have already too much of my freedom."

This sounds very much like the unmeaning gallantry which was the tone of the day; high-flown compliments were looked upon as the current coin of conversation, little value being attached to them—still, we may be allowed to doubt the prudence of such constant intercourse between a young and lovely girl and a man so versed in all the arts that win a woman's affections as was Chesterfield. In all this we cannot help wondering how the young lady's friends allowed such an intimacy to continue, knowing, as they must have done, the reputation Lord Chesterfield had as a man of indifferent morals, whose friendship and attentions were in the last degree undesirable, not to say dangerous. Witness the case of Lady Fanny Shirley, the beautiful daughter of Lord Ferrers, who had sacrificed everything—position and reputation, and a good establishment to her love for the fascinating Stanhope.[1]

Eleanor was not likely to risk her good name; although she was virtuously proud of her conquest she in all ways

---

[1] Lord Chesterfield addressed the following lines to Lady Fanny, who was ever after known as "the blooming fair":—

> When Fanny, blooming fair,
>   First caught my ravished sight,
> Struck with her shape and air
>   I felt a strange delight.
> Whilst eagerly I gazed,
>   Admiring every part
> And every feature praised,
>   She stole into my heart.

Pope also addressed some complimentary verses to the beauty.

jealously guarded her reputation, keeping well within the limits of platonic friendship. Nor does she seem to have aroused the jealousy of Lady Chesterfield, who, for the rest, was pretty well accustomed to the wandering fancies of her lord, who had ceased to care for her (if he ever had done so). A quarter of a century had gone by since he had married her, and whatever of beauty Melusina had once possessed, was a thing of the past. She was now old and fat, and, in addition, was subject to periodical attacks of St. Anthony's fire in her face. She was, however, good natured, a lover of music and of eating, but earnest in her desire to help her husband in his effort to conciliate the people over whom he ruled. She was popular in her own way, and, when the weavers were in distress, gave balls, to which everyone was commanded to come dressed in woven stuff or material ; this she likewise wore, although it must have been unbecoming to one of her figure. She was very intimate with Mrs Delany [1] and paid her visits at Delville to inspect the japanning and shell work in which the Dean's lady was such a proficient. Lord Chesterfield's

likening her to Minerva and Venus, and concluding with the following lines, in which he supposes the lady to speak and address him :—

> Come, if you'll be a quiet soul,
> That dares tell neither truth nor lies,
> I'll list you in the harmless roll
> Of those that sing of those poor eyes.

Thomas Coke, Earl of Leicester (Lord Lovell) was one of Lady Fanny's many admirers, and would have married her despite what the world said of her relations with Chesterfield, but she would not listen to him. "That foul fiend Chesterfield has bewitched her," wrote the unhappy lover to his friend, Lord Essex ; "and under pretence of serving me has entirely defeated me, and is in full possession of the lady's soul." Lady Fanny lived to repent the error of her ways. In her later years she lived in great privacy at Twickenham ; she was a follower of Whitfield, who, it is hoped, gave her consolation. Horace Walpole wrote some unkind verses about her in the Twickenham register :—

> " Here Fanny, ever blooming fair,
> Ejaculates the graceful prayer ;
> And 'scaped from sense with nonsense smit
> For Whitfield's cant leaves *Stanhope's* wit."

[1] It is somewhat singular that in Mrs. Delany's gossiping and very delightful letters she never names Miss Ambrose, or makes any mention of Lord Chesterfield's admiration for " the dangerous Papist." This may be accounted for by the line of demarcation already alluded to as existing between the two religions.

Viceroyalty came to an end in 1749. His term of office made an epoch in the history of the country he had governed with so much prudence, and his departure caused a universal feeling of sorrow. He had been in earnest in his efforts to improve the condition of the unfortunate people, and in return he was beloved to a degree quite unparalleled. The beautiful verses which were written in his praise more than twenty years after he had returned to England show his memory dwelt in the hearts of those he had tried to serve :—

> " Cheered not with one benignant ray
> Since Chesterfield's unclouded day ;
> That day, to fond remembrance dear,
> Still honoured by a grateful tear,
> When first an happy people knew
> From Stanhope's care what kings should do.
> When last perhaps was clearly shown
> The bright distinction of a throne." [1]

Miss Ambrose must have shared in the general sorrow felt for the departing Viceroy. She now, perhaps for the first time, recognized that his attentions, which were so pleasing for the moment, were evanescent as a puff of wind, and nothing tangible remained to console her for the loss of her charming friend. It was altogether a mistake, as such friendships always are. Her other admirers seemed coarse and vulgar in

---

[1] These verses appeared in Barratariana, and were by Henry Grattan. Swift also has left on record an equally beautiful tribute to Lord Chesterfield's character :—

> " Stanhope has gained one point of fame
> To which I'll prove he has no claim.
> Say they, his favors he extends
> Without regard to place, or friends.
> *Nothing* prevails with him but merit,
> Nay, he'll dispense with merit, too,
> When modest want can reach his view.
> Meer prejudice—tis plain to see
> No man takes sweeter bribes than he.
> To clear the point from any doubt
> A parable shall help me out :
> The noble Fulvia spurns at gain ;
> Freely she heals the lover's pain ;
> But surely you'll allow me this
> That when she grants she shares the bliss.
> So Stanhope in each generous action
> Shares more than half the satisfaction."

contrast to the elegant Stanhope's refined wit and many
accomplishments,[1] nor was she spared the malicious laugh of
jealous friends who had envied her the favour she had
enjoyed, and now took occasion to point out how foolish had
been such a loss of time. " Why, poor Eleanor was growing
an old maid ! " etc. etc. Eleanor was above such contemptible
taunts, although it would not be in female nature not to feel
them. Moreover, as long as her glass continued to tell a
flattering tale, she had no need to care, especially as lovers
continued unabated in their devotion. It was not, however,
until she had nearly reached her thirtieth year that she made
her selection. It was in 1751, the year when the lovely
Gunnings had burst upon the town, and by their youthful
charms distanced all competitors. Miss Ambrose must
indeed have felt herself dethroned. Her choice was nevertheless by no means of the sort vulgarly called *pis aller*, while
the manner in which the event is announced in the monthly
magazine is a testimony that she still was looked upon as a
reigning beauty :—

" The celebrated Miss Ambrose of this kingdom has, to the
much envied happiness of one, and the grief of thousands,
abdicated her maiden empire of beauty, and retreated to the
Temple of Hymen. Her husband is Roger Palmer, Esq., of
Castle Lacken, Co. Mayo."

The remaining portion of the life of " the dangerous Papist,"
has little of general interest. We hear of her occasionally as
visiting Bristol hot-wells to drink the waters, and if we
choose, we can imagine that she visited London and saw her
former admirer, and obtained through his influence, the
baronetcy which was conferred upon her husband in 1777.

---

[1] Chesterfield showed the best side of his character during his all too
short viceroyalty ; he was accused of being hollow in his profession of
wishing to serve the country, but his acts show that he was at all events
in some instances sincere. He got a grant of five hundred pounds for
the Royal Dublin Society. Sheridan, who was one of his accusers, used
to tell a story of how, when he was in Ireland, the courtly Viceroy feigned
a desire to institute an academy, but that when some years later he
waited upon him in London he had forgotten all about it. On the other
hand, his letters to Faulkner the printer are evidence that for many
years he continued to interest himself in the prosperity of Ireland.

She had a long life, and in her old age (she lived to be ninety-eight) could talk to her grandchildren of all the splendours she had seen in her early youth. She knew enough of this world's history. " Queen Anne was only six years dead when she was born, and Queen Victoria came into the world the same year that Lady Palmer died. Sir Robert Walpole, Chatham, Voltaire, Burke, Fox, Grattan, Goldsmith, Johnson, Canning, Peel, and O'Connell were among her contemporaries. She was in her teens when Pope was writing his " Moral Essays," and she lived to know personally, Byron and Moore. Chesterfield died nearly half a century before her, and she survived to see twenty-seven Viceroys after him, holding their state in the Castle of Dublin. The fair faces that had been eclipsed by her surpassing loveliness, the gallant *beaux* that had fluttered round her—all had long gone to their last home; and three generations of their descendants had passed through the Vice-Regal drawing-rooms." [1] In her extreme old age Shiel paid her a visit, and has left so sparkling a description of " the dangerous Papist " in the last year of her life, that I cannot resist giving it here as a suitable conclusion to this passing notice of one of Ireland's most memorable Court beauties.

" The admiration which Lord Chesterfield is known to have entertained for this lady induced me," says Shiel, " to seek an introduction to her. Although rich, she occupied a small lodging in Henry Street, where she lived, secluded and alone. Over the chimney-piece of the front drawing-room was suspended the picture of her Platonic idolater. It was a half-length portrait and had, I believe, been given to her by the man of whose adoration she was virtuously vain. I was engaged looking at this picture while I waited, on the day of my introduction, for this pristine beauty of the Irish Court. While I gazed upon the picture of a man who united so many accomplishments of manner and of mind, and observed the fine intellectual smile which the painter had succeeded in stealing upon animated canvas, I fell into a somewhat imagina-

[1] Burke's *Vicissitudes of Families.*

tive train of thought, and asked myself what sort of a woman 'the dangerous Papist' must have been, in whom the Master of the Graces found such enchanting peril. 'What a charm,' I said, 'must she have possessed, upon whose face and form those bright eyes reposed in illuminated sweetness—how soft and magical must have been the voice, on whose whispers those lips have hung so often—what gracefulness of mind, what an easy dignity of deportment, what elegance of movement, what sweet vivacity of expression, how much polished gaiety and bewitching sentiment must have been united.' I had formed to myself an ideal image of the young, the soft, the fresh, the beautiful, the tender girl, who had fascinated the magician of so many spells. The picture was complete. The castle in its quondam lustre rose before me, and I almost saw my Lord Chesterfield conducting Lady Palmer through the movements of a minuet, when the door was slowly opened, and in the midst of a volume of smoke, which during my phantasmagoric imaginations had not inappropriately filled the room, I beheld, in her own proper person, the being in whose ideal creation I had indulged in a sort of Pygmalion dream. The opening of the door produced a rush of air which caused the smoke to spread out in huge wreaths about her, and a weird and withered form stood in the midst of the dispersing vapour. She fixed on me a wild and sorceress eye, the expression of which was aided by her attitude, by her black attire, her elongated neck, her marked, and strongly moulded, but emaciated features. She leaned with her long arm and her withered hand of discoloured parchment upon an ivory-headed cane, while she stretched forth her interrogating face, and with a smile, not free from ghastliness, inquired my name. I mentioned it; and her expression, as she had been informed I was to visit her, immediately changed. After the ordinary formulas of civility, she placed herself in a huge chair, and entered at once into politics. She was a most vehement Catholic, and was just the sort of person that Sir Harcourt Lees would have ducked for a rebel and a witch. Lord Fingall and the Catholic question were the only subjects in which she seemed to take any interest. Upon the wrongs done to her country she spoke not only with energy, but with eloquence; and with every pinch of snuff, poured out a sentence of sedition, 'S'death, sir, it is not to be borne!' she used to exclaim, as she lifted her figure from the stoop of age, with her eyes flashing with fire, and struck her cane violently on the ground. Wishing to turn the conversation to more interesting matter, I told her I was not surprised at Lord Chesterfield's having called her 'a dangerous Papist.'. I had touched a chord which, though slackened, was not wholly unstrung. The patriot relapsed into the woman, and passing at once from her former look and attitude, she leaned back on her chair, and drawing her withered hands together, while her arms fell loosely and languidly before her, she looked up at the picture of Lord Chesterfield with a melancholy smile. 'Ah,' she said —But I have extended this note beyond all reasonable compass. I think it right to add after so much mention of Lady Palmer, that although she was vain of the admiration of Lord Chesterfield, she took care never to lose his esteem, and that her reputation was without a blemish."

The writer of the present memoir remembers seeing some twenty years ago, at a portrait exhibition held in Dublin,[1] a picture of Miss Ambrose in pastel. It was a face to haunt the memory; a patrician style of beauty, with long seductive eyes, dazzling complexion, and *espiègle* expression. The lips parted in a half mocking smile—one might almost fancy she was about to give expression to some of the bright repartees which delighted Chesterfield. This picture was in the possession of a descendant of the Ambrose family, More O'Ferrall of Ballina, Co. Kildare. A fire took place there a few years ago, in which several valuable pictures were burned, amongst them the portrait of Miss Ambrose. The present owner of Ballina, Mr. Ambrose More O'Ferrall, is of opinion that no portrait of the once famous beauty is in existence. This opinion is confirmed by Mr. Traynor of Essex Quay, Dublin, through whose hands most of the best engravings in Ireland have passed.

[1] The National Portrait Exhibition, 1872.

Beauty, however, is an inheritance. Sometimes, with a sort of caprice very unfair to those who are nearest in descent, it skips a generation, and appears in a great grand-daughter, or grand-niece, who will present a curious reproduction of some bygone belle. In this way the families of Seagrave, Higgins-Brabazon and Campbell at different times and in greater or less degrees, have proved their claim to a share of the beauty bequeathed to them by " the dangerous Papist."

Who has not heard of the two Irish girls who, less than 150 years ago, crossed the Channel which divides the sister countries, and came to seek their fortunes, with only their lovely faces *pour tout potage*. The surpassing beauty of the two sisters has become matter of history, nor is there a parallel instance of mere beauty exciting so extraordinary a sensation as that produced by these portionless girls.

Horace Walpole, writing his usual chronicle to his friend, Sir Horace Mann, at Florence, first mentions the Gunnings in 1751, in these words :—

"The Gunning girls have no fortune and are scarce gentlewomen, but by their mother (she was the Honourable Bridget Bourke, third daughter to Theobald, sixth Viscount Mayo) the Bourkes," he adds, "have Plantagenet blood enough to compensate for the inferior tap of the Gunnings."

In making this statement, the cynic of Strawberry Hill wrote with that reckless disregard of actual facts which marks many of his stories, delightful as they are. Far from being of "an inferior tap," Mr. Gunning was the equal of his wife in good birth. The Gonninges of Tregonning, an ancient Cornish family, had a long look back, and in common with most old families, their branches spread octopus-like in different directions.

There were Gunnings of Langridge, of Swanwicke, Tregarthyn, Trendsburg, and Ashe near Meopham.

The Gunnings in whom we are interested, descended originally from the Gunnings of Ashe, one of whom settled in Kent in the time of Henry VIII., and acquired large estates, situated in the Lath of Shepnay. The family seat was called Gunnings Brook. From this pleasant dwelling-place they were driven, by the persecutions Queen Mary instituted against her Protestant subjects; the Gunnings of Ashe, at this time, returned to their original quarters at Meopham.

In Elizabeth's reign, however, we find Peter Gunning comfortably established as Vicar of Hoo and Gravesend, in Kent. Of his two sons, Peter, the elder, likewise entered the Church, where he had a brilliant, although somewhat chequered, career. Beginning life as tutor to Lord Hatton, he made his way to high posts, being a man of learning and of uncompromising character. He had been presented to a prebend in Canterbury Cathedral and made Bishop of Chichester, when it was demanded of him that he should sign the Covenant. Sooner than go against his conscience he refused, and lost all his benefices, which, however, were restored to him under Charles II., with the additional honours of Chancellor of Oxford and Bishop of Ely. He never married, and seems to have been possessed of considerable wealth. He made no less than seven or eight wills,[1] with numberless codicils.

His brother Richard, who was the immediate ancestor of the Irish branch of Gunnings, was a soldier of fortune, and came to Ireland in the early part of the reign of Charles I., when the Irish plantation, as it was called, was still in full swing. Sir Charles Coote, who had done great service in subduing the rebellion led by Tyrone, had been granted large possessions in Connaught, which he divided amongst his followers; Richard Gunning received a good slice of land close to the Castle of Coote, which Sir Charles, who was Provost Marshal, had erected to protect his property and to be a defence against the constant raids made upon the English settlers by the natives. Under these circumstances the Governor's hands needed to be strengthened by faithful adherents close by. The Castle of Coote, and that of Athleague, which was held

---

[1] The bishop's last will was made at Ely House, Holborn. He left 200*l.* for paving the "*quire*" of the church with marble stone. He is buried in Ely Cathedral. He was born 1613—died 1680. (For Peter the Bishop and Sir Robert Gunning, see Appendix.)

by Richard Gunning, stood several sieges led by Con O'Rorke and John Burke, nicknamed Shane O'Tlevij; the settlers occupying the lands of the natives may be said to have held their lives in the hollow of their hands, living as they did in a wild, desolate region, surrounded with tracts of moor and bog where the miserable peasants, who had been driven from their homes, found shelter and revenged their wrongs by every species of outrage, the lawlessness of the district giving rise to the saying " to Hell or Connaught."

Richard Gunning did his part manfully in helping Sir Charles to repel the attacks of the aborigines. Athleague Castle, which he held for many years, was constantly the scene of hard fighting, but, by degrees, more peaceful times succeeded to these stormy days. As years went on, Richard seems to have taken kindly to his adopted country. Like many of the English settlers, he grew more Irish than the Irish themselves. He married an Irish lady, by whom he had several strong sons and handsome daughters, and before his death he had begun the house which later on became the family residence, and where a distant branch of the family is now living.

In the succeeding generation we find the same conditions repeating themselves until we come to Bryan Gunning, who more nearly approaches our heroines. He married Miss Catherine Gerathy—not an euphonious name albeit intensely Celtic. I am not at all sure whether the Gerathys were chieftains; at any rate, they were of a large clan, and their nationality can never be one moment in dispute.[1]

---

[1] In the church at Roscommon there is a monument erected to Mr. and Mrs. Gunning, with the following epitaph :—

P.M.S.

Here lyes interred the Bodye's of Bryan Gunning. Eqre., of Castle Coote, and Katherine Gunning *alias* Gerathy, his only wife.

They were happily joyn'd together in life
Nor were they long divided in Death ;
She departed this life 13th November, 1715,
He departed this life 22nd January, 1717,
They were the parents of sixteen children,
Of which number
Five sons and five daughters survive
To bewaile the loss of their affectionate care and tender love.

Mrs. Gunning presented her affectionate husband with no less than sixteen pledges of their mutual affection. Of this patriarchal number, John, the second, was destined to have a small niche—in the temple of Fame, I was about to say, but that is decidedly too big a word. It would be more appropriate if I were to place him on a foot-stool near the niche, where his two daughters, whom we shall come to presently, are for all time enshrined.

Their beauty, a divine gift, has placed them there; and some of this beauty came to them from the Gunnings, who were, we are told, a fine race,[1] John, the father, being handsome. His good looks, for it was not his fortune—he being a briefless barrister of the Middle Temple—won him the love of Bridget, daughter to the 6th Viscount Mayo, her mother being a Browne of the Sligo family. The young pair would have their way, and so married on slender means in October, 1731. After a little we find them relegated to the country village of Hemingford Grey, in Huntingdonshire. What brought them into this secluded place is not clear, unless it might be that Mr. Gunning's noble father-in-law had made interest to procure him some small post (inland revenue, or the like), which helped him to live better than did his legal pursuits. Here four children were born, Maria in 1731, Elizabeth in 1732,[2] Lucy and Charlotte in 1740. The two

[1] One of Mr. Gunning's sisters, Margaret Gunning, was the second wife of Theobald, Viscount Mayo. This lady married no less than four times—1stly J. Edwards, Esq.; 2ndly, William Lyster, of Athleague; 3rdly, Captain Houston; 4thly, in 1731, Viscount Mayo. Her picture, which is at Palmerstown, the seat of the present Earl, shows us a pleasant, thoroughly Celtic face, with a sly touch of humour about the mouth, but has no trace of the refined beauty of the Gunnings. After Lord Mayo's death his widow was given the post of housekeeper to Somerset Palace. Another of his sisters married Mr. Nugent, of Carlingford, Westmeath.

[2] The account of this undistinguished portion of the family was written by an ancient parish clerk in a letter to a Mr. Madder of Fulham :—

"I take this freedom," says this document, which is dated from Huntingdonshire, "in *wrighting* to you from an information of Mr. Warrington that you would be glad to have an account of my Townswoman the Notefied, the Famies, Beautifull Miss Gunnings, born at Hemingford Grey, tho' they left the Parish before I had knoledge enough to remember them and I was born in '32. But I will give you the best

last named died and were buried in the chancel of the old church, under a black mavel, upon which there is a simple and pretty inscription.

In 1740, news came that the elder brother of Mr. Gunning was dead—his father had died some years previously—hence he was the owner of the family place and such property as still remained out of the original grant; this, however, had considerably dwindled, as was only natural. Sixteen in a family would make a considerable hole in the largest estate; the claims of his sisters, cousins and aunts did not leave much for John Gunning's family, which was duly increasing, Lizzie having been born in 1741, and a few years later another girl, Catherine, and a boy, John.

With so many children to provide for, Mr. Gunning did not find much benefit from his accession to his father's property, burdened as it already was. While Mrs. Gunning, who had the hard task of trying to make both ends meet, must have often regretted her imprudent marriage, as year after year went by in the dull seclusion of Castle Coote.

Country life in Ireland was a very rough-and-ready sort of affair. "You cannot picture to yourself anything more deplorable," writes Arthur Young; "men of 5000*l.* a year live in houses a man of 700*l.* a year in England would disdain to occupy. Neatness and order is wanting in a surprising degree, and there are a number of small country gentlemen,[1] who hunt all day, and get drunk at night."

account I can, which I believe is better than any man in the country beside myself though I have not the Birth Register for so long a Date and since Dr. Dickens is dead I don't know where it is," but he adds, "there were two more which perhaps you don't know anything about, which I will give you the true Mortalich Register off from a black mavel which lies in our chancel.—(From "Kings and Queens of an hour," FitzGerald.)

[1] At this time there were in Ireland three descriptions or grades of gentlemen.

    1. The half mounted.
    2. The gentleman every inch of him.
    3. Gentlemen to the backbone.

The first were the descendants of Cromwell's soldiers, who were admitted grudgingly into society; if they were good riders, they were called Buckskin Breeches, or Squireens, and had the right to keep the course clear at races. The second class were descendants of some of the

Drink was, in every way, the curse of the whole country; nine gentlemen in ten were impoverished by the great quantity of claret, which, from mistaken notions of hospitality and dignity, they thought it necessary should be drunk in their houses. Horse racing was such a passion that, in 1739, Parliament framed some laws to check, throughout the country, the day labourers taking part in this exciting amusement. A like passion for gambling, sporting, drinking, cockfighting and dancing prevailed, together with a

JOHN GUNNING.

rude but cordial hospitality, and a genuine love of ostentation and extravagance.

John Gunning was precisely the man described in Young's vivid picture ; to the last day of his life he was boastful, extravagant and pretentious ; he took no thought for the morrow, but, when a lucky stroke of fortune gave him the handling of a little money, he spent it at once as a gentleman should.

---

old families, whose estates had paid forfeit, and whose children had been forced to *degrade* themselves by taking to a trade or profession. The last named were the *real old stock* who, although reduced, lived on in the family place.

He knew he was pretty safe in contracting debts, as once at home in his native bogs he could defy his creditors to harm him. The approach of any officer of the law was at once the signal for the whole countryside to rise, and the unfortunate process-server would be hunted down and either sunk in the bog or shot like a dog.[1]

It was amid scenes like these that the future peeresses grew up, with little or no education beyond what they could obtain from the common, or as he was called, hedge school-master. What manners they had, they learned from their Plantagenet mother, who had her reminiscences of her early days to go back upon. It must have gone hard with the poor lady who had been accustomed to better things in her youth, to find herself now unable to give her daughters any of the advantages to which their position entitled them. There is no doubt that the want of proper education was, later on, to be a sad stumbling block in the otherwise successful career of the beauties, and, amidst their signal triumphs, was the cause of many and bitter mortifications. Neither of them could spell decently, and the expressions they made use of, the solecisms and mistakes into which they constantly fell, afforded infinite amusement to the fashionable circles of the society to which their high rank gave them admission.

As their beauty gradually unfolded, the mother's ambition began to awake; stories of Miss Ambrose's success and Lord Chesterfield's admiration for her, filtered down to Roscommon, and stirred in Mrs. Gunning's heart a longing to show to the world the loveliness that was blushing unseen in the wilds of Connaught. Prompted by maternal vanity,

---

[1] The writer remembers hearing an old lady describe an exciting scene she had once witnessed in her father's house. A process server had ventured into the wilds of Roscommon to serve a writ; he failed, however, to accomplish his purpose, and the indignant debtor threatened to shoot him dead and have his body thrown into the bog. The unfortunate man threw himself on the protection of the ladies of the house, who managed to conceal him somewhere until daylight came, and then the eldest daughter, a girl of 17 (who narrated the story) walked across the country road to the nearest village, in company with the frightened wretch, who clung to the skirt of her dress. It was four o'clock of a summer's morning, and the scene was never forgotten by her.

she made a last rally of all her resources, and removed herself and her five children to Dublin, to partake, as far as they were able, of the gaieties of the capital. Her energy is highly to be commended. Without some such stroke of management, Maria and Elizabeth might have done as she herself had done, married some illiterate fox-hunting squire, and gone to their graves unknown and uncoroneted.

It was in the year 1750 that Mrs. Gunning took this first step on the road that was to lead to fortune. It was in the height of the season that she arrived in Dublin and settled herself in Brittain Street, a locality which is now a mean quarter of the town, occupied by small provision shops and a large hospital. In 1751 it was, however, well considered; its proximity to Rutland Square [1]—then the principal square in Dublin—on one side and the Mall—now Sackville Street —on the other, making it a fashionable locality. Many persons of rank occupied houses, amongst others Lord Kingsland, Lady Alice Hume, Mr. Putland, etc.

The moment for the arrival of the young beauties was well chosen. The town was unusually full, and a brilliant season was expected. Dublin, in spite of its manifold drawbacks, was a city of many fascinations; there was a wealthy earl as Viceroy, successor to the courtly Chesterfield, and himself of the house of Stanhope; his court, if not quite so distinguished for hospitality, was brilliant; there were balls and ridottos, and a constant stream of witty, gifted, titled people coming to and fro, and causing a stir and racket. There were good chances in the matrimonial market, and Mrs. Gunning may be credited with building many an airy castle, for had not her beautiful daughters, with their connections, every chance of success? Alas! in a few days her airy fabrics were for the time dissolved, an untoward incident bidding fair to defeat all her fine anticipations. The story has been often told, but it is so dramatic that it bears repeating.

If Dublin had its attractions it had also its temptations,

---

[1] The houses in Rutland Square are large, commodious mansions; they were occupied almost exclusively by the nobility, who later removed to Merrion Square, the West End of Dublin.

especially for a man like Mr. Gunning, pompous, wishing to appear what he was not, and desirous to take his part in all the fashionable vices of the day, gambling, racing, drinking. It was easy for him to gratify his tastes in these directions, and to lay more burdens on the already heavily mortgaged estate. Whether it was in this way that the incident occurred, or whether some former creditor unexpectedly turned up, we do not know, in either case the result was the same.

A friendly hint was given to Mr. Gunning that the sheriffs' officers were likely to put in an appearance in Brittain Street, and that it would be wise for him to go, as the phrase went, into retirement. The bailiffs, finding their prisoner flown, took possession of the furniture and effects, while Mrs. Gunning in vain tried to move their stony hearts. Her children, in tears, clung round their distracted mother; their cries reached the ears of a lady who chanced to be passing; this was George Ann Bellamy, a young actress, whose beauty and histrionic talent were causing a furore at Sheridan's Theatre, in Smock Alley. Without a moment's hesitation, this impulsive creature obeyed the thought which prompted her to assist anyone in distress, and as the hall door stood open, she went in, and found in the parlour an agitated but elegant lady, surrounded by four lovely girls and a sweet cherub of a boy. Mrs. Gunning received her visitor politely, complimenting her, in the high-flown language of the time, upon possessing such sentiments; she then entered upon the reason why she found herself in such a situation. Mr. Gunning was away, and Lord Mayo, her brother, was likewise out of reach. She introduced his name, and that of several of her high connections many times. The interview ended by the actress promising to send her man-servant, as soon as it grew dark, with directions to stand under the drawing-room window and catch any light articles which could be thrown to him with safety. Miss Bellamy did more; she received the whole family into her house, keeping them until some arrangement could be made with the creditors. After a time the two younger children went to reside with their mother's sister, Miss Bourke, the rest of the family still remaining as the guests of their generous friend. It was during this visit that the three girls, for Ann Bellamy was hardly out of her teens, went by way of a frolic to consult a famous fortune-teller, who was then astonishing all Dublin by her wonderful skill in reading the future, and recounting the past of those who visited her in her mysterious den in Capel Street. The girls were frightened when they were introduced to the prophetess, who sat in a curtained recess, her head enveloped in dark draperies, while her piercing eyes seemed to penetrate the inmost soul of her timid visitors. The seer, however, was all gentleness to the sisters; she held their pretty hands in hers, and gazed admiringly at their eager, lovely faces, which were suffused with blushes and happy smiles, as she unfolded to them a future laden with golden prospects. Maria was to marry an earl and be loved exceedingly, Elizabeth to soar even higher, and be destined to wear on her brow two coronets, both of strawberry leaves. The delighted beauties withdrew to make way for their companion. Now it happened that the actress, by way of testing the powers of the prophetess, had placed upon the third finger of her left hand the golden symbol of matrimony, but this attempt at deception drew down upon her the wrath of the gipsy.

In a voice utterly different from that in which she had addressed the Gunnings, the prophetess exclaimed, "Take off that wedding ring! You never were, you never will be married." Then, bending over the frightened actress, she whispered in her ear a few words of terrible import, and vanished into Cimmerian darkness.

Strangely enough, before long these prophecies came true. In the case of the Gunnings, it probably laid the foundation of their future fortunes, as it kindled in their minds the ambition to rise to greatness. Ann Bellamy [1] drifted off to London and

---

[1] GEORGE ANN BELLAMY.

The career of this unfortunate woman who was by birth Irish, can only be glanced at. It would serve no useful purpose to give it in detail. Her beauty was of the most attractive kind, and from her first

there began the wild career which made her notorious in a time when female virtue was at a low ebb. Her story is a sad record of the good things of fortune recklessly bartered for the pleasures of the moment. The intimacy between the beauties and their benefactress diminished as such incongruous friendships generally do, but in the first warmth the following ill-spelt, ill-written letter from Maria Gunning has been preserved :—

appearance on the stage she captivated her audience. She had likewise powerful protectors, her father, Lord Tyrawley, not only paid for her education but induced his sister, Mrs. O'Hara, to look after the young girl and take her out in society. When she came to Dublin she had troops of friends, and the story of her triumph over Garrick and how she filled the house when he had to play to a thin one, is amusing reading. Unfortunately she fell into the hands of her scheming, good-for-nothing mother, an actress also, who had married Mr. Bellamy an actor of small parts, many years younger than herself. For a long time George Ann behaved with much propriety, and her reputation was so unblemished, and her friends so powerful, that she surmounted the rather dubious incident of being carried off from Smock Alley Theatre by Lord Byron, a wild young nobleman. After this Miss Bellamy distinctly stated her terms were marriage, a coach, and two footmen. The first seemed quite possible, her beauty and simplicity winning her many honourable lovers. She was, however, her own enemy. When in the zenith of popular favour and playing good parts at Drury Lane, one night when her turn came she was nowhere to be found; after a time the curtain drew up and Quin appearing informed the audience that their favourite had eloped with Mr. Metham, an admirer of hers, who would certainly provide her with the coach and footmen. From this time her downward course began. She returned to the stage, but had lost her beauty and youthful simplicity. She was all but hissed off; she tired out all the friends she had by frequent applications for money, and finally found her way to the Queen's Bench. The actors, always generous to those of the profession who are in want, got up a benefit for her, and Miss Farren then in the height of her popularity, spoke the address :—

> " But see, oppressed with gratitude and tears !
> To pay her beauteous tribute she appears."

The curtain then drew up and discovered Miss Bellamy seated in an arm-chair, from which she in vain tried to rise, but her tears overcame her, she managed to utter a few words, and then the curtain descended. After this came years of misery until death closed the scene. Before her death she published the story of her life under the name of "An Apology;" it is an uninteresting, ill-written record of no value. In it she states, with perhaps no ground of truth, the ungrateful treatment she received from her quondam friend (then Lady Coventry), who in the height of her triumphant career, came one night to Drury Lane, and when Miss Bellamy was acting some tragic part burst into a scream of laughter and quitted the theatre. This would not seem to be in keeping with Maria's good nature on ordinary occasions.

"I receid my dearest Miss Bellamy's letter at last after her long
silence indeed I was very Jealous with you but you make me amens
in Letting me hear from you now, it gives me great joy and all our
familey to hear that y⁺ dear mama and y⁺ Dearest Self are in perfect
health to be sure that y⁺ Relations where fighting to see which of them
shod have you the Longest with them. I am very unfortunate to be in
the country when our Vauxhall was. . . If I was in Town I shod be
thear and I believe I should be more delighted than at a publicker diversion. . . . . . I don't beleive it was Mr. Knox you read of at Bath for he
is hear;
"Dublin is the stupites place. . . . I beleive Sheridan can get no one
to play with him is doing all he can to get funds for him sef to be sure you
have heard he is marrd for sirtain to Miss Chamberlain—a sweet pare—
"I must bid a due and shall only say I am D⁺
"Your ever affe⁺ᵗˡʸ
"M. Gunning."

Not only the orthography, but the whole tenour of this
letter, with its local gossip, marks the ill-educated mind of the
writer; such deficiencies are not easily overcome; it is a fact
that has been often noticed, that a want of early training, although it may be sufficiently veneered to pass muster for one
occasion, is sure to break out in unlady-like words or actions,
under provocation or excitement.

During the dark days that followed on her expulsion from
Brittain Street, Mrs. Gunning must have lost heart, for her
brilliant anticipations seemed as far off from realization as
when she was pining in the wilds of Connaught. Her husband
being still in retirement, her beautiful daughters had no
opportunity of exhibiting their charms to the world. Despair
seized upon her, and it was said she seriously contemplated the
idea of placing them on the stage, where their beauty would
be certain to make its mark. This, however, rests solely upon
the testimony of Walpole, who circulated the story amongst
his friends. The small grain of truth that it did possess was
probably due to the fact that, through Miss Bellamy, Sheridan,
then manager of Smock Alley Theatre, had become a friend of
the mother and daughters, and warmly admired them. Mrs.
Gunning's Irish pride, however, would never have stooped to
such a lowering of the family dignity as would have been involved in allowing her children to do anything towards maintaining themselves, neither had she relinquished the hope that
their beauty might yet win for them a high position. Already

people had begun to talk of some wonderful beauties who had
been seen at the theatre and at Ranelagh. Mrs. Gunning's
connections began to take notice of them, and a lady, probably
Mrs. Butler, who lived in Stephen's Green, and was one of the
great leaders of fashion, interested herself to procure a card
for the Birth-night Ball at the Castle. Here was Cinderella's
glass coach coming round.

Tradition has it that the fairy god-mother on this occasion
was Sheridan, who lent the young beauties the tinsel finery
from the theatrical wardrobe of Smock Alley. Here again a
glance at the illustrations in *Bell's Theatre* or any other theatrical magazine of the time is enough to prove the absurdity
of this story. The costumes worn by Mrs. Woffington, or Mrs.
Yates, as Monimia, or Belvidera, would hardly have been
suitable for a young lady's ball-dress ; the loan may have consisted of some ornament for the hair or neck, which the good-
natured manager was only too pleased to supply. In whatever
guise they appeared, the two sisters saw and conquered ; their
success far surpassed their mother's most sanguine expecta-
tions. The ball which was to be the turning point in the lives
of our heroines, was given in honour of the King's birthday.
The dancing was in the new room, commenced during Chesterfield's viceroyalty. " Between the dances the company retired
to the long gallery,[1] where, as they passed slowly through,
they stopped at shops elegantly formed, where was cold eating
and all sorts of wines and sweetmeats, and the whole most
beautifully disposed by transparent paintings through which
a shade was cast like moonlight. Flutes and other soft
instruments were playing all the while, but, like the candles,
unseen. Fountains of lavender water diffused a grateful odour
through this fairy scene, which certainly surpassed everything
of the kind in Spenser."[2]

We may imagine how this seeming Paradise must have
delighted our two beauties and made them unconscious of the
effect they were producing. Fascinatingly coy, with all the

---

[1] This must have been the throne room. St. Patrick's Hall was not
begun until 1777, and was finished in 1783.
[2] Victor : History of the Stage.

timidity of untutored country lasses, yet bold at the same
time with all the daring of their perfect simplicity, artlessly
captivating by the ingenuous ardour of their enthusiasm for
the gay sight in which they found themselves for the first
time, they, the unknown nobodies, *entéred*, so to speak, the
spectators and won an easy victory over the established
beauties of the town, amongst whom were Mrs. Madden, then
the toast of Dublin, Miss Ambrose, still reckoned a beauty,
and supposed to be wearing the willow for the departed
Chesterfield. There was no lack of pretty women, and one
of the great English beauties, Lady Caroline Petersham,
lately married to the Viceroy's eldest son, was there. She
was one of the Beauty-Fitzroys mentioned in Horace Walpole's
poem of "The Beauties." Luckily for the Irish girls, she
was of a singularly generous and unselfish nature, so we
gather from the numerous anecdotes which are to be found in
Walpole's wonderful collection of gossip. Lady Caroline
was more inclined to help these unknown girls, whom she
did not look upon as rivals, than to be jealous of their
youthful charms. Of the kindly Viceroy they made a complete
conquest. We can imagine how joyful was the return from
this, their first taste of real triumph. Their reign was now
beginning; by the next morning the whole town rang with
their names, and the fame of their beauty travelled to England.
"All you have heard of the Gunnings," writes Mrs. Delany,[1]
"is true, except their having a fortune, but I am afraid they
have a greater want than that, which is discretion." One
does not know what this stricture was pointed at, probably
some youthful gaiety which offended the Dean's lady; for the
rest, discretion was unfortunately lacking to Maria all through
her career. And now they were to appear on a larger stage,
where argus eyes would be on the watch for any lapses of
decorum. Lord Harrington, the kind-hearted Viceroy, had
spoken words of wisdom to the proud and happy Mrs. Gunning,
advising her to take her lovely daughters to London, where there
would be a proper field for the display of charms like theirs.

---

[1] Mrs. Delany's letters to her sister, 1750.

He likewise offered her introductions to good houses. Mrs. Gunning was not loth to follow his counsel which coincided with her own ambitious views; the girls too, were eager, they had drunk of the intoxicating waters of success, and wished for a deeper draught; and had not also the fortune-teller prophesied one should be a duchess and the other a countess, and was not London full of dukes and lords? The only obstacle lay in the want of funds, but this seems to have been got over in a miraculous manner. Where there's a will there's a way—and, as we have seen, Mrs. Gunning was a woman of determination. Small sums were got from relations, and for some *unexplained* reason, Mrs. Gunning, probably through Lord Harrington's influence, received a grant of £150, upon the Irish Establishment.[1] She likewise undertook the charge of a young lady, Miss Plaistow[2] who wished to visit London and enjoy its gaieties under proper chaperonage, and as she was wealthy, this probably added to Mrs. Gunning's means of living. The party set forth in the highest spirits; it was a long journey at that time to London, it took four days and perhaps longer if the passage to Chester was made in bad weather. Persons of distinction generally travelled in the

[1] The Irish Establishment was a real grievance and most justifiable cause of complaint. Pensions were given to all manner of persons of doubtful reputation, whose names could not appear on the civil list of England. Catherine Sedley, James II.'s mistress, had a grant of 5000*l*. a year; the Walmoden and Schulenburg were provided for in a similar manner, in George I.'s and II.'s time. George III. saddled the Irish list with 3000*l*. a year for his sister, the unfortunate Caroline Mathilda. In Mrs. Gunning's case, however, the grant was merely a piece of jobbing.

[2] Catherine Plaistow, daughter of General Plaistow was of Dutch extraction. She was very pretty, and being seen with the Gunnings was considered a "third beauty" of course in a minor degree; she married Cyrus Trapeaud, a relation of Marshal Turenne. At the battle of (1743) Dettingen he saved the life of George the Second, whose horse had run away with him. Ensign Trapeaud seized the bridle and when the King alighted he said, "Now, if my horse will run away my legs shall not!" the young officer got rapid promotion to reward him for his service. He was made General Trapeaud 1783, and was alive in 1800, living in one of the Adam houses in Mansfield Street, where Paoli and other distinguished personages visited him and his wife, who retained much of the beauty handed down in her picture by Sir Joshua Reynolds. The General, who was blind and 83 years of age, died in 1801 and is buried at Chelsea Hospital. Mrs. Trapeaud then removed to Welbeck Street, where she died in 1805. They had no children, but had adopted a nephew of hers.

Lord Lieutenant's yacht, for which they paid five guineas each to the captain. It was, however, a mark of favour to get a passage, as the sailing vessels that plied from Dunleary to Chester were rough in their accommodation; from Chester there was a road journey, either by posting or coach.

All things taken into consideration, it was a bold venture which only ultimate success could justify, failure would indeed have been disastrous; nothing, however, "succeeds like success," and the triumphant career of the Gunnings has given them a place in history. It must, however, be remembered, when considering their good fortune, that in the day in which they lived beauty was all powerful. There never was a period when so much homage was paid to female loveliness. Men went down in worship before their mistress, fought duels to get possession of a ribbon or a flower she had worn, and threw all prudence to the winds to obtain her. Women taken from the lowest classes and from what was, in those days, thought to be the lowest of all, the stage, were raised to the highest positions, so that the actual rise of the Gunnings taking into account that they were of good birth, is not a matter that should excite astonishment. There is, however, in their career certain elements of dramatic interest which makes their story always fresh and interesting.

It was in the spring of the year 1751 that Mrs. Gunning arrived in London. Maria was then in her nineteenth, Elizabeth in her eighteenth year. Both being lovely, it would be difficult to say which was really the lovelier. Judging from their portraits, one would say that Maria had the more delicate features and the sweeter smile, while Elizabeth's face wears a composed and yet arch expression. The character of their beauty is much the same; both have the long, seductive eyes, delicate mouths, exquisite colouring, and oval faces; the features harmoniously set.

The moment of their appearance was well chosen; the world of fashion, which Thackeray describes so graphically as embroidered, be-ruffled, be-laced, snuff-boxed, red-heeled, and impertinent, was always on the look-out for novelty. The *beaux* were in the humour to elect the Irish girls to the dignity of standard beauties—a word to which our "Professional beauty" answers. We find from garrulous Walpole that their names were in every one's mouth. They were said to be the handsomest women alive, "although for my part," he adds, "I think their being two so handsome and such perfect figures is their chief excellence, for *singly* I have seen much handsomer women than either of them." There were others who supported this view; the Duchess of Somerset found them too tall, and Selwyn thought their faces too long. Mrs. Delany considered Maria had a silly look about her mouth, and again asserts that both young ladies were wanting in discretion. Dr. Carlyle raved of Elizabeth.

In all these criticisms we can read between the lines. It was the old story. The beauties who had been "standards" were not minded to lower their colours, and *their* friends and admirers backed them up. When we look into the chronicles of the time, it is amazing what a galaxy of lovely faces present themselves. Lady Stafford and "lovely Mrs. Pitt![1] Miss Chudleigh, afterwards the too famous Duchess of Kingston—and at this very time secretly married to Lord Hervey—the charming Miss Bishops, the beautiful Peggy Banks, with whom the Duke of Cumberland—hero of Culloden—was madly in love, Lady Diana Spencer,[2] Lady Caroline Petersham, and Lady Rochford, "with whom all the royals" were in love.

The Gunnings possessed the charm of novelty; they had a certain freshness and natural wit, born of their Irish nature, which attracted the graver Saxon, as did likewise the soft Celtic voice, tinged with a decided brogue, which to English ears has a certain music. Their somewhat hoydenish manners, which occasionally degenerated into vulgar boldness, were pronounced to be youthful gaiety, and their rather doubtful remarks were called the naïveté of extreme innocence. This innocence, however, exposed them to

---

[1] This lady, a celebrated beauty, was the daughter of Sir Richard Atkins. Her husband, who treated her badly, was made Lord Rivers.

[2] 1st married to Lord Bolingbroke; 2udly, Topham Beauclerk.

rather an unpleasant adventure. Being a great deal too frank, the girls imprudently confided to some of their new friends the visit they had paid in Dublin to the wonderful fortune-teller, together with the great things that were to befall them. Said the simple Maria, " Shure Lizzie is to be a duchess twice over, and I am only to be a countess, but I am not one bit jealous, for shure my lord is to love me, and that is what I care for most."

It can hardly be believed that this simplicity should have been taken advantage of, and that two men—they cannot be called gentlemen—actually employed a low fellow, to whom they paid a sum of money, to personate one of the noblemen for whom the sisters were sighing. Mr. Thrale, the rich Southwark brewer, at this time not married to the lovely Esther Salusbury, was one of the conspirators, and brought the pretended lord to introduce him as an admirer to Maria. Mrs. Gunning, with wonderful acumen, saw there was something suspicious in the whole matter. She quietly kept a watch on the proceedings, and, having satisfied herself that the supposed nobleman was an impostor, she ordered both him and his companions to leave her house. One cannot but feel pleased that this meanness should have been circumvented. This was not the only proof the beauties received to show them that their success was raising up a horde of enemies who would stop at no nasty trick " to drive rivals from the field." The story is well known of the Duchess of Bedford's [1] masquerade, to which all the world was going, and towards which the Gunnings, mother and daughters, cast longing eyes, but, like the Peri outside the gates of Paradise, had no chance of admission. With their usual silly frankness they again confided in their friends, and were again hoaxed by receiving a sham card of invitation. Once more they were saved from what would have been " social damnation " by their mother's quick intelligence. Scanning the card curiously, she detected some erasures which excited her

[1] Gertrude, daughter to the 1st Earl Gower, married 1737, John, Duke of Bedford. She was a well-known figure in the latter half of the last century, and was strangely mixed up in the Gunning history.

suspicion; the application of a chemical exposed the fraud—another name was written underneath. With great courage and ready wit, Mrs. Gunning turned this trick, which was intended for her discomfiture, into a cause of triumph. Card in hand, she waited upon the duchess—with whom she had no previous acquaintance—taking care to be accompanied by one of her lovely daughters. While the mother discoursed upon the ill-natured hoax, the eyes of her hostess travelled over the fair face and elegant figure of the young girl. She was a well-established leader of society, and knew the value of such attractions. Needless to say she substituted a genuine invitation for the mock card.

In all the early history of the beauties there are but meagre details. One would wish for more specific information as to where they lived, and many other minor circumstances of interest which have not been handed down. Thanks, however, to the indefatigable flow of gossip that was kept up in the last century, when the letters to friends at a distance took the place of "society papers," we are kept pretty well *au courant* of what concerned people in the world. In this way we catch constant glimpses of our heroines as they went on their triumphant progress.

Society in 1751 did not differ essentially from society in 1894; there may have been, perhaps, more easy freedom in intercourse, for it was then a more restricted circle. There was a great deal of card playing; "there were cards everywhere." Reading was considered ill-bred. "Books! don't talk to me of books," said the old Duchess of Marlborough; "the only books I know are men and cards." Even the great "dungeon" of learning, Dr. Johnson, regretted he had never learnt how to play games of chance. There was also a flagrant display of wickedness, and, in spite of Mrs. Lynn Linton's declaration of the great purity and sweetness of the women of the eighteenth century as compared with those of the present day, the reading of the old memoirs would incline one to suppose that all this goody behaviour was put on. It might have existed in the country, but it was speedily lost sight of in town, where an extraordinary license of manners prevailed. Ladies of the rank of the Duchess of Ancaster,[1] with Mrs. Bouverie and Mrs. Crewe, aspired to be pretty fellows, and went to masquerades attired as *men*. We are more surprised to find that Mrs. Damer, the "infanta" of Walpole and the friend of Mary and Agnes Berry, adopted this fashion, but it was in her young days when example was contagious. Her cousin, the fast young wife of Lord Grandison, Gertrude Conway,[2] the queen of beauty, beat the record for eccentricity, to call by a mild name a total want of decorum. It was her custom to be present at the suppers given at break of day after the masquerades were over. These suppers, which "no lady need leave save those who are too immodest to stay" (so ran the formula), were marked by hard drinking and singing; and it was the custom to fling open the windows and pelt the eager, hungry, thirsty, howling crowd below with half empty bottles. It was not surprising that when ladies of rank so lowered their standard, men should treat them much as they did their "Delias from Drury Lane."

To return to the Gunnings. We can follow them through all the gay scenes of this brilliant London season. To Ranelagh on a water party with Lady Caroline Petersham, all the fashionable lords in attendance; to St. James's Palace one Sunday afternoon, when they were presented to the old King George II., and kindly received, an event duly chronicled in the *Dublin Journal*. Then we see them at the theatre surrounded by admirers, and at Vauxhall, where an admiring crowd, growing larger every minute, followed them wherever they went. This also happened when they walked in the Mall. Lord Clermont describes how, one Sunday, when the young ladies were in the Park, such crowds collected to gaze at them, and so violent and impertinent was their

---

[1] The Duchess of Ancaster was not to the manner born, being the daughter of Joe Panton, a well-known jockey. The Duchesses of Ancaster were all singular. Says Horace Walpole, "the three last were never sober."

[2] Gertrude Conway, daughter to Lord Hertford, elder brother of General Conway, married the Earl of Grandison, now an extinct Irish title.

curiosity, that he, as well as the other gentlemen who escorted the ladies, had to draw their swords in order to protect them from the too bold admiration of the mob, while they made a precipitate retreat to Lord Harrington's house at the corner of St. James's stable yard.[1]

The girls were more frightened than flattered at these proofs of the power of their beauty, for at this stage of early girlhood they were singularly modest and simple. The public, however, are never restrained by any feelings of delicacy, and continued to follow and stare at their favourites whenever they showed themselves in the streets or parks. Here is a little scene which reads as if it happened only yesterday :—

"'Tis a warm day," writes George Selwyn, from Whyte's to Lord Carlisle, "and some one proposes a stroll to Betty's fruit-shop ;[2] suddenly the cry is raised, 'the Gunnings are coming,' and we all tumble out to gaze and to criticize."

Walpole too, has their names for ever at the end of his pen, prompted, one would say, by a petty feeling of jealousy that mere women should usurp so much attention. He says, writing to Sir Horace Mann at Florence, "You, who knew England formerly, will be surprised to hear that the 'folly' at White's,[3] together with the famous beauties, are more talked of than the change in the Ministry." And in

---

[1] In 1751 the now fashionable region of Hyde Park and Belgravia was a country suburb, and London proper was confined to Mayfair. St. James's Park was the fashionable promenade, and a woman of fashion or recognized beauty never failed to show herself there, accompanied by as many gallants as she could muster.

[2] Betty's fruit-shop, facing St. James's Park, kept by Mrs. Elizabeth Neale, better known by the name of Betty. She kept, for many years, a house in St. James's Street as a fruit-shop, and had the first pre-eminence in her occupation, and might be called the "Queen of Apple-women"; her knowledge of families and characters of the last and present age was wonderful; she was a woman of pleasing manners. Mason introduced her name into the Heroic Epistles :—

> And patriot Betty fix her fruit-shop there.
>
> "Selwyn's Memoirs."

[3] The "folly" was a dinner of seven young men, who bespoke it to the utmost extent of expense; one article was a tart made of Duke's cherries, from a hot-house, and a rule was made that only one glass of champagne was taken out of each bottle.—"History of White's Club."

the next letter, " They make more noise than any one
of their predecessors since Helen of Troye; a crowd follows
them wherever they walk, and at Vauxhall they were driven
away, but," he adds, " this mobbing is a sure sign of success,
although now and again it be attended with a certain amount
of inconvenience as when they went to see Hampton Court.
As they were going into the 'Beauty Room' another company
arrived; the housekeeper called out 'Ladies, here are the
beauties,' upon which," adds Walpole, " the two Gunnings flew
into a passion and roundly abused the woman, telling her they
had come to see the Palace, not to be made part of the show."

MISS GUNNING.
(*Watch-paper portrait.*)

Another proof, if indeed proofs were wanting, of their growing fame was now given by the appearance of their portraits
in print shops. Sayer, who was the fashionable engraver of
the day, issued a small vignette engraved from a picture
by Cotes.[1] This little print was intended for a "watch-
paper," which was then a fashionable necessity, most men
carrying about with them the portrait of some standard
beauty, which was made of the size and shape to carry inside

---

[1] Through the kindness of the Hon. Gerald Ponsonby, I am able to
present my readers with an engraving of this interesting little print,
now exceedingly rare.

the lid of the large sized watches of the day, with their highly chased cases.

This evidence of the general appreciation of her daughters' beauty, although, no doubt, gratifying to Mrs. Gunning, was not the form most pleasing to her maternal heart. She very rightly considered that admiration to be worth having needs the seal, or trade mark of brilliant matrimonial success, just as a good sale marks the real value of all purchasable articles. It was true that some of the best matches of the season had fluttered round the sisters ; Lord Coventry had been dangling after Maria; a Scotch Earl beset Elizabeth, besides an infinite number of smaller fry: but the season had come to an end without either of the girls receiving an offer worth acceptance. Their father who had now joined them, was no doubt a detriment to them, his loud-voiced pomposity being singularly discordant to English ears.

With spirits somewhat lowered—and no wonder, for God help the poor souls, they must have had a fine load of debt by this time—the mother and daughters betook themselves to Bath. Everyone went to Bath in those days, and drank the waters there, instead of going, as they do now, to Homburg or Royat—it was London over again—just as we go abroad now and find Lady C——, and Lady D——, and H.R.H. mixed up with the Tuggs' from Ramsgate, and the Ledburys' from Brighton. Only there was a little more gossip and scandal, and general wickedness. We may give the rein to our imagination about the Gunnings at Bath, for we know nothing ; Walpole wasn't there this autumn, or he would have written to some of his cronies, and filled up the vacuum by chronicling every doing of the girls ; poor things, they must have had heavy hearts, for what was to happen if nothing came of all the fashion and the mobbing, the extravagance, and the fortune-teller's prophecy. Something, however, was coming, the Pumpkin was going to turn into the carriage and four white ponies, and the Cinderellas were to be real, great ladies ; it was only a question of a very few weeks before all London would be talking of their triumph. Christmas saw them once more in the Park, looking more beautiful than ever. "I saw these goddesses of Gunnings," writes Mrs. Montague, "wrapped in quilted satin pelisses, their lovely throats hid by rich furs, which set off the brilliancy of their complexions. In this garb, the beauties took their noble admirers' hearts by storm and fairly beat down and extinguished every remnant of prudence."

By that strange law of contrast which seems to govern all love affairs, the Duke of Hamilton, a wild, boisterous, hard-drinking, dissipated man, damaged alike in fortune and in health, attached himself to Elizabeth, attracted no doubt by her demure and rather sober gravity, while the Earl of Coventry, pompous and proud, was more than ever infatuated by the somewhat hoydenish manners of the lovely Maria. Both men were desperately in love, but the Duke's wooing was in a more advanced stage. His courtship was watched by a hundred curious, unfriendly eyes, and supplied gossip for as many tea-tables. It shows infinite tact upon the part of the young girl that she should have played her game as she did, with open cards, while the audience looked on, making their bets as to the result almost within her hearing. Elizabeth's demure, composed nature carried her through this trying situation. She appeared everywhere with her admirer, sitting beside him when he moved an address in the House of Lords. In this month of December, Lord Chesterfield, who was now living in the retirement of private life, busy with his letters to his son, threw open Chesterfield House,[1] which was just finished, and inaugurated the occasion by a splendid entertainment. The nobility of the eighteenth century practised, it may be to an excess, the motto of *noblesse oblige*, a motto which, by the way, has fallen very much into disuse. Except in very rare cases, noble birth imposes now-a-days no obligations upon the holder of the dignity; this may be as well—especially as we are gradually approaching a Commonwealth—but when we come to reflect upon the men who played such a part in the history of the Georges, we cannot refrain from admiration. In spite of their many grave defects, their loose morality, their extravagant habits, they had some grand

[1] Chesterfield House now belongs to Mr. Magniac.

qualities, and there was nothing petty about them. They patronized men of letters and artists with a generosity that was admirable, their houses were palaces, their entertainments princely ; and so we come back to Chesterfield House, where every person of distinction was bidden, and where all the world went.

"The assembly at my Lord Chesterfield's was made to show the house, which is really magnificent," writes Walpole next day to Sir Horace Mann, and then he goes on to give him an insight into Elizabeth Gunning's chances of being " duchessed." " The Duke of Hamilton, having already fallen in love with her six weeks ago at a masquerade, made such violent love to her to-night at one end of the room, while he was playing at Pharaoh or ' Faro ' at the other, that he saw neither the bank nor his own cards, which were of three hundred each, and soon lost a thousand. I own I thought that all this parade looked ill for the poor girl, and could not conceive if he was so engaged with his mistress as to disregard such sums, why he played at all."

Lord Chesterfield was of the same opinion, and confided to Selwyn, he did not think it looked well for the *lady's honour.* The bets made as to the probable issue of the courtship now ran into large sums. Elizabeth Gunning, however, was just the girl who could keep so bold a lover within proper limits ; her coldness of temperament standing her in good stead. She never lost her head, as when, two evenings later than the Chesterfield entertainment, being left purposely at home whilst her mother and Maria went abroad, she so inflamed the duke's passion by a due mixture of coquetry and coyness, that in an access of love he swore they should be married that very night; Mrs. Gunning returning at the proper moment, a parson was sent for and the party, repairing to Mayfair chapel, this strange wedding took place at midnight on February 14th, 1752.

The next day all London was in a tumult. Stories flew like so many windmills ; the " Benjamin Backbites " and the " Mrs. Candours " wagged their tongues in every drawing-room ; the women were furious, " Mad," says Walpole, " that so much beauty had its effect. The event, " he writes to Sir Horace Mann, " which has made the greatest noise since my last is the extempore wedding of the two Gunnings,[1] who have made so vehement a noise. Lord Coventry, a young lord of the patriot breed, has long dangled after the eldest virtuously for her honour, not very honourably with regard to his own credit. About six weeks ago, Duke Hamilton, the very reverse of the earl, not debauched, extravagant, fell in love with the youngest at a masquerade." Then he goes on to give an account of Lord Chesterfield's assembly, adding, " I own I was so little a professor of love that I thought matters looked ill for the poor girl, but two nights later, when her mother and sister were at Bedford House, a sudden ardour, either of wine or love, seized upon him, a parson was promptly sent for, but on arriving refused to officiate without the important essentials of license or ring. The duke swore and talked of calling in the Archbishop. Finally the parson's scruples gave way, the licence was overlooked, and the lack of the traditional gold ring was supplied by the ring of a bed curtain ! " He does not say what was really the case, that the party set off at midnight in a coach to the church in Mayfair, where the marriage took place.

One of the first results of the marriage was that the duke's example incited Maria's graver and more dignified lover to a declaration, fearful that he would lose her. Lord Coventry made up his vacillating mind, and three weeks later, on March 1st, 1751, led the more fascinating of the two sisters " to the hymeneal altar." A poem was published at the time entitled the "Charms of Beauty, or the Grand contest between the fair Hibernians and the English Toasts."[2] It was occasioned by the marriage of his Grace the Duke of Hamilton with Miss Elizabeth Gunning, and the expected marriage of her elder sister with a certain noble earl, and is a most amusing picture of the excitement caused by the success of the Irish girls.

---

[1] This is a curious mistake. Maria was not married till the following March.
[2] The sisters were painted as " the fair Hibernians." See Appendix.

Ye British fair, whom Envy may excite
To blast the Gunnings with envenomed spite,
Can these fair breasts such rancour entertain,
Those eyes so brilliant sparkle with Disdain ?

Hibernian land amid its bogs and Fens
Has cultivated Beauty, Wit and Sense.
How widely have we erred from the truth
To call the Irish wild and scorn their youth.
By foreign fashions they are not disguised,
What Heaven gives, by them is choicely prized.

Long have the Gunnings, both divinely fair,
Unrivalled shone on Beauty's glorious sphere,
Long been the Toasts amongst the gay and great,
And daily conquests prostrate at their feet.

The noble Hamilton confessed his Flame,
A name recorded in the books of Fame ;
Eliza's virtue clothed with Beauty's robe
He loves beyond the riches of the Globe.

The noble C——y tho' *sage* and *wise*
Above his years, and good without disguise,
Feels the most soft impression on his heart,
And yields himself a Captive to desert
Etc., etc.

MARIA, COUNTESS OF COVENTRY.

[To face page 87.

MARIA, COUNTESS OF COVENTRY.

BORN 1731, DIED 1760.

IN the old-fashioned three-volume novels marriage generally
concluded, as it were, the heroine's adventures, the curtain
being supposed to drop upon an existence of never-ending
felicity. This misleading picture of the realities of life has
in our generation been considerably modified, and our authors
(especially the women writers) present their heroine either on
her wedding day or immediately after, their portrait of
married life being as uninviting as the former one was
imaginative. In biography the real story has to be told, and,
curiously enough, the same features are generally to be found
in the record of most lives. It is a true saying that it is what
we ourselves put into life that generally makes or mars our
happiness. We all have our burdens to carry, our dark hours
to pass through. If the first were shouldered with a strong
will and the second supported by a good heart, the weight
would be lessened and the gloom lightened.

We are now about to follow our heroines whom we left
standing on the threshold of a new and wonderful life. They
had fitted on the glass slipper, and, like their prototype
Cinderella, all had changed in a moment. Good-bye to debts,
difficulties, the poor shifts of gentility, and the slights of the
rich and the fashionable. It must have seemed to them like
some enchanting dream from which they feared to awake to
find all vanished—the prince, the glass slipper and the coach.
This feeling would be in the first blush of delighted surprise;
but by-and-by time and habit (which stales the infinite variety
of all things) will take off the first enchanting gloss, and then
we shall see how they passed over the burning ploughshare

of that wicked, but delightful world of our great grandmothers, and how Maria made a disastrous failure and Elizabeth enjoyed tranquil domestic happiness.

"'The world is still mad about the Gunnings," writes the indefatigable Walpole. "When the Duchess of Hamilton was presented last Sunday, the excitement was so great that even the noble crowd in the drawing-room stood upon the chairs and tables to look at her. There were mobs at the doors to see her and Lady Coventry get into their chairs, and people go early to get places at the theatre when it is known they were to be there. Doctor Sacheverell never made more fuss than did these two beauties."

After a brilliant season, we hear of their retiring to their husbands' country seats, and of no less than seven hundred people sitting up all night in and about a Yorkshire inn to see the Duchess of Hamilton get into her postchaise; and then the world is silent about the beautiful sisters for a little time—only Gossip Horace keeps his eye upon them. He and the famous *partie-carrée* which met at stated periods at Strawberry Hill—George Selwyn, Gilly Williams, Dick Edgecombe—constituted what Walpole was wont to call "his out-of-town party." What a debt of gratitude we owe these men, scandal-mongers though they were; as Thackeray says, "In their correspondence with one another one almost hears the voices of the dead past, the laughter and the chorus, the toast called over the brimming cups, the shout at the racecourse or the gaming table, the merry joke frankly spoken to the fine lady." Our great English writer seems to give the palm to the published letters of George Selwyn, from the fact that these are the work of so many hands. You hear more voices speaking, as it were, and they are more natural than Horace's dandified treble or Sporus's malignant whisper. It is in Selwyn's correspondence that we grow acquainted with Gilly Williams, whose voice has an especially kindly ring, in talking of poor, silly Lady Coventry, who seems to have shown great kindness to her husband's friends, thereby gaining their regard for herself and her children.

It must be owned that with all her faults Maria Gunning

was far the more attractive of the sisters. Her weakness was vanity and love of admiration. She was a poor, foolish thing, a foreshadowing of the French heroine who dies in the lovely tea-gown. Looking at her picture, you can gather an idea of those wonderful charms which bewitched so many men. There is something bright, dazzling, more spiritual than in the calmer and colder Elizabeth ;[1] ever ready to smile or to cry was Maria, with an extraordinary play of expression. " She has a thousand dimples," says Mrs. Delany, "and a thousand prettinesses in her cheek, her eyes a little drooping, but fine for all that ; she has a thousand airs, but with a sort of humour that diverts me."

This is a good picture of the Irish girl, who was indeed weighted with fearful disadvantages, for her husband was not a man to help, being somewhat of a prig ; some people called him a solemn fool. Walpole said of him that in his wise way he was quite as ill-bred and ignorant as his Countess, besides being jealous, a prude and scrupulous. To judge from the evidence of his intimate friends, one would say his lordship was ill to live with from his affected superiority and disputatious assertiveness.[2] He and his beautiful wife quarrelled like a pair of children, she complaining to everyone, with a charming pout, that it was so odd my lord should treat her in such a way, when she knew he would die for her, and had been so kind as to marry her without a shilling. They were, in fact, an ill-matched couple, although by no means so in appearance. The picture of Lord Coventry by Ramsay shows us a charming face with a sweet expression and that grand-seigneur air which marked the nobleman of the day. Looking at it, one is inclined to discredit the ill-natured stories told of " Covey " by his friends—and yet the judgment of contemporaries is

[1] She is well described in a magazine of the day :—

" Maria every care beguiles,
She glances rapture in her smiles ;
To all the beauties of her mind,
She adds the beauty to be *kind*."

[2] The character Lord Coventry bore at White's Club was that of a disputatious man, "who was opposing and arguing with some person every night."

generally accurate, and, at all events, it is the only guide we have of knowing those who lived a hundred years before our time.

Poor, silly Maria! her foolish talk and stupidity made her the jest of the town, which in itself must have been galling to a man of Lord Coventry's nature. It did not mend the matter that many of her *bêtises* were the additions of some sprightly wit. In all this the jealousy which her good fortune had excited had to be taken into account, while her want of education, due to the early Roscommon training, and which she had not the art to conceal like her cleverer sister, made her a mark for the ill-natured. Society, in fact, indemnified itself for its insane admiration of her face by circulating her " Sprospositos,"[1] to quote the name given to her odd sayings by Horace Walpole, who diligently collected them for the amusement of his correspondents.

" I cannot say her genius equals her beauty," he writes to the Countess of Ossory ; and then he pays a tribute to her good humour. " If she were not," he said, " the best-tempered creature in the world, I should have made her angry." This was at a supper at Lord Hertford's, and the beauty, being asked to take more wine, answered, with a strong Irish accent, if she drank more she would be " muckibus." " Lord ! " said Lady Mary Coke, " what is that ? " " Oh," cried Mr. Walpole, " it is only Irish for sentiment." On another occasion, the King, asking her if she were not sorry there were no masquerades, she said, No, she was tired of them ; she was surfeited with most sights, there was but one she wanted to see, a coronation. The old King told this himself. He was very partial to the pretty creature, and forgave her unintentional *gaucherie.*

The first check her vanity received was in Paris, where Lord Coventry took her soon after their marriage. They went with a party which included the still beautiful Lady Caroline Petersham ; their adventures on their journey are amusing

---

[1] These Sprospositos recall similar sayings of a well-known lady who figured in the " fifties." Mrs. Hudson was, however, more of a Mrs. Malaprop than Lady Coventry.

reading, but some of Lady Coventry's "sprospositos" on this occasion do not bear repeating. There was a natural want of refinement in her, due to the early training: for the rest, in the last century it was the custom to call a spade a spade. The Parisians were by no means impressed by any of the party, and paid no homage to the wonderful beauty which had so bewitched the English. So far Walpole's opinion is borne out that, taken singly, the goddesses were ordinary handsome women.

"Our beauties are returned," he writes to Sir Horace. "The French could not conceive that Lady Caroline *ever had been* handsome, or that Lady Coventry had much pretence to be so now; indeed, all the travelled English allow there is a Madame Brionne handsomer and of a finer figure. Poor Lady Coventry," he goes on to say, "was under disadvantages, for, besides being very silly, ignorant of the world and breeding, speaking no French and suffered to wear neither red nor powder, she had that perpetual drawback, her lord, who speaks French just enough to show how rude he is."

Rude he certainly was (possibly driven wild by the hoydenish behaviour of Maria), doing all manner of ill-bred *gaucheries* which excited the amusement and contempt of the Parisians, then the most refined people in Europe. The husband and wife made themselves infinitely ridiculous by their quarrels; while his absurd jealousy rendered him a sort of butt, and incited the gallant Frenchmen to pay additional court to his lady. One can imagine how such a scene as took place at Sir John Bland's must have afforded food for mirth; when the grave English "milor" was seen chasing his beautiful countess round the dinner table, and, having run her to earth in a corner, proceeded to rub with a napkin all the raddle and powder [1] off her face, telling her that since she had broken her

---

[1] Lord Coventry was not singular in his dislike to the white lead and raddle. *The World*, to which Lord Chesterfield contributed largely, in its issue of October, 1756, makes an earnest appeal to the fashionable ladies of society to lay aside "the shameful piratical practice of hoisting false colours upon their top gallants in the mistaken notion of captivating their countrymen. Be it known to them that there is not a man in England who does not prefer infinitely the brownest natural to the whitest artificial skin."

promise to him and got herself painted, he would carry her
back to England forthwith. Another time he made a scene
about her presenting the Marechale de Lowenthal with a fan
that lady had admired. The next morning, however, arrived
an ill-written letter asking for it back as her parting with
it would make an irreparable breach with my lord, because
he had given it to her before marriage. She begged her
accepfance of another fan, which turned out to be old and
shabby.

These were a few of the stories that were circulated from
one to another in the French capital. To complete the poor
beauty's discomfiture, one night at the Opera " the lovely Mrs.
Pitt "[1] appeared in a box opposite. She wore some arrangement of a red veil which increased her beauty so much that
the *parterre* rose up in admiration of this real English belle.
Lady Coventry's cup being now full, she, according to Mr.
Thackeray, quitted Paris in a huff. She would not wait for
the grand *fête* at St. Cloud, nor for the reception at Madame
Pompadour's, her lord giving as an excuse that he would miss
a music meeting at Worcester. So the pair returned to
London somewhat discomfited, but with " new cloaths for
the drawing-room." Mrs. Delany saw her that year at a
party where the Duke of Portland wore a coat of dark mouse-
coloured velvet and a vest of Isabella velvet, and described
her as looking in high beauty. We get constant glimpses
of husband and wife in that wonderful collection of letters
which passed between the *partie carrée*.

" We eat and drink well, and the carl is in the best of
humours," writes Gilly. " He holds a faro bank every night,
which we have plundered considerably. There is a certain
captain mentioned as studying pretty attitudes for the countess,
who is in high spirits," he adds, " and great beauty. You
may write to your friends that our London journey will be
early this year to meet our sister Grace from Scotland, and
that the loss of one child will soon be repaired, God willing,
by the birth of another."[2]

[1] Mrs. Pitt's beauty is spoken of in all Memoirs of the time.
[2] This piece of information "to be given to friends," has more signi-

It is easy to read between the lines of the correspondence, how, by degrees, the husband began to tire of his girl wife. Maria was not a woman likely to hold the affections of a man like Lord Coventry, who was especially fond of his own way and liked to hear himself talk. We can imagine that she laughed in her hoydenish manner at his preachings and teachings, and put her fingers on her pretty ears not to listen to his sermons. They were a pair somewhat after the pattern of "Lord and Lady Towneley," and we can imagine her saying, "Lord, my lord, what could I possibly find to do at home?"[1]

She now added the fashionable vice of gambling to her other distractions. In the days of the Georges cards were a favourite diversion. Everyone played cards; and Thackeray

---

ficance than at first appears. From the extracts lately published from the betting book of White's Club, it would seem that more than 240*l.* was staked upon which of the sisters should first present her lord with a child. Lord Hobart bet Lord Ducie ten guineas, Mr. Jeffries ten guineas, and Mr. Vane twenty guineas that the Duchess of Hamilton would have a child born alive before Lady Coventry, and Lord Montfort bet Lord Hobart twenty guineas to ten guineas that the Duchess of Hamilton or Lady Coventry should have a child born alive before Lady Rockingham. Again on February 25th, 1753, there was a sweepstakes of one guinea each person, as to which of the following ladies should give birth to a child first:—

Lord Hobart	Lady Coventry.
Lord Montfort	Lady Hilsbury.
Sir R. Bertie	Lady Car Duncannon.
Mr. Maxwell	Lady Di Egerton.

Lord Montfort then wagered Mr. Maxwell thirty guineas to twenty that either he or Lord Hobart should win the sweepstakes. Mr. Maxwell won.

Lord Montfort was one of the most reckless gamesters. In an early betting book at White's he registered no less than sixty bets amounting to 5000*l.* The events were entirely of the nature of births, deaths, and marriages. His death came about in the most tragic manner. He had wagered with Sir John Bland a sum of one hundred guineas that Beau Nash, the King of Bath, would outlive Colley Cibber, the once popular actor, both men being ill and likely to die; but underneath the wager there is written in a different handwriting, "Both Lord Montfort and Sir John Bland put an end to their lives before this bet was decided." Lord Linden's comment on this awful circumstance was typical of the times. "Well, I am very sorry for Lord Montfort, but it is the part of wise men to make the best of every misfortune. I shall now have the best cook in England."

[1] The provoked husband.

says that when we try to recall social England in the last century we must fancy it playing at cards for many hours every day. Even Mrs. Delany, who set herself, or rather I should say was set up as a sort of pattern for all to imitate, held a commerce table for the amusement of the visitors of her friend Mrs. Clayton. Quadrille was the favourite game in George the Second's time. It was a gambling game, but that was all the better for one of Lady Coventry's spirit. In 1757 Lady Elizabeth Walpole writes to the Duke of Bedford:—

"Pray tell the Duchess of Bedford the height of Lady Coventry's ambition is to play at quadrille, at which she plays four hours a day to be worthy of your parties at your return. She says she likes it immensely and prefers it to all other diversions."

Lady Coventry was soon proficient enough in quadrille to drop twenty or thirty guineas at a sitting. She was, indeed, a mere butterfly, running here and there in search of pleasure and admiration; but in all this we must consider her youth and extreme beauty. In 1755, Horace Walpole finds her handsomer than ever, and Mrs. Delany gives a charming picture of the young beauty who was brought by the Duchess of Portland to feast her friend's eyes. And a feast she was. "She has a thousand airs, but with a sort of innocence that diverts one. Her dress was a black silk sack made for a large hoop, which she wore without any, so that it trailed a yard on the ground; she had a cobweb laced handkerchief, a pink satin long cloke lined with ermine mixed with squirrel-skins. On her head a French cap, that just covered the top of it, of blond, standing up in the form of a butterfly, with the wings not quite extended; frilled sort of lappets crossed under her chin, and tied with pink ribbon—a head-dress that would have charmed a shepherd! She has a thousand dimples and prettinesses in her cheeks, her eyes a little drooping at the corners, but very fine for all that."

About this time the Duke of Norfolk gave an entertainment especially for her, and danced all the evening with her, "So there was one happy woman for at least two or three hours."

A very pretty story is told by the same *raconteuse* of little Miss Allen, Lady Carysfort's sister, a lively, unsophisticated fairy who had a great desire to see Lady Coventry. At the great masquerade given at Somerset House, this little girl went up to the beauty, who was unmasked, and stared earnestly into her face, then said, "I have heard a great deal of this lady's beauty, but it surpasses what I have heard."

"What!" cried Lady Coventry with adorable simplicity, "have you never seen me before?"

Her original freshness seems never to have deserted her, and, in spite of the amazing amount of homage she received and the admiration her beauty excited, she preserved her good name, which was all the more wonderful as her husband had grown careless about his beautiful wife, or was probably weary of her whims and oddities. She did not, however, escape altogether the censorious tongues of the Sneerwells and Backbites who made up her world, nor was she wise in allowing men of doubtful reputation, such as the Duke of Cumberland and Lord Pembroke, to pay her open attention. Horace Walpole, whose argus eyes nothing escaped, writes to a lady friend :—

"The Duke of Cumberland has appeared in form in the Causeway in Hyde Park with my Lady Coventry. It is the new office where all lovers now are entered. How happy she must be with Billy and Bully."[1]

This last was Lord Bolingbroke, who was also an ardent admirer of Lady Coventry's. He was young, handsome, devoted, ever at her side, while her husband made the most absurd spectacle of his jealousy, for, although he had ceased to care for her, he was exceedingly mindful of his own honour. He went about talking loudly and consulting friends as to whether he should get a divorce, which, says Walpole, "has put my Lady North into a terrible fright lest Bolingbroke might marry Maria." This inveterate old gossipmonger concludes the tale of scandal which he has been writing to his friend at Florence with a *bon mot* at poor Lady

[1] Walpole adds that "Lady Coventry would be stupid enough to call her admirers by the wrong nicknames."

Coventry's expense. Says he, "'T'other night they danced minuets for the entertainment of the King, George II., who sent for Lady Coventry to dance. If he had offered her a boon she would have asked the head of St. John. I believe I told you of her passion for Lord Bolingbroke. All the talk and the scandal came, however, soon to an end, as did likewise Lord Coventry's vapouring as to divorce, for presently Lord Bolingbroke, who was susceptible, fell desperately in love with the lovely Lady Di Spencer, and, marrying her in all haste, set out on a sea of domestic troubles on his own account." [1]

This was in 1757,[2] and the desertion of her admirer did not seem to affect Lady Coventry, who was in high beauty and spirits the next season, and of course set the world talking of her. It was said she complained to the old King with whom she was a favourite, that she could not walk in the Park because of the mob who crowded round her, and who, no doubt incited by the silly airs she gave herself, made disrespectful remarks upon her. The King promised to send her a guard to protect her, an honour a more sensible person would have declined. The sequel of the story is well known. The Honourable Sackville West, another of the gossip tribe, writes off to Lord Nuneham an account of what happened :—

"June 20th, 1759.

"Will it be any news to inform you that last Sunday se'night your friend, Lady Coventry, was mobbed in the Park,

---

[1] The way in which this marriage was brought about is a type of the manners of the day. The young pair were together at Vauxhall with a large party entertained by the Duke and Duchess of Bedford. The company were teasing Lord Bolingbroke to marry ; he turned quickly upon Lady Diana, and said,—
"Will you have me ?"
"Yes, to be sure," she replied.
It passed off that night as a joke, but with consideration of the lady's merit, which they say is a great deal, and the persuasion of his friends, he made a serious affair of it, and was accepted. 1500*l.* a year jointure and 500*l.* a year pin money has cast a veil over the past. If he has any sense they may be happy, for he must then see what an absurd figure he has hitherto made, so long the dupe of beauty and folly.
[2] It was said her flirtation with Lord Pembroke gave great uneasiness to his lovely wife. The Ambassador of Morocco was also in Maria's train.

and that to prevent it, last Sunday twelve sergeants of the guard were ordered to disperse themselves about in case of a riot, and a sergeant and twelve men were ready in case of wanting assistance? This her ladyship knew, and went to the Park and *pretended* to be frightened, directly wanted the assistance of the officer on guard, who ordered the twelve sergeants to march abreast before her, and the sergeant and twelve men behind her; and in this pomp did this *idiot* walk all the evening with more mob about her than ever, as you may imagine; her sensible husband supporting her on one side and Lord Pembroke on the other."

Walpole too, scribbled off an amusing ballad on the incident, which was handed round amongst his *coterie* and convulsed the Ladies Ossory, Ailesbury, and the rest of the clique:—

I sing not of wars nor invasions,
  I tell you a merrier tale,
How Fisher [1] and Covey were mad, Sir,
  And sent all the people to jail.
But Covey could not bear a rival,
  She thought it a terrible case
That first they should gaze on Kate Fisher,
  And then come and stare in *her* face.
"Indeed, if I were but Miss Gunning,
  They might have done just as they chose,
But now I am married to Covey,
  They shall not tread on my toes.
I'll make my case known to the King,
  The Monarch I know he adores me,
And won't suffer any such thing."
  Then straightway to Court she betakes her,
"I'm come, Sir, to make my complaint,
  I can't walk in the Park for your subjects,
They stare without any restraint.
  Shut, shut up the Park, I beseech you,
Lay a tax upon staring so hard,
  Or, if you're afraid to do that, Sir,
I'm sure you will grant me a guard."
  The boon thus requested was granted,
The warriors were drawn up with care,
  "With my slaves and my guards I'm surrounded,
Come, stare at me now, if you dare!"

Tune, "Kitty Fisher's Jig."

One cannot help thinking that it was beneath a man of

---

[1] Kitty Fisher, a famous courtesan of the day. She was painted several times by Sir Joshua Reynolds. She shared the admiration of the mob.

Walpole's undoubted ability to thus lampoon a young creature whose vanity was so transparent as to be almost a mania. All through, however, Horace seems to have grudged the Gunnings their success. A petty feeling of jealousy in regard to his own beautiful nieces may have prompted this. All the same, it was unworthy. This year his niece, the lovely Maria, married the Earl of Waldegrave, and poor Lady Coventry (who seems to have been surrounded with persons on the watch to record her frank but singularly foolish admiration of her own beauty) unguardedly said to Lady Anne Conolly that "now she had seen the new beauty she was easy." This was repeated in every drawing-room.

Her reign was, however, to be a short one. Her follies and the gibes and sneers of an ill-natured world were soon to come to an end. Already she was showing some symptoms of the family disease, consumption, but would take no heed, pursuing her "boisterous, racketing" life, turning night into day, and adding the fashionable vice of gambling to her other excitements. This love of pleasure was, however, the outcome of her malady. In March, 1759, she was looking in high beauty at the Duchess of Hamilton's wedding,[1] and in November of the same year, she was again in town, and showed George Selwyn (always her kind friend) her new clothes for the drawing-room, blue with spots of silver the size of a shilling, and a silver trimming, "and cost—my lord will know what." She asked Selwyn with her usual simplicity how he liked them, and the wit answered, "Oh! you will be change for a guinea!" Neither the beauty and novelty of her blue and silver, nor the white and red raddle which she now used *ad libitum*—her lord no longer caring what she did—could conceal the ravages her fatal illness had already made on her bright loveliness. She looked old, faded, a ghost of her former self.

In January, 1760, she seems to have made a short rally. Walpole saw her at the trial of Lord Ferrers [2] in that year,

---

[1] Married to Colonel John Campbell.

[2] Laurence, 4th Earl Ferrers, although not actually insane, evinced, as the courteous Burke tells us, strong symptoms of *constitutional violence of temper*. In one of the paroxysms of rage habitual to him, his lordship killed an old gentleman, Mr. Johnson, who acted as his

and reports, " that she surprised her friends by looking as well as ever. I sat next but one to her, and should not have asked her if she had been ill; yet they are positive she has but a few weeks to live." Then he adds his malevolent sting, " She and Lord Bolingbroke seemed to have different thoughts, and were acting all over again the old comedy of eyes." [1] This was her last appearance in the world which had such keen eyes for her coquetries and foolish want of decorum. This very January she fell seriously ill, but lingered on for some months, as is the course of this fell disease, and was sometimes at the point of death, sometimes recovering. The doctors thought she would not live over the spring, and when that passed, pronounced autumn would be the critical period.

It must be owned that now that she was actually dying, the world, as seen through Walpole's glasses, seems to have been really concerned, and to have followed the fluctuations of her illness with extraordinary anxiety. In June he writes: "The pretty Countess is still alive, was thought dying on Tuesday night, and *I* think will go off very soon."

On August the 8th she nearly verified this prediction. The poor beauty was alone at Crome, where it is probable she spent many lonely days. What sad thoughts she must have had as she lay on her couch, away from the gay world, where her place was already filled, and where she would never again receive those tributes of admiration which had been so dear to her foolish heart. We must hope she thought of better things. We know that Parson Brooke rode over constantly on his pony to visit her, but it was hard to reconcile her to die. She was hoping to live on this very 7th of August, when the fatal letter came from her sister, the duchess, to Lord Coventry, who was up in London, where presently a messenger followed him, riding day and night to fetch him back if he wished to say farewell to his dying wife.

land steward. For this act of " constitutional bad temper " he was tried by his peers in 1760, and being condemned by them to suffer the extreme penalty of the law, was hung at Tyburn in May of the same year.

[1] Lord Bolingbroke was much affected when the news of her death reached him. He could not bear to hear her name mentioned, and always left the room to hide. Walpole says that he was *not* crying.

She did not, however, die this time. Doctor Wall, the family physician, kept faithful George Selwyn posted up in all the details of the poor lady's illness, making "no excuse for being minute, because I believe that it would be most agreeable that I should be so." Here we have the whole story set forth in these simple letters, their minuteness being their real attraction—the touch as to " using the terms of art " is delightful.

[1] " Crome, August 8th, 1760.

" SIR,—I have spent almost all my time at this place since my lord went to London ; and, indeed, Lady Coventry has been so extremely ill, so much worse than when you saw her last, that she wanted all the attendance I could give her. For two or three days the oppression on her breast and the sickness at her stomach were excessive ; but these were at last happily removed by some medicines, which, indeed, operated a little roughly ; but it was a necessary severity, for she could not have lived without it. She has now for two or three days complained of a pain in her side and across the breast, which I look upon to be muscular, and a sort of spasmodic rheumatism. Excuse me for using terms of art, but I don't know how to express myself without them. Her pulse, notwithstanding this, has for three days last past been very remarkably slower, her feverish heats less than usual. She is extremely weak. Yesterday morning a letter came from the Duchess of Hamilton, directed for Lord Coventry. She knew the hand, and unluckily opened it.

" Hinc illæ lachrymæ !

" The duchess had too plainly explained her sentiments of Lady Coventry's condition ; had lamented her as a sister whom she should never see ; had entirely given her up, expressing her concern as for one already in the grave.

" You, who know how apt Lady Coventry is to be affected, may easily conceive the anguish which such a letter would occasion. Indeed, it did almost kill her. I was called to her, and found her almost fainting and dying away. How-

---

[1] Crome seems to have been the old spelling of the word, therefore I have not altered it where it appears.

ever, she soon after recovered, and I took my leave; but after I was gone the same scene was several times renewed. Her attendants thought her expiring. In their hurry they despatched an express to my lord, who, I suppose, will, in consequence of that, be here this evening. However, she has had a very good night, and is tolerably well this morning."

The improvement seems to have continued, for in September there were hopes of her recovery, and Walpole writes hopefully of her condition to General Conway, who had a sincere regard for the countess. "She may yet appear as your Roxana," he says.[1]

There was, however, no chance of her ever appearing again on the stage where she had played so brilliant a part. The hopes of recovery were speedily dashed, and the end drew rapidly near. It is painful to read how, at this last dread moment, her vanity, the master-passion of her life, came to the front, although in this, as in many other incidents of her life, there is probably an amount of exaggeration in the tradition of Lady Coventry's last moments. As a matter of fact, the story of her keeping the pocket glass under her pillow, and watching the change in her face all day long, has never had any authenticity, but it has, however, marks of truth from the internal evidence of her character; from long habit she had grown to regard looks as the first object, and even in our more enlightened generation we will find many women who hold the same opinion. Years previously Pope had depicted a similar scene to the one said to have been enacted round Lady Coventry's death-bed.

> "Odious in woollen! 'twould a saint provoke,"
> Were the last words that Narcissa spoke.
> "No; let a charming chintz and Brussels lace
> Wrap my cold limbs and shade my lifeless face;
> One would not sure be frightful when one's dead,
> And, Betty, give this cheek a little red."

And thus the end came. She died October 1st, 1760, being twenty-nine years of age.

[1] General Conway was planning private theatricals.

It has been always the prevailing idea that Lady Coventry's death was, if not actually caused, hastened by the profuse use, which like all fashionable women of her day, she made of cosmetics. Those who lived in her time seemed to have been persuaded of this fact. Mrs. Delany, who was not very devoted to the pretty creature, writes shortly before her death :—

"What a wretched end Lady Coventry makes after her short-lived reign of beauty. Not contented with the extraordinary share Providence has bestowed upon her, she presumptuously and vainly thought to mend it, and by that means, they say, has destroyed her life, for Doctor Taylor says the white she made use of for her *neck and face was rank poison*." One who is very nearly connected with her has, however, contradicted this statement. Lady Russell,[1] writing to the author, says, "It is a popular fallacy that Lady Coventry died from the use of cosmetics. She died, as did her sister (Lizzy)[2] and the young Duke of Hamilton, from consumption." This disease was, no doubt, in the family. Several of John Gunning's sisters had died of it, and the Duchess of Argyll showed symptoms of it after Lady Coventry's death ; but this fact ought to have been an additional reason for caution, as in such cases the danger of introducing white lead into the system is intensified. I am afraid, taking into account the prevailing fashion and the vanity of poor Maria, one cannot quite acquit her of injuring her health in more ways than one. Lady Coventry had been married only eight years and a few months ; years of feverish excitement, triumph, admiration, mixed with much domestic unhappiness, ending in estrangement from her husband. She must have felt his coldness, for she was of an affectionate disposition and easily touched by kindness. It may be remembered that when the fortune-teller in Dublin prophesied the greater fortune that was to come to Elizabeth, Maria was consoled by being

---

[1] Lady Russell's grandmother, Lady Charlotte Bury, *née* Campbell, was the second daughter of John, Duke of Argyle, and Elizabeth Gunning.

[2] Lizzy, whose beauty excelled that of her sisters, died in Dublin, 1751.

assured "that *her* husband would love her." That this prophecy failed of its promise was possibly her own fault, her whims and follies wearing out her lord's patience. Still, allowance should have been made for so young a creature, exposed as she was, without any previous training, to so many temptations; neither were her follies the outcome of a bad heart. Her parents (especially her father) loved her more than their other children, and her husband's intimate friends showed a loyalty to her memory which is a strong testimony in her favour. The world, generally ill-natured to the dead, had not a harsh word to say of her, and even Walpole has a touch of feeling at the end of his pen, as he records that "the charming countess is dead at last; she was only twenty-seven." The Rev. Richard Mason, one of the Strawberry Hill clique, wrote a beautiful monody on Maria's death, which the sentimentalists of the time repeated with handkerchiefs to their eyes. The lines in which he describes her peculiar loveliness are singularly happy :—

> Yes! Coventry is dead. Attend the strain,
>   Daughters of Albion! ye that, light as air,
> So oft have tripp'd in her fantastic train,
>   With hearts as gay, and faces half as fair.
>
> For she was fair beyond your brightest bloom
>   (This Envy owns, since now her bloom is fled);
> Fair as the forms that, wove in Fancy's loom,
>   Float in light vision round the poet's head.
>
> Whene'er with *soft serenity* she smiled,
>   Or caught the *orient blush of quick surprise,*
> How sweetly mutable, *how brightly wild*
>   The liquid lustre darted *from her eyes!*
>
> Each look, each motion waked a new-born grace,
>   That o'er her form a transient glory cast;
> Some lovelier wonder soon usurped the place,
>   Chased by a charm still lovelier than the last.
>
> That bell again! It tells us what she is;
>   On what she was no more the strain prolong;
> Luxuriant Fancy, pause; an hour like this
>   Demands the tribute of a serious song.
>
> Maria claims it from that sable bier,
>   Where, cold and wan, the slumberer rests her head;
> In still small whispers to Reflection's ear
>   She breathes the solemn dictates of the dead.

She left three children, two girls and a boy, the eldest,

Lady Anne, being seven at the time of her mother's death. She was an object of the greatest interest to that strange being, George Selwyn, whose character presents such a bundle of contradictions, a passionate love of children going hand in hand with a revolting desire to witness the sufferings of dying criminals. The letters that passed between him and Gilly Williams on the subject of Lady Coventry's motherless children show both men in the most amiable light, and prove that, despite their frivolous mode of life, they had feeling hearts.

" Your child Nanny," writes Gilly, " is all the better for the sea air. The little boy has just come up to school, and says his sister is the admiration of the place. This you will believe, although the father neither knows nor cares anything about it." When Nanny had the chicken-pox and violent inflammation in her eyes, they were all anxiety lest her beauty should be spoiled, and Gilly confided to Selwyn his suspicion that the fault lay with the stamina of *our dear* friend, " her children have not had one hour's health since I have known them." In 1763 he writes that Lord Coventry has returned to town, and talks of setting out for France :—" his errand is to buy furniture, to talk of tapestry and glasses, and to pay for importing worse things than an English courier would have helped him to. He told us last night his estate is worth £10,000 a year with a debt of fifty. I suppose you would be willing to add to the incumbrance for your little girl. I have sent them the dolls, and their father visits them on Friday. They are both better for the sea water ; but," he adds, " I look upon his visit to have been as much out of form as affection, and, having satisfied the public, he leaves the rest to Almighty God. Nanny is looking remarkably handsome, but their father never lets them see any other children, though there are some of their own condition." All through the correspondence there is this ring of honest indignation against the father's neglect. What a stir and commotion took place when it became known that his lordship contemplated a second marriage, which, considering he was a young man and four years a widower, was a matter to create no surprise. His choice likewise was a suitable one. Gilly, however, writes in all excitement to break the news to George Selwyn, at that time on his travels :—

"July 30th, 1864.

" My dear George,—This packet brings *very serious advice* indeed. I received a notification *in form* last night that Nanny would soon have to bow the knee to Bab St. John [1] as her mother-in-law. God grant this woman may have long life, or the poor children will have more odd uncles, aunts and cousins than any people of their condition in Europe. I shall see *him* in a few days and hear more particulars, but I was not willing this ship should sail without your knowing as much as I do."

The marriage was altogether a strange affair, having somewhat of the same embarrassment that accompanied that of the Duke of Hamilton to Elizabeth Gunning. "An odd event," writes a lady to her son, "happened the day they were to have been married. His lordship had not got a license ; they were at Lady St. John's house in the country—my lord was obliged to come up to Doctors' Commons to swear to his own age and that of Miss St. John, and then to send to Lambeth for the license. Unfortunately his Grace was not at home. So it was agreed that they had better eat the dinner rather than that it should be spoilt, so to dinner they went and sat all the afternoon dressed in their white and silver, expecting every moment an express from Lambeth. But nothing came. The same reason held good for eating a supper as for eating the dinner, and, in short, they supped and sat till two, and then by mutual consent dismissed the parson, and all retired. About four in the morning the license came , but they were not married until mid-day."

Gilly, of course, has his word to say about the pair, and writes full details to his *Fidus Achates*, Selwyn, who was abroad still :—

" My dear George,—You may talk as you please of what

---

[1] Barbara, daughter to John, tenth Lord St. John, of Bletso.

you have seen and heard since we parted, but I would not have given up my last night's supper for the whole put together. The earl brought his new countess to Margaret Street. You know him so well that I daresay you are perfectly master of his words and actions on such an occasion; and as for her ladyship, it was all prettiness, fright, insipidity, question and answer, which neither gold stuffs, diamonds, a new chair with a very large coronet in the centre, like the Queen's—neither of these, I say, had power to alter; and as my friend was never cut out for decent and matrimonial gallantry, a very awkward air made them both as entertaining a couple as ever I passed an evening with. They are to be introduced at Court next Sunday. The King has told him she was the wisest, prudentest, handsomest of women. And they go to Crome next day."

The King proved himself in the right, the new countess making an excellent wife and mother. She came of a good family, had a slender provision and much prettiness. Walpole says, " She was elevated above the first countess for a few weeks and then, with equal injustice, placed infinitely below her. At Saturday's opera," he goes on, "she didn't make near noise enough, but sat quite private and pale faced." Poor bride. . . with the eyes of the world of fashion upon her. She was in poor health besides, and Gilly notices she has a cough and "expects old Brookes will be trotting over with a prayer-book in his hand." This was when he dined with her at the Duchess of Argyll's, who affected a tear at the sound of her voice. " Coventry has given us one dinner at Margaret Street, and has been most excellent in his old way of disputation; he has bought Sir Henry Hunlock's house in Piccadilly for ten thousand pounds."

In another letter we hear of Mrs. Gunning, who was now getting old. She had a comfortable sinecure as housekeeper of Somerset House, a good appointment procured for her by one of her noble sons-in-law. " I met mother Gunning " says Gilly, " in Soho. She told me although she could not go to see *the woman* she would be glad to see the children, and desired me tell Lord C. so. . . It is feared old Gunning will die, and defeat all the finery smuggled by the earl and countess for the next birthday."

The mention of the children recalls his account of their reception of their new mamma.

" You will certainly want to know how the children relish their new relation. I will give you a trait of Nanny that pleased me. When mademoiselle broke it to them, Maria cried, and the little one said : ' Do not cry, sister. If she is civil to us, we will be civil to her ; if not, you know, we can sit up in our own rooms, and take no notice of her.' There is a degree of philosophy in this infant that I do not think age can improve."

Nanny, in spite of her philosophy, " seemed as much frightened as when she was delivered over to mademoiselle from Kitty. I wish she may fall into as good hands, for I believe Mdlle. Le Comte's [1] reign is short—he has already told me her French is impure, and her orthography worse."

After their first introduction, the children were sent to Brighthelmstowe, with Gilly to look after them, for he writes complaining to Selwyn of the father's coldness, " he leaves them to Providence, and me—but at the end of the month they are to go with their stepmother to Crome," whither their kind friend accompanied them, and has left a really diverting account of his visit.

" I like," he says, " the behaviour of the children much, and likewise the propriety of Bab's behaviour to them ; but you would have laughed to have seen what a hearty kiss the little one would often give mademoiselle (their governess), as looking upon her as the only real friend she had in the family. . . Of the new Madam there is no possibility of saying more at present, than that she is very pretty—the rest is all grimace. But as to his lordship, he certainly surpasses all you can conceive of him ; his plantations, his house, his wife, his plate, equipages, etc., etc., are all topics that call forth his genius continually. We went to church with them, and the curiosity of all the neighbouring parishes would not have displeased you. I thought I could hear among the crowd some

[1] The children's governess.

odious comparisons, and these were all in favour of *our old friend* who lies very quietly in the neighbourhood. I do not love to deal in horoscopes, but his lordship will certainly tire of this plaything as he has done of all he has hitherto played with, and be plagued with the noise of the rattle when he is no longer pleased with blowing the whistle. He means to instruct, by *lectures* in his table talk, and by drawing pictures of good and bad wives; you know how he succeeded in his last. God grant him better success in his present plans."

This pious wish was fulfilled; the new Countess succeeded perfectly in that wherein the other had failed. She made her husband happy, "although she was a most unworthy successor to the bustle and uproar which followed the name in the first venture." After a few years Gilly declares he likes her better and better every hour "I am with her. Indeed, she is the best thing in petticoats I ever saw in my life." To the children of her predecessor she was only too kind, for they had inherited the high temper of the Gunnings. Judicious restraint would have been of use. They, especially Nanny, grew more ungovernable from want of contradiction. Even Gilly has to report unfavourably to Selwyn of his favourite—

"Nanny grows so intolerably passionate that I wish, some time or other, she may not hurt her sister. She constantly throws the cards in her face if she is not satisfied with her hand, as if she were the daughter of the Bishop of London. Pray send her some serious admonition, her spirit is much beyond that of her late Mamma's. There is seldom a night that she does not fight us all round; the very last night she hit me a box on the ear, and told her good-natured stepmother not to be so impertinent as to trouble her head about her. Her father talks to her out of Halifax's advice to his daughters, which God knows comes too early in the day for *our* comprehension, so I fear she will be outdone before she knows she is to blame."

And yet this same little termagant had a kind heart. Here is a letter of hers which her friend, George Selwyn, preserved as a proof of her fine disposition.

LADY ANNE FOLEY.

(To face page 78.)

" March 4th, 1770.

" MY DEAR NURSE,—This is the only opportunity I have of writing you a line to let you know we are all well. I am sorry I have not time to write a line to your poor Polly. My love to her, and tell her I shall not forget her when I grow up. I will remember you likewise you may depend upon it. I long to see you, but longing will not do. I had not time to write to you that time you went to Mr. Burgess. He told me you were very well. If I can know in two or three days how you are, I shall be contented, so adieu.

" I am your ever-loving friend,

" ANNE COVENTRY.

" To Mrs. Shelton at the Earl of March,
" Piccadilly."

Poor little Lady Anne, spoiled on one hand, lectured on the other, her life fulfilled Gilly Williams' prophecy. She married, when only seventeen, Colonel Foley, but, soon afterwards was divorced and re-married to Captain Samuel Wright. She died in 1784. . . .

As Thackeray says, " Poor painted mother, poor children ! "

ELIZABETH, DUCHESS OF HAMILTON AND ARGYLL.

BORN 1732, DIED 1791.

THE record of this woman's life presents a most unusually even run of good fortune, which stands out in singular contrast to the strangely different fate of her less fortunate sister. These contrasts are often to be met with, and although we believe all events of importance are regulated by Providence, still we cannot but observe, in considering the accidents which have either marred or made the fortune of those who have journeyed along the road we are now travelling, how very much their own actions and mode of treating the opportunities given them are allowed to influence their success in life.

Elizabeth was cast in a totally different mould from Maria. Those who knew her in the flesh may not have cared for her in the same degree. We who look at her from a long way off, cannot but feel infinitely more respect for her fine character: it surmounted the same defects of education and early training which Maria never made any effort to supply.

We get only occasional glimpses of her Grace during the short period of her first marriage. After her elevation to the rank of Duchess she seems to have taken very little share in the doings of the gay world, but to have lived mostly in Scotland, showing, in this, wonderful wisdom in withdrawing her rakish husband from the attractions of town life. In 1755 she accompanied the Duke on a visit to Ireland, remaining some time in Dublin, where they put up at the Eagle

Tavern,[1] Cork Hill, the approaches to which were rendered impassable by the vast crowds thronging to see their beautiful countrywoman, whose attractions had caused such a sensation in England. It must have been a curious feeling for the Duchess, returning in such an exalted position to the place wherein she had suffered so many buffets of ill fortune. Under such conditions, however, the human mind is very elastic, and, especially in youth, accustoms itself easily to altered circumstances.

In their Highland home the Duke and Duchess kept up almost regal state. "They walk in to dinner," says Walpole, "before their company, sit together at the upper end of their own table, eat off the same plate, and drink to nobody beneath the rank of an Earl. Would you not wonder," he adds, "how they would get anyone either below or above that rank to dine with them?"

After six years of this royal state the Duke died (1758) leaving his duchess, a beautiful and well-endowed widow, with two baby sons to carry on the ducal line, and one daughter. Before her year of widowhood was out Elizabeth was surrounded with suitors, her "very proper behaviour" conducing as much to the admiration she excited as did her beauty, which had increased rather than diminished. She had her choice of titled husbands, the Duke of Bridgwater being madly in love with her.[2] Her second marriage was, however, evidently dictated as much by affection as by ambition. It was no bad stroke of luck to secure a man she could love as she did Colonel John Campbell,[3] and who moreover, was heir to a Dukedom, thus

[1] The Eagle Tavern on Cork Hill was the home of that strange institution, the Hell Fire Club. It has been sometimes doubted if this ever had any existence. The report however, of the Lords' Committee dealing with it, which is to be found in Madden's periodical Irish literature, is convincing. From this report we learn that the club was not invented by a native, but was due to one Peter Lens, a German or Dutch artist.

[2] The Duke made it a condition that all intercourse with Lady Coventry should be at an end; to this the Duchess would not agree, and the marriage was broken off.—"Nat. Biography."

[3] Colonel Campbell was the eldest son of Mr. Campbell of Mamure, who in 1761 succeeded Archibald, 3rd Duke of Argyll, as 4th Duke. His mother was the famous beauty, Mary Bellenden, maid of honour to Caroline of Anspalle.—"Douglas's Scottish Peerage."

fulfilling the fortune-teller's prophecy. Elizabeth's sense of propriety would not, however, allow her to make her lover happy until more than the full year of mourning had expired. Her wedding did not take place until the summer of 1759. "It is a match," writes Walpole, "which would not disgrace Arcadia. Her beauty has made sufficient noise, and in some people's eyes has even improved. He has a most pleasing countenance, person and manner, and like the antediluvian lovers they reconcile the great houses of Hamilton and Campbell, and all this brought about by a Gunning!"

From this remark, it is evident Walpole adhered to his idea as to the inferior tap of the Gunnings; indeed all through his life he seems to have had a latent grudge against that family. Later on we find him writing to Sir David Dalrymple in another tone: "I don't doubt but in Scotland you approve what is liked here almost as well as Robertson's History. I mean the marriage of Colonel Campbell and the Duchess of Hamilton; if her fortune is singular so is her merit; such uncommon noise as her beauty has made has not at all impaired the modesty of her behaviour." We must remember that here he was writing to *a Scotchman.* In his correspondence with his *fidus achates,* General Conway, he lets out his real sentiments: "It is the prettiest match in the world since yours, and everybody likes it but the Duke of Bridgwater and Lord Coventry. What an extraordinary fate is attached to these two women. For my part I expect to see Lady Coventry Queen of Prussia? I would not venture to marry either of them for these thirty years, for fear of being shuffled out of the world prematurely to make room for the rest of their adventures. The first time Jack carries the Duchess to the Highlands I am persuaded some of his second-sighted subjects will see him in his winding-sheet with a train of Kings behind him as long as those in Macbeth."

This caustic although pleasantly put piece of writing was not a correct prophecy. Poor Lady Coventry instead of being Queen of Prussia was, as we know, at the very time of writing, beginning her descent towards her grave, while "Jack" survived his Duchess many years. She had undoubtedly prolonged the life of her first disreputable spouse, and now made as good a wife to an excellent husband. Their marriage was eminently successful, the Duchess's conduct being remarkable throughout for great good sense, than which there cannot be a better possession. Unlike poor silly Maria, she gave no reason for the ill-natured to throw any malicious stones at her, and if in her advanced age such malicious throwing was attempted, it fell very short of its object.

She bore her honours meekly enough, although in her inmost soul there must have been a tumult of exultation as she took her place in the front rank of Peeresses at the Coronation ceremony,[1] which poor Lady Coventry had so desired to witness. "She looked," said an eye-witness, "the picture of majestic modesty."

Her sister's death was keenly felt by her. They had never lost their affection for one another. Report said that the Duchess was likewise attacked by the fatal disease, which it seemed was hereditary. Walpole writes to Sir Horace Mann, 1760: "The Duchess of Hamilton is in consumption, and going abroad; perhaps you may see the remains of these prodigies—you will see but little remains. Her features were never so beautiful as Lady Coventry's, and she has long been changed, though not yet six-and-twenty. The other was but twenty-seven."

The Duchess, however, recovered both her health and her good looks. We hear of her at the time of the Wilkes' and Liberty riots, when the excited mob, triumphant at their champion's victory, paraded the streets at night, ordering everyone to illuminate their windows in honour of the popular candidate's return as Member of Parliament. The Duchess was at Argyll House expecting her confinement. Lord Lorne was absent, so she was alone, but her haughty spirit would not bend to the orders of any mob. She obstinately refused to allow a light in the windows. The crowd, furious at this

---

[1] Another honour is said to have been conferred upon the Duchess by selecting her to accompany the Princess Charlotte on her journey to England on the occasion of her marriage to George III. This, however, would seem to be a mistake, as it was *the Duchess of Argyll* who was chosen for the office.

aristocrat's contumacy, brought crowbars to force the iron gates, which had been shut to keep them out. They tore down the railings, and forced an entrance. Still she would not give in. They battered at the house for three hours. The key of the back door could not be found, so no help could be sent for. The troops, however, at last arrived, and saved the situation. This was of course sheer obstinacy on her Grace's part, and highly imprudent, as the consequences might have been serious, as once the mob had scored a success, their appetite for plunder would have increased; to say nothing of the risk to herself in the situation in which she then was.

The duke succeeded to his father in 1770, eleven years after his marriage with the duchess. During these years many of her old ties had been severed by death. She had lost her sister, Lady Coventry, her father and mother, and also her eldest son, the young Duke of Hamilton, who had succumbed to the family malady.

From this time she resided principally in Scotland. One of the most pleasant incidents in Boswell's delightful tour through the Hebrides is the account of his and Dr. Johnson's visit to Inverary Castle. Boswell, who had good reasons for thinking Duchess Elizabeth disliked him,[1] was still anxious to get himself and his august friend invited by the duke, so accordingly waited upon his Grace at the moment when he supposed the ladies would have retired from dinner. Having received an invitation for the following day, he was about retiring when the duke said, "Mr. Boswell, won't you have some tea?" "I thought it best to get over the meeting with the duchess, so respectfully agreed. I was conducted to the drawing-room by the duke, who announced my name, but the duchess, who was sitting with her daughter, Lady Betty Hamilton, and some other ladies, took not the least notice of me. I

---

[1] Her dislike to Boswell was based on the share he had taken in the celebrated Douglas cause, which excited the attention of Europe. The claim of Lord Archibald Stewart, son to Lady Jane Douglas, was disputed by the Duke of Hamilton. The Duchess, who supported her son's claim, went to Paris in 1763 to collect evidence. Horace Walpole says the French thought her no beauty, and had the bad taste to admire the Duchess of Ancaster.

should have been mortified at being thus coldly received by a lady of whom I, with the rest of the world, have always entertained a very high admiration, had I not been consoled by the obliging attention of the duke." He then goes on to give an account of the next day's entertainment where Dr. Johnson was an honoured guest and in excellent humour. He was placed at table next the duke, and the duchess made much of him, so did Lady Betty Hamilton (her daughter by the first marriage), who, like many girls, was attracted by the elephantine graces of the sage. She brought her chair close to his, listening eagerly to all he said. Boswell relates his own mortifications in his usual frank manner. "I was in fine spirits, and, though sensible that I had the misfortune of not being in favour with the duchess, I was not in the least disconcerted, and offered her Grace some of the dish that was before me. . . . I knew it was the rule of modern high life not to drink to anybody, but that I might have the satisfaction for once to look the duchess in the face with a glass in my hand, I, with a respectful air, addressed her: 'My Lady Duchess, I have the honour to drink your Grace's good health.'" He adds that he repeated the words audibly and with a steady countenance, but he does not tell us with what countenance the duchess received the attention. The only words she addressed to him were when on making some observation on second sight she said, "You *will* be a Methodist," the use of the verb betraying her early training, as it is common phrase in the west of Ireland. Boswell makes allowance for his hostess's rudeness in consideration of the warm part he had taken in the Douglas cause, but he confesses that the manner in which she said to Dr. Johnson "*I know nothing* of Mr. Boswell," was too severe. When, however, he recollected that his punishment was inflicted by so dignified a beauty, he had "that kind of consolation which a man would feel who is strangled by a silken cord!"

In 1773 Lady Betty Hamilton [1] was married at Argyll House to Lord Stanley, heir to the title and large estates

---

[1] Elizabeth Hamilton, only daughter of James, sixth Duke of Hamilton and Brandon, born 1753.

of the Earl of Derby, his grandfather, then in his eighty-fifth year.

The festivities on the occasion were almost regal in their magnificence. At Lord Stanley's seat in Surrey, The Oaks, a *fête champêtre* was given on the 9th June, a fortnight previous to the wedding, which caused a sensation in fashionable circles. The entertainment is elaborately described in the *Gentleman's Magazine* as being the first of the kind given in England.[1]

The festivities began early, the afternoon being employed by guests in sauntering on the lawn and witnessing a pastoral scene on a stage improvised on the grass. When it was dark the masque of "The Maid of the Oak," composed for the occasion by General Burgoyne (Lord Stanley's uncle by marriage),[2] was led by Lord Stanley, supported by Lady Betty Hamilton, the Queen of the Oak, and Miss Stanley, the rest of the company following two and two through the beautiful octagon hall with transparent windows painted suitably to the occasion. At the end of the great room hung six superb curtains of crimson satin with gold fringe, *supposed* to cover the same number of windows. Colonnades appeared on each side of the room, with wreaths of flowers running up the columns. The whole building was lined, chair-back high, with white Persian and gold fringe. Here the company amused themselves by dancing minuets and cotillons com-

---

[1] All the arrangements were under the supervision of those wonderful artists, the Adam brothers, who may, with justice, be called the universal providers of their time.

[2] Colonel, afterwards General, Burgoyne, had run away with Charlotte, daughter to the eleventh Earl of Derby. In 1777 he commanded the British army in America, and was afterwards made commander-in-chief of the army in Ireland. Horace Walpole says that after the great people had enjoyed General Burgoyne's composition, "The Maid of the Oak" was dished up by Garrick at Drury Lane in the following November; it had only a short run. Another play written by the gallant general was more successful. The *fête* at The Oaks was made the subject of two pictures painted on panels by Antonio Zucchi in Lord Derby's house in Grosvenor Square which was built and decorated by Robert Adam. The pictures are now at Knowsley Park. The principal figures are portraits, the two entering the supper room and leading the dance being unquestionably Lord Stanley and Lady Betty Hamilton.—From the Knowsley Catalogue.

posed by the Earl of Kelly. Lord Stanley, in the costume of " Reubens," and Lady Betty as " Reubens' wife," opened the ball, and the rest of the nobility danced in their turns, until supper, which was served at half-past eleven, when an explosion, similar to a large number of rockets going off, put the whole lively group into consternation.

After supper the masque of " The Glory of the Oak " was presented to the company. A Druid of the Oak, personated by Captain Pigott, summoned fauns and wood-nymphs to attend the ceremony. These then entered, led by Cupids and Sylvans, and sang a grand chorus, and the whole concluded with a device in transparency with two hymeneal torches lighted on the top, and a shield representing the Hamilton crest (an oak with a saw through it) and a ducal coronet.

George Selwyn, who was present, and who evidently thought the whole thing a bore, says it appeared to him as if Colonel Burgoyne had planned it and Lord Stanley had paid for it. The Druids, he adds, had Lord March for their speaker, which " fl̃ame says was not very *desent*." As we may imagine, the *fête* gave plenty of food for talk and gossip to the world of " Powder and Patches," which was even more ill-natured than our world of Belgravia, and did not relish such homage to be paid to other than themselves, and that other " Betty Gunning's daughter ; " so they called the *fête* a splash made to mortify a certain young lady who had shown the bad taste to reject Lord Stanley only a few weeks previously. " All the world was there," writes that funny old lady, the Dowager Lady Gower, " except the Bloomsbury lot, who that old hoyden, the Duchess of Bedford, would not let go, or go herself, I suppose, because of his recovering her niece's rejection so soon."[1]   Horace Walpole hears the entertainment will cost five thousand pounds, and remarks with a sneer that Lord Stanley has bought all the orange trees round London, and supposes hay-cocks will be

[1] Lady Gower was a most pleasant letter writer. She possessed wonderful vitality, continuing to ride when over seventy years of age. She was sister-in-law to the Duchess of Bedford, and no love was lost between the ladies.

made of straw-coloured satin. Gentle Mrs. Delany has nothing but praise for everything and everybody. People, she says, in "general wore costume and were elegantly dressed, but not masked, the very young were attired as peasants, the next in age as Polonaise (?), the matrons and men in dominoes; but some of the latter were disguised as *gardiners* (surely a simple make up)." The affair would seem to have been too long, and must have engendered a certain weariness; and for the young Lady Betty, the principal performer in the show, it was heavy work. The Duke of Argyll said, "nothing but Betty could have stood it," and one is inclined to agree with this definition of the day's amusement. It was reported the very following morning that Lord Stanley's match was off, the lady disliking him. "Sure," says Lady Gower, "she should have known her mind before she accepted ye entertainment." Whether there was any truth in this bit of gossip or not, we only know that the wedding took place at Argyll House on the 23rd June. It was in all respects an ideal marriage, the young couple having youth, good looks, exalted rank, splendid fortune, everything, excepting, perhaps, lasting affection. They had both married hastily, only to repent for twenty odd long years. The young wife seems to have been of a sweet and loving nature, with a touch of her aunt, Lady Coventry's, lightness of character. The picture painted of her in the year of her marriage by Sir Joshua Reynolds shows us what a pretty creature she was. The portrait represents her in her character of bride, wreathing with flowers the inevitable Altar of Hymen, on which (possibly to give a touch of colour to the picture) perched Sir Joshua's macaw, a stock property piece.

The following letter, written by the Duchess to Sir William Hamilton,[1] is full of interest. It shows that Lady Betty was *persuaded* into marrying Colonel Stanley, a mother's prudence "talking down a daughter's heart." This gives the key to the future position and explains the short duration of the happiness upon which the Duchess dilates :—

---

[1] Sir William Hamilton then residing at Naples as Ambassador.

ELIZABETH, DUCHESS OF HAMILTON.

[To face page 8*.

"Argyll House,
"August ye 12th, 1774.

"I have with the greatest pleasure received your congratulations upon my daughter's marriage. It is an event that gives me the greatest satisfaction. Lady Betty might have taken the name of Stanley long ago if she had chose it. A very sincere attachment on his side has at last produced the same on hers, and I have the comfort of knowing that she is really happy. You will do her great injustice if you imagine that her great vivacity prevents her thinking when it is of real consequence, *R.* I am confident she will make a good wife, she has all the ingredients necessary, having the very best temper in the world, a good understanding, and I am sure you would easily excuse me if you could guess to what a degree I love her.

"The Duke of Argyll desires me to say many kind things for him—you must imagine them—but pray give my best compliments to Lady Hamilton, and believe me, etc." [1]

Lord Stanley succeeded to the title and estates of his grandfather in 1776, and it soon became evident that he and his young wife did not, as the saying goes, hit it off. The slender amount of mutual liking with which they had set out dwindled away in a few years to *nil*—the story of Lord and Lady Coventry repeating itself. The Earl indeed was not so pompous or contradictious as Lord Coventry. He was an accomplished man with a taste for the drama. The intimacy between him and Miss Farren unfortunately widened the breach between him and his wife, but already there had been differences between the young pair. Betty, although gentle and sweet, had somewhat of the lightness of character of her Aunt Maria, and had inherited very little of the good sense remarkable in her mother. She affected to be indifferent to her husband's coldness. She went everywhere encouraging a train of admirers round her. We hear of her at a ball given by a Mrs. Onslow in St. James's Square, a locality just made the fashion by the brothers Adam. She stayed until five o'clock

---

[1] This letter is published for the first time from Morrison MS

in the morning; her chair not coming for her and no chairmen to be had at that hour, two young bloods of the day, Lord Lindsay and Mr. Storer, undertook the charge of carrying her pretty ladyship home in Mrs. Onslow's chair. On their way they met her own chair and chairmen, but,

COUNTESS OF DERBY.
(Lady Betty Hamilton.)

says the chronicler of this bit of news, they would not give up their fair burden, only halting to furnish themselves with the chairmen's straps, that they might finish their task more steadily.

These sort of escapades would not be pleasing to a man of Lord Derby's character, tenacious of his own self-respect, and when, in the next year, his wife's name was coupled with that of the Duke of Dorset, a report went about in society that Lord Derby meant to take the matter up seriously. Lady

Gower heard he had announced to Lady Derby on a certain Friday that the divorce had actually begun. Another report said the Duke of Dorset had waited on her brother, the Duke of Hamilton, and declared his intention of marrying Lady Derby as soon as the law allowed him. This ill-natured story was all nonsense. There were no divorce proceedings, the matter was tided over for the time, and next season Lady Derby appeared under her mother's wing, the gayest of the gay. " Her mother is fonder of her than ever," writes one of Mrs. Delany's correspondents, " and says the Duke of Argyll has wrote to her to come to Scotland, but she will not leave Lady Derby." This year she was at Admiral Keppel's [1] trial looking lovely, and soon after this, in 1779, a separation was arranged on friendly terms between her and Lord Derby, whose devotion to Miss Farren had now become a matter of notoriety. Considering the great anxiety of the actress to secure for herself the position occupied by the Countess, and the equally strong desire on the part of her noble lover to meet her wishes, there can be no more convincing proof of Lady Derby's innocence of anything which could have given a chance of procuring a divorce; for the rest, her conduct was undoubtedly open to censure, on one occasion she ran away from her husband's house, and was brought back by her brother the Duke of Hamilton.

To return to the Duchess of Argyll. As she advanced in life distinctions were showered upon her. In 1776 she was created a Peeress in her own right, with the title of Baroness Hamilton of Hambledon, rather an unnecessary distinction for a double duchess, but which gave rise to Dr. Johnson's " douce expression " that she was a duchess with three tails. [2] Again, in 1778, fresh honours came to her. She was appointed

[1] Admiral Keppel was tried upon some charges brought against him by his Vice-Admiral, Sir Hugh Palliser, for misconduct at the battle of Ushant. He was unanimously acquitted, the mob showing their satisfaction by breaking all the windows in the house of his accuser. Visitors to the National Gallery are acquainted with Sir Joshua's magnificent portrait of the Admiral.

[2] The Duke of Argyll, who was against the Duchess quitting her post, dictated the letter of resignation in a cautious manner. The Duchess added this postscript:—" Though *I* write this letter the Duke dictated it."

Mistress of the Robes to the Queen. Her Majesty, however, did not like her, and on one occasion invited Lady Egremont to take her Grace's turn of office, upon which the duchess ("Betty Gunning," says the old Duchess of Gower, "has a spirit of her own ") at once tendered her resignation, which however she was induced to rescind. She was at this time in her forty-seventh year, and was still a beautiful woman. Sir Nathaniel Wraxall, who saw her a few years later, says that even then, when her health was broken by a trying illness, she presented a form, figure, and complexion which it would have been vain to seek elsewhere. He adds:—"She seemed, indeed, composed of finer clay than the rest of her sex."

It was said that the Queen was jealous of this beautiful matron, and the gossips set about a story that the duchess was endeavouring to attract the King. She who had all her life escaped the tongue of scandal, was now in a measure its victim. The Burneys, Goldsworthys and Schwellenbergs, the Horace Walpole clique, and others repeated the absurd tittle-tattle of how the duchess chatted to the King in church, behind the Queen's back and so on. There could not have been much harm supposing she had done so. The truth lay probably in the state of the poor King's mind, which was for ever travelling back over the spell of years since his coronation; he forgot, as in the case of Lady Pembroke, the lapse of time, and saw youthful charms in some ci-devant beauty and paid her antiquated although perfectly harmless compliments.[1]

It is the drawback of Court life to be ever on the watch for the slightest indications of royal favour, and to transform the simplest action into a desire to obtain undue influence. No one, however, gave for a moment any credence to these idle tales against the duchess. Later on there were stories as to the admiration of the Prince of Wales for her eldest daughter, Augusta, who in her early youth had much of her mother's

[1] The poor old King's penchant for Lady Pembroke, was very distressing to the object of it, then a mature matron. The Queen too was evidently uneasy, and tried to prevent his speaking to her, but his Majesty would watch his opportunity and slip away to the end of the room where Lady Pembroke was sitting, she being annoyed at his coming.

beauty, still she could not, said one who saw them both, be addressed as " O matre pulchra filia pulchrior." Her youth, her rank, her face, which was very charming though not intelligent, compensated for the defects of her shape and figure, she possessed, however, neither accomplishments nor mental qualities to retain her Hamlet in lasting bondage ; [1] the poor Ophelia had rather a melancholy fate. Harassed by the *on dits* flying about as to the Prince's sudden coldness, Lady Augusta took a summary way of cutting short all the annoyance she was enduring. She had other admirers ready to avail themselves of her state of mind, and with one of these, Mr. Clavering, she eloped one night from the Duchess of Ancaster's ball.[2] Miss Burney, who mentions the circumstance, is full of horror at a duke's daughter being guilty of an action only fit for a housemaid. Her mother was much of the same opinion. A lively scene took place when the duchess was hiring Lady Tweeddale's house on Twickenham Green, for the family of her brother, General Gunning. Lady Tweeddale, who probably knew where to run a malicious needle into her visitor, wished her joy on Lady Augusta's marriage, to which the other answered, with all Betty Gunning's spirit, " No great joy, madam. There was no occasion for Lady Augusta Campbell to marry." [3]

[1] The Court had nicknamed the poor girl Ophelia, mad for love of the Prince Hamlet. The Duke of Argyll was Polonius.

[2] " His being only twenty-two and she some years older, makes people imagine that she rather ran away with him, than he with her. They went away from the Duchess of Ancaster's, who saw masks that night. The Duchess of Argyll went home, and thought that Lady Augusta would soon follow her ; but after sitting up till five o'clock, and no Lady Augusta returning, she sent in search of her to the Duchess of Ancaster's. No tidings were to be learned there of the fair fugitive. She, it seems, as soon as her mother went home, left the Duchess's with Mr. Clavering, and went with him to Bicester, in Oxfordshire, where they were married ; she, it is said, was married in her domino. Lady Augusta had leisure to repent her foolish marriage. She passed a long and obscure life far from the splendour of Courts or capitals, within the walls of an antique castle in a severe climate, by no means in affluence, after having undergone the humiliation of seeing her husband, General Clavering, committed to Newgate for prevarication in attempting to defend the Duke of York's conduct as Commander-in-Chief."—" Wraxall's Memoirs."

[3] Lady Augusta Campbell's portrait by John Benwell, was engraved by Bartolozzi, and is well known under the name of a " St. James' Beauty." The original is in the possession of H. H. Almack, Esq.

"Lord, my dear!" returned her ladyship, with a sarcastic laugh, "I wonder to hear you say so, who have been already twice married."

The Duchess's health had long been failing. In 1784, Charles Greville writes to Sir William Hamilton: "The Duke of Argyll has gone with his whole family and Lady Derby to the South of France. The Duchess is very weak and low, and would not follow the advice of the faculty unless attended by her *whole* family. I fancy we shall not see her again." She did, however, return, and was said to have had a hand in writing to bring about a marriage between her niece and the Marquis of Lorne. This does not seem probable, although the Duchess was devoted to her own family. She fell ill again, and died[1] at Argyll House on the 3rd March, 1790, at the comparatively early age of fifty-eight. She was buried at the collegiate church of *Helmore* in Argyllshire.

We cannot conclude without a word as to her second daughter, Lady Charlotte Campbell, one of the beauties at the beginning of the present century. She was a most gifted woman. Some people still alive can recall her brilliant talents and charm. She was the friend of Walpole, of Mrs. Damer, of the Miss Berrys, and was a remarkable feature in society both in Paris and London for many years, having a reputation as a beauty, a wit, and an authoress. In the last named category she took a high position, her books having a first place in her own day, and even now being read with pleasure, as they bear the test of time better than most works of fiction written in another phase of society. "The Divorced," and the "Memoirs of a Peeress," will always hold their own, if only as pictures of a bygone age, while the "Life and Times of George IV." is of value to all readers of Court life. This last is, however, a very severe and biting commentary on her own time. Lady Charlotte

---

[1] In connection with the Duchess's death there is, in the Hamilton and Nelson MS. before mentioned, an interesting letter from Emma Hart (Lady Hamilton) to her former admirer, Charles Greville, in which she bears testimony to the Duchess's true kindness of heart. "I never had such a friend as her," writes Emma ungrammatically, but gratefully.

married twice ; first her cousin, Colonel Campbell—secondly, Mr. Bury.

Literary talent is hereditary, although, like beauty, it some-times skips a generation. The present Duke of Argyll is a cultured writer, with a certain grace of style that re-minds one of Lady Charlotte. The Marquis of Lorne and Lady Frances Balfour have likewise a share of the literary gift, and possess decided originality.

We must now take a glance at the remaining members of the Gunning family, giving first place to Mr. and Mrs. Gunning, who have dropped out of their position in this narrative. This is due to the fact that, having played their part in securing so much good fortune to their beautiful daughters, they probably took their ease for the rest of their days—at least, very little is said about them. One can imagine that Mr. Gunning was somewhat of a thorn in the flesh of his noble sons-in-law, resembling, as he did in many ways, Captain Costigan, with his rich South of Ireland brogue and general pompous manner. His constant boasting would have been tiresome, "Me daughter, the duchess," and "Me daughter, the countess," being for ever on his lips. The latter seems to have been good to him. There is a letter in verse written by him to his grand-daughter, Lady Anne Coventry, aged two years old, "On the recall of the French Ambassador, from her affectionate Grandpapa." It was just in keeping with his character to write to a mere baby on such a subject.

His miniature, engraved by Houston from Leotard's miniature,[1] is a proof of his absurdity ; underneath the likeness there are four verses in Latin. The picture has, to the left, six circles enclosing Love, Peace, Tranquility, Mildness, Temperance, Joy ; to the right, six circles enclosing Hatred, Variance, Pride, Wealth, Drunkenness, Despair. Two doves (three doves were the Gunning crest), are on each side with eight verses transcribed below them

[1] This engraving is very rare. There are only two known. One is in the National Gallery. Dublin, in the fine collection presented by Lord Iveagh.

beginning, "Now on the verge of three score and ten praise ye the Lord." Below there is a circle with an account of his preference for doing works of charity in preference to hearing Miss Brent sing.

Round his neck hangs a medallion with a portrait of Lady Coventry.[1] He died in 1767 at Somerset House,[2] where Mrs. Gunning had for many years enjoyed the lucrative appointment of housekeeper. This was a sinecure office involving no trouble and bringing in a good income. Here she likewise died in 1770.

It will be remembered that beside the two elder sisters there were three other children, two girls and a boy. Lizzie, the eldest of the three, died of consumption in 1753. Her promise of beauty was even greater than that of her sisters. Her mother used to say that had she lived, the blaze of her beauty "would have set the world on fire." In view of such a calamity it was as well she died so young.

Catherine, the youngest girl, was fortunately not so dangerously handsome. From the portrait of her by Cotes we can see how nearly she resembled both the beauties, Lady Coventry perhaps the most. The smile is almost identical, and she has the same expression of most engaging frankness. Houston engraved three half-lengths of the sisters in one

---

[1] From the time of Lady Coventry's death Mr. Gunning wore this medallion suspended round his neck. In his account of the Duke of Richmond's famous masquerade in 1763, Horace Walpole says, "Old Gunning was there, habited as a running footman with a miniature of his late daughter hung, like the Croix de St. Louis, round his neck."

[2] All manner of romantic histories are connected with old Somerset House, which took its name from the Protector. Queen Anne of Denmark made it her palace, and it was called Denmark House in her honour. Inigo Jones beautified it exceedingly, for his good friend and patroness, and here some of his lovely masques were given. Henrietta Maria, who likewise annexed it, banished all carnal amusements, and filled it with Capuchin Friars, who, in their turn, were banished. It was said that the Pretender was secreted in Somerset House. Under the Georges it was constantly occupied by royal guests. Christian of Denmark and the Duke of Brunswick lodged there at the time of their marriages with the royal princesses. Under George III. it was demolished, and rebuilt by Sir William Chambers, when the front wing, looking on the Strand, was devoted to the Royal Academy of Arts. The office of Housekeeper seems to have been almost hereditary in the Gunning family. It was enjoyed by Lady Mayo (Bridget Gunning) for many years after the death of Lord Mayo.

frame, side by side. On the left hand is Maria (after Cotes's watch-paper miniature). Underneath is written some doggrel :—

> "In other conflicts numbers may prevail,
> In Love alone you'll find this maxim fail."

MISS KITTY GUNNING.

In the centre of the frame is a copy of the head of Elizabeth, after Hamilton. Underneath, the lines :—

> "The sister Graces when we view apart,
> Each thus resistless captivates the heart."

To the right appears the copy of a head, after Cotes, of "Miss Kitty Gunning." Underneath the lines :—

> "But if the Graces we together see,
> Not knowing which to chuse, they set us free."

This is a proof of how like the sisters were. Their fates were, however, very different. As is often the case when the elder members of a family succeed beyond all expectation, Miss Kitty considered she had only to go in and win. Perhaps she soared too high, or that there had been enough of the Gunnings. It is impossible to reckon on luck, it being all the world over a most capricious mistress. The story goes that Catherine was of a sweet and retiring disposition, and at the very outset of her career made a love match with a young Irish gentleman, Travis by name, and they lived happily ever afterwards in their remote country home.

The facts of the case, however, have not this romantic setting, Miss Kitty not marrying the man of her heart (if he were thus distinguished) until she had reached, according to the prevailing opinion of the day, the very verge of old maidenism. She was in her thirtieth year when she gave her hand to Robert Travis on the 6th May, 1769; neither did she retire to the country, to live happily ever after.

We find that on her mother's death, which took place a few months after Mrs. Travis's marriage, the office of House-keeper to Somerset House was transferred to her, and that here she died after four years of marriage, in 1773, at the early age of thirty-three. Her portrait, after Cotes, was engraved by Houston and sold by John Bowles at the " Black Horse," on Cornhill. Underneath are the lines :—

> " This youngest of the Graces here we view,
> So like in beauty to the other two ;
> Whoe'er compares their features and their frame
> Will know at once that Gunning is her name."

GENERAL GUNNING AND THE STORY OF HIS DAUGHTER GUNILDA.

It will be remembered that when Miss Bellamy came to the rescue of the family in the obscure lodgings in Britain Street, she was struck with a sweet boy of three years old. This sweet boy, growing to man's estate, reaped considerable advantage from the aristocratic marriages of his sisters. It was the day when interest was all-powerful, and young Gunning, being drafted into the army, passed rapidly from one grade to another, until he was gazetted a full-fledged general. It is due to him, however, to state that he was not altogether a feather-bed soldier; he did some good service at the Battle of Bunker's Hill. Those who knew him considered him like his father in being somewhat pompous, and he was evidently inflated with a notion of his own importance, for on one occasion he published a pamphlet, claiming to be 32nd in descent from Charlemagne.

In spite of his handsome face and many advantages, he married, in 1769, to disappoint his family. His wife was a Miss Minifie, of Fairwater, in Somersetshire. It does not appear that she was either rich or beautiful, but she was an authoress, having already written two novels. The marriage was not a happy one. Mrs. Gunning was deficient in tact; she was always doing something to annoy her husband. Horace Walpole was of opinion that there was madness in the Minifie family, and if so, the poor lady was surely not accountable for her mistakes. There were two children of this marriage—girls both. The mother found them in her way and sent them out to nurse, as was the custom in those days. The younger, Helen, was adopted by a lady, who brought her up as her own child.' The other, Catherine, christened later on "Gunilda" by Horace Walpole, has a singular story of her own, which is now forgotten, but which in its day caused more stir than perhaps it merited. It is strange enough to bear repeating here.

The young lady, it appears, was ambitious; from her childhood she had heard of the good fortune of her aunts, who had come to London with only their beauty as their fortune, and being fired with a laudable desire to follow their example, she too, resolved to be a duchess. She forgot, putting aside the fact that there is no heredity of good luck, that the important factor of beauty being wanting in her case, the difficulty would be all the greater. Catherine was far from handsome; some people called her plain. She had a fine complexion, the long eyes of the Gunnings spoiled by the long nose of the Minifies, but no one could deny that from the same source she inherited the most beautiful hand and arm, charms which, in the days of our great grandmothers, were held in consideration. We are told, on the authority of Dr. Whalley, "that her manners were most pleasing, and her temper and disposition excellent."

Casting about for strawberry leaves, Miss Gunning, in the first instance, selected her cousin, Lord Lorne, and bestowed upon him her youthful affections. She had ample opportunities for securing his, as the Duchess of Argyll, her aunt, was very kind to her brother's family, and had them constantly with her. It got whispered about that a marriage between the cousins would be probably the event of the season. Doctor Whalley, who lived near the general, and was intimate with the family, writing to his sister in May, 1788, says :—

"The Gunnings are leaving Langford Hall next month,

' This story rests on slight grounds. It was stated by a writer in the *Argosy* of 1891, with the addition that Helen married the son of Mrs. Farleigh, the lady who adopted her. Miss Hamilton also mentions in her diary calling for the *two* Miss Gunnings, and taking them in Mrs. Boscawen's coach to see "ye vase at her uncle Sir William Hamilton's." On the other hand, we have Mrs. Gunning's oft-repeated declaration that she had only one child, her darling Catherine.

and the new tenants take possession of it at Midsummer. Saving *their dirt*, we should like our old ones best. It is said, but this is strictly *entre nous*, that Miss Gunning is engaged to her cousin, the Marquis of Lorne, and that the marriage will take place on his return from the Continent. He is handsome, amiable, clever, exclusive of titles, riches, and God knows what. Has she not provided well for herself? But I must, in justice, say that she merits and will grace the highest exaltation ; she is totally uncorrupted by the gay and great, and as humble, affable, and benevolent as before she mixed in the splendours and dissipations of the Great City."

Here we have a testimony to Gunilda's virtues ; it smacks somewhat of the sprouting strawberry leaves, which the clergyman saw already on her youthful brow, and which made him condone even " THE DIRT." The contemplated marriage, however, came to nothing, there being, in fact, no ardour on the part of the supposed bridegroom, who laughed at the notion. The " uncorrupted " Gunilda, nothing daunted, turned her battery against another dukeling, Lord Blandford,[1] son of the Duke of Marlborough, and here her imagination would appear to have run riot. Whether she had any grounds for the assertion which she made boldly, that he was her lover, must always remain amongst the undiscovered secrets, but it seems more than probable that the wish to be Duchess of Marlborough was the parent of the whole invention.

Some two years after the Lorne disappointment, in the month of January, 1790, we find the Gunnings living in good style in St. James's Place, the family consisting of the general, his wife, daughter, and " Auntie Peg,"—a sister of Mrs. Gunning. They kept a carriage and a household of servants, and Miss Gunning had her chair and her own footman, as befitted her future dignity; for it was now universally said that she had made a conquest quite equal to

---

[1] George William, eldest son of the Duke and Duchess of Argyll, born 1768, consequently 23 years of age. He married in 1810 a daughter of Lord Jersey, and died without issue.

that of her beautiful aunts. Of course Horace Walpole has
the story, and writes it all round to his correspondents.

"She is to have the same jointure as the Duchess of
Marlborough," he writes to Miss Berry, "but Lady Clackmannan,[1] who has, you may be sure, questioned both the
duke and Lord Lorne, says the former answered coolly:
'They tell me that it is to be'; the other said, '*He* knew
nothing of the matter.'"

The Duke of Gloucester believed there was nothing in it,
but General Conway[2] asserted the truth of the report so
peremptorily that Mr. Walpole was fain to believe in a
second blossom of dukes to the Gunnings, but again thought
it was due to the semi-dotage of the old Duchess of Bedford,[3]
who was still harping upon "conjunctions copulative."
Mrs. Gunning was very distinct on the subject to her intimate
friends. She told her cousin, a certain Mrs. Bowen, on the
20th of January, that the marriage was fixed and the settlements signed . . but that it was still a secret—even from
the general. She also confided in the Duke of Argyll,
although not to the extent of the settlements. . . Presently,
however, the young lady declared to the receiving of constant
love letters from the marquis, who, she averred, was all anxiety
to marry her, but was coerced by his family, although in the
beginning they had given every encouragement to the match.
Thereupon, the Duchess of Argyll took up the cudgels for
her niece, and went about saying that the general, her brother,
was not a man to be trifled with. The general, to show that

---

[1] Lady Clackmannan was a name for a lady much given to gossip.
[2] "You asserted so peremptorily Miss Gunning's match with Lord
Blandford that though I doubted it *I* quoted you. Lo! it took its rise
solely in poor old Bedford's dotage, that still harps on conjunctions
copulative, but now disavows on a remonstrance from her daughter."—
Horace Walpole's letter to Hon. H. Conway, August 9, 1790.
[3] This was Gertrude, the old Hoyden of Bloomsbury (see page 87).
Her daughter had married George, Duke of Marlborough, in 1762; the
Marquis of Blandford was twenty-five. The old duchess had still wit
enough to be exceedingly mischievous. She was a scandal-loving, be-
rouged, card-playing old dame, such as Richardson loved to paint.
When she was vice-queen in Dublin she would go to anyone for a game
of quadrille, and she was never so happy as when in the midst of an
intrigue or match-making.

his family was equal to that of the descendants of a soldier
of fortune like Churchill, published in the papers that he was
32nd in descent from Charlemagne.   Walpole, in his sarcastic
way, comments on this act of folly :—

> He had better like Priors, Madam,
> To cut things short, go up to Adam.

" GUNILDA " GUNNING.

At last it entered the head of the " Carlovingian Hero," as
Walpole styles the general, to suspect that *something* was
wrong.   It was either a trick, or they were the compositions
of his wife, the Minifie novelist.[1]   He inclined to the latter

---

[1] Miss Minifie and her sisters had been joint authoresses of several
sentimental novels. Mrs. Gunning, after the *dénouement* of her
daughter's extraordinary history. gave the world a novel in four
volumes called " Mary." This is written after the manner of " Evelina,"
in letters, but without the charm that makes that obsolete style
bearable. " Mary," however, owing to the circumstances under which
it saw the light, ran into three editions.

supposition, and on another supposed love letter arriving, he examined it closely, and found that it had been altered and interlined; whereupon, thinking this was confirmation of his suspicions, he, in his impetuous Irish fashion, took the matter into his own hands, and sent off the whole packet to Lord Blandford, who immediately distinguished the two kinds, owned the few letters that were his, and disavowed the others.

The rest of the story is best told in the words of the Prince of Raconteurs, who in his own inimitable fashion, sets it all before us in so life-like a manner, that one can fancy it news of yesterday, instead of its happening one hundred and three years ago.

Letter to Miss Berry.

" 13th February, 1791.

" The following narrative, although only the termination of a legend, you know by the foregoing chapters, is too singular and too long to be added to my letter, therefore you will receive two by the same post, and you will not require. . . . The *Gunnihiad* is completed, and not by a marriage like other novels of the Minifies'. *Voici* how the *dénouement* happened. The general and his ducal brother-in-law of Argyll thought it expedient that Miss Charlemagne's [1] character should be cleared as far as possible; she still maintaining the prodigious encouragement she had received from the parents of her intended *sposo*, she was ordered to draw up a narrative which should be laid before the Duke of Marlborough, and if allowed by him, it was to be shown for her vindication. [2] She obeyed,

---

[1] It now came out that the Charlemagne letter was another forgery. The general had never heard of his royal descent. " It is true I am well born," he said, " but I know no such family in Ireland as the *Charlemagnes*."—Horace Walpole to Miss Berry.

[2] LETTER FROM GENERAL GUNNING TO THE DUKE OF MARLBOROUGH.

" St. James's Place, 3rd February, 1791.

" MY LORD,—I have the honour of addressing this letter to your Grace not with the smallest wish after what has passed of having a marriage established between Lord Blandford and my daughter, or of claiming any promise or proposal to that effect, but merely to know *whether* your Grace or the Duchess of Marlborough have it in recollection that your Graces, or Lord Blandford, ever gave my daughter reason to think a marriage was once intended.

" My motive for giving this trouble arises merely from a desire of

and her former assertions did not suffer by the new statement, but one singular circumstance was added. She confessed, ingenuous maid, that though she had not been able to resist so dazzling an offer, her heart was still her cousin's—the other Marquis (of Lorne). Well, this narrative, after being laid before a confidential Junto at Argyle House, was sent to Blenheim by the general's own groom. Judge of the astonishment of the Junto when Carloman laid before them a short letter from the Duke of Marlborough, declaring how delighted he and his Duchess had been at their son's having made choice of so beautiful and amiable a virgin for his bride, how greatly they had encouraged the match, and how chagrined they were that from the lightness and inconstancy of his temper the projected alliance was quite at an end.[1]

removing any imputation from my daughter's character, as if she had entertained an idea of such importance without any reasonable foundation.

"For my own satisfaction, and that of my particular friends who had been induced to believe the reports of the intended marriage, I have desired my daughter to draw up an accurate narrative of every material circumstance on which that belief was founded.

"This narrative I have the honour of transmitting to your Grace for your own perusal, and that of the Duchess of Marlborough and Lord Blandford, thinking it highly suitable that you should have an early opportunity of examining it—and I beg leave to request that your Grace will, after examination, correct or alter such passages as may appear either to Your Grace, the Duchess of Marlborough, or Lord Blandford, to be erroneously stated. . .

"I have the honour to be,

"With the greatest respect, my Lord,

"Your Grace's most humble and

"Most obedient servant,

"JOHN GUNNING."

[From Captain Bowen's affidavit.]

[1] ANSWER FROM THE DUKE OF MARLBOROUGH TO GENERAL GUNNING.

"Blenheim.

"SIR,—I take the earliest opportunity to acknowledge the receipt of your letter, and to answer it with that explicitness you are so much entitled to. From the first of the acquaintance of the D——s of Marlborough and myself had with Miss Gunning, we were charmed with her, and it was with infinite satisfaction we discovered *Blanford's* sentiments similar to our own. It had been long the wish of both to see him married to some amiable woman. Your daughter was the one we had fixed on, and we had every reason to suppose the object of his tenderest affections, and, from the conduct of both himself and his family, yourself and Miss Gunning had undoubtedly *every* right to look on a marriage as certain. Indeed, when I left town last summer, I

" This wonderful acquittal of the damsel the groom deposed to have received half an hour after his arrival at Blenheim, and he gave the most natural and unembarrassed account of all the stages he had made coming and going.

" You may still suspect, and so did some of the Council, that every word of this report and this letter was not Gospel, though *I* [1] thought the epistle not irreconcilable with other parts of the conduct of their Graces about their children, still I defy you to guess a thousandth part of the marvellous explanation of the mystery.

" The first circumstance that struck me was that the Duke in his own son's name had forgotten the D in the middle—that was possible in the hurry of doing justice. Next the wax was black, and nobody could discover for whom such illustrious personages were in mourning. Well, that was no proof one way or the other; unluckily, someone suggested that Lord Henry Spencer was in town, though he was to return next day to Holland. A messenger was sent to him late at night, to beg that he would repair to Argyle House. He did; the letter was shown to him ; he laughed, and said it had not the least resemblance to his father's hand. This was negative detection enough. But now comes the most positive and wonderful unravelling. The next day the general received a letter from a gentleman [2] confessing that his wife, a cousin of

---

regarded her as my future daughter, and I must say it is with sorrow I relinquish the idea. The actions of young men are not always to be accounted for ; and it is with regret that I acknowledge my son has been particularly unaccountable in his. I beg you will do me the justice to believe that I shall ever think myself your debtor for the manner in which you have conducted yourself in this affair, and that I must always take an interest in the happiness of Miss Gunning. I beg, if she has not conceived a disgust for the whole of my family, she will accept the sincerest good wishes of the Duchess and my daughters.

" I have the honour to remain,
" Sir,
" Your much obliged and
" Most obedient, humble servant,
" MARLBOROUGH."

[From Captain Bowen's affidavit.]

[1] This *I* would lead one to suppose Mr. Walpole was one of the *Junto.*

[2] This was Captain Bowen, who was married to Lisetta Lyster,

Miss Charlemagne's, had lately received from her a letter from the Duke of Marlborough in her favour, and begging the gentlewoman's husband would transcribe and send it to her, as she wished to send it to a friend in the country.[1] Her husband had done so, but had taken the precaution to write 'copy,' and before the signature had written 'signed M,' both which words Miss Charlemagne had erased, and then delivered the gentleman's identic transcript to the groom to be brought back as if from Blenheim, which the steady groom, on being examined anew, confessed; and that being bribed he had gone but one post and invented the rest.

"You will pity now the poor general, who had been a dupe

daughter to W. Lyster of Athleague Castle, Co. Roscommon. She was niece to General Gunning.

[1] MISS GUNNING'S LETTER TO MRS. BOWEN.

"8 o'clock, Tuesday.

"You will, my dear Mrs. Bowing, be surprised at receiving a note from me so early, but when I tell you my motive you will, I am sure, intercede with Mr. Bowing to pardon the liberty I am going to take, and grant my request. I will tell you in a very few words the situation I have, for some time, been in. Mama weded to Lord Blandford thought everything he did right, while I was merely a cypher in the whole affair; and, indeed, to tell you the truth, that was the only light I wished to be considered in; for though I acknowledged him to be very aimiable, my heart refused him any share in it, as it has long been devoted to another.

"Within this week I have gained papa so far of my side as to represent to him that I was displeased with the conduct of Lord B.; and as he has a natural affection for the person interested in my application, he the more readily joined me, and three days ago wrote, at my positive request, to the Duke of Marlborough to tell him that I was not satisfied with Lord B., and in the most handsome manner wished to break off all further connection. The Duke of M. wrote a letter which he received yesterday, and of which I enclose you the copy, and beg you will have the goodness to ask Mr. Bowing to write it off fair for me; as I wrote it from memory, and wish to send it to a friend of mine this evening by the post. Pray tell him my story, but save me as much as you can. If I could present Lord Lorne to you he would be an apology for everything I have done. Neither papa or I have courage to tell mama this, for she detests the person dearest to me on earth. I am sure I may depend on your not telling her any part of this letter. I should have spoken to you last night, only found I had not courage. Do not send any note or message to this house about the contents of this letter. I will send to you about two o'clock for the copy I hope Mr. Bowing will have the goodness to send me. I would call, but that I am to be all the morning at Argyle House. I write in such a hurry, I do not believe you will be able to read this.

"Ever yours affectionately,

"E. GUNNING."

from the beginning and shed floods of tears—nay, has actually turned his daughter out of doors,[1] as she is also banished from Argyle House, and Lady Charlotte (Campbell) to her honour, speaks of her with the utmost indignation; in fact, there never was a more extraordinary tissue of effrontery, folly, and impertinence. You may depend upon the authenticity of this narrative, and may guess from whom I received all the circumstances." We are at liberty to guess also, and his informant, no doubt, was Mrs. Damer, who was the dear friend of Lady Charlotte Campbell, the daughter of the Duke of Argyll and cousin to Gunilda.

While sharing the indignation that all honourable people must feel at such a series of deception, one cannot help a certain measure of pity for the wretched girl who had thus disgraced herself, when one thinks of the Junto sitting upon her conduct, and the betrayal of her cousin, Mrs. Bowen, together with the shame of being branded as a liar and a forger. Still, to the last she would confess nothing. The whole matter might have died away had it not been for the want of tact and prudence of her friends who certainly did not act upon the advice given in the French proverb as to private family washing. To say nothing of the extraordinary action of General Gunning in violently expelling his erring wife and daughter from his house, Mrs. Gunning on her side had the folly to take the public into her confidence by publishing a letter to the Duke of Argyll which highly diverted fashionable society, and must have made the fortune of the printer.

The lady who, as we know, was an "authoress," filled pages in the high-flown language of the time; she imposed on the Duke the task of searching for this mystery in the very deepest recesses of its "dark recess." The spotless innocence of her "glorious child" had everything to hope and nothing to fear; the foes of her soul's treasure might be multiplied as the sands of the sea shore. Let them be dragged out of their lurking places. She does not scruple to drag out of its hiding place *her* domestic unhappiness, she unveils the faults of the

---

[1] The Duchess of Bedford lent the mother and daughter Lord John Russell's house.

general, his neglect, infidelities, stinginess. She denounces him as the author of the plot to disgrace his own child, and she stigmatizes as human monsters Captain and Mrs. Bowen, who, she avows, were paid by him to forge the letters. She gives no reason for this insane desire on his part to degrade himself and his family, and the impression left on the mind of the reader of these 147 pages coincides with that of Horace Walpole, that the whole Minifry—meaning the mother, daughter and aunt—were in the plot to secure for Miss Gunning a ducal husband.

One of the human monsters now entered the field. On the 10th April, a month after Mrs. Gunning's pamphlet had appeared, Captain Bowen addressed the Duke of Argyll a statement of facts in answer to Mrs. Gunning. He published likewise all the affidavits and documents which were laid before counsel.[1] These are of such a nature that no one

---

[1] AFFIDAVIT OF THE GROOM.

William Pearce, groom to General Gunning, aged fifty or thereabouts, maketh to oath and saith that a pacquet and a letter were delivered to him by General Gunning, on the morning of the day he was directed by General Gunning to go to the Duke of Marlborough's and that he was directed to carry them to the Duke of Marlborough's at Blenheim, that immediately after the pacquet and letter had been so delivered to this deponent by General Gunning, Hannah Hales, who was at that time Miss Gunning's maid, came to this deponent and requested him to go to Miss Gunning; that he accordingly went to Miss Gunning who was then in her bedchamber. That it was about 10 o'clock in the morning that Miss Gunning met the deponent at the door of her room and said, "You are going to the Duke of Marlborough's," deponent answered "Yes." That then Miss Gunning said to this deponent, "You must not go." That this deponent answered, and said, "Miss Gunning, it is a matter of trust," I must perform my trust," upon which Miss Gunning said, "I would not have you go for five thousand pounds;" and that she insisted upon his not going time after time, and said that the business he was going upon was concerning a letter which she had had two or three days. And that she knew what the paper was which he had from her papa, and that it was of her own handwriting. And that this deponent saith that Miss Gunning desired him to leave the papers which had been delivered to him by General Gunning with her which she many times insisted upon. And this deponent saith he went downstairs and brought the papers which he had received from General Gunning and delivered them into Miss Gunning's own hand. That when the witness had delivered the papers which he had received from General Gunning to Miss Gunning she delivered to him a letter which she said was a letter from the Duke of Marlborough, and which she told this deponent she had opened and sealed it again with the Duke of Marlborough's arms.

[From Captain Bowen's affidavit.]

could have any reasonable doubt that Miss Gunning had tampered with the groom, and exchanged her own letter for that written by her father to the Duke of Marlborough. It would take up too much space to go into the various details of this very remarkable document which deals with all the numerous lies and deceptions of the fair Gunilda. In face .of this accumulated evidence even the greatest partisan of the fair Gunilda was obliged to be silent in her defence, a very noticeable fact being that no rebutting statement was even attempted.' The old Duchess of Bedford, who remained steadfast to her protégée, now wrote to Lord Lorne, begging him to intercede for his cousin for his dear mother's sake who doted upon her. Miss Gunning likewise posed as a persecuted victim, declaring that it was her mother's aversion to Lord Lorne which had prevented his declaring himself as her lover. They also, both mother and daughter, set about a story that a duel was to be fought between Lords Lorne and Blandford; but as this never came off, we may suppose it was another falsehood. It is difficult to imagine what object could be attained by so much deception, unless that in some natures there is such a moral warp that the mere pleasure of lying compensates for all the risk of exposure.

Another concoction was probably the letters which were said by the ladies to have passed between the father and daughter, and which appear in Mrs. Gunning's pamphlet.

GENERAL GUNNING TO HIS DAUGHTER.

" Monday evening.

" From a heart that still feels most sensibly the afflictions of a

---

' " After the groom's confession, and after Captain Bowen had been confronted with her and produced to her face her note to his wife, which she disowned resolutely, she desired the Duke of Argyll to let her take an oath on the Bible of her perfect innocence; he would not allow it. Next day, taking two of the Duchess of Bedford's servants, she went before a Justice of Peace and swore to her innocence, and said to the magistrate, "Sir, from my youth you may think I do not know the solemnity of an oath, but to convince you I do, I know my salvation depends upon what I have now sworn." It is but a burlesque part of this wonderful tale that old crazy Bedford exhibits Miss every morning on the Causeway in Hyde Park, and declares her protégée some time ago refused General Trevelyan."—Horace Walpole to Miss Berry.

father for her, who was dearly belov'd, proceeds this letter. That afflicted father desires an interview with his unfortunate daughter, in which she may depend on having no more to fear than the workings of an anxious and perhaps over-indulgent parent. The time and place of meeting is left entirely to her who is even now

"dear to

"(Signed)   G. GUNNING

" Send an answer sealed with red wax by the bearer. I have opened the note and made it up in the form of a letter. I sup to-night at Soho Square. I lodge at No. 13, Norton Street, Portland Place."

COPY OF ANSWER OF MISS GUNNING TO HER FATHER.

" Monday evening.

" Turn'd from your door defenceless, pennyless, and robb'd by you of what is and ever will be dearer than my life—my character—stigmatized for forgeries which those who really did forge the letters, and you, sir, must know I am as innocent of as heaven is free from fraud, you who I never in my life offended in thought, word or deed, to cast me out upon the wide world as a guilty creature, when you know my heart would not have harboured a thought that could have dishonoured you, myself or my sex, and after you had thrown me off, to pursue me as you would the bitterest of your enemies, to raise up false witnesses to crush that child whom you should have protected with your life, innocent as I am, and as I again repeat *you* know me to be ; even if I had been guilty, which God be praised I am not, still you should have screened me, and your chastisements should have been softened by pity. You call me unfortunate, I am unfortunate, who has made me so ?

" This unfortunate will not appear in your presence till you announce, and that in the most publick and unequivocal manner, to the whole world, how much she has been wronged by scandalous contrivances and unheard-of calumny.

" (Signed)   E. GUNNING."

There is a very theatrical ring about this letter, which would give the idea that it was written for the public. The world was indeed deluged with Gunning papers. A curious pamphlet now appeared entitled " The strange incidents in the family of General Gunning." In this the theory is started that the young lady was really in love with her cousin Lorne, and thought that by raising up an imaginary rival, she might supply the proper stimulant to quicken his addresses. In this effusion we learn a great deal of the domestic relations of General and Mrs. Gunning and the total want of harmony in their lives. Mrs. Gunning had been ordered by her husband to quit his house some time before the discovery of the forged letters. From the high falutin style in which the document is conceived, one would say it was written by Mrs. Gunning, although her identity is carefully concealed.

Meantime, Gunilda's name began to be dragged through the kennels of the press. A print appeared called "The New Art of Gunning," which represented her astride on a cannon, firing a volley of forged letters at Blenheim Castle, and the old Duchess of Bedford, " emaciated, withered, and very like," lifting up her hoop to shelter injured innocence.

An imaginary letter to the Duke of Argyle appeared next. The frontispiece presented a medallion of Gunilda, supported by two Cupids (not marquises), her name, and four verses underneath. This was soon after followed by a very amusing satirical parody of the " House that Jack Built," which was handed about privately, but which finally got into print. It was supposed to be written by the Honourable J. Fitzpatrick. Walpole, writing to his dear Berrys, sends them a copy. "This is not at all news," he says; "I have heard it once or twice imperfectly, but could not get a copy until now; and I think it will divert you for a moment, although the heroines are as much forgotten as Boadicea : nor have I heard of them since their arrival at Dover, whither they have gone terrified by Captain Bowen's threat of prosecution for libel. The town is very dull without them," adds this invincible gossip.[1]

[1] " Lord Ossory has just been here and told me that Gunilda has

I

THE PARODY ON THE HOUSE THAT JACK BUILT.

This is the note
That never was wrote.

This is the groom
That never was sent
To carry the note
That never was wrote.

This is Minifie Gunning
Who used all her cunning
The groom to prevent
That never was sent
To carry the note
That never was wrote.

This is Ma'am Bowen
To whom it was owing
That Minifie Gunning
Has used all her cunning
The groom to prevent
That never was sent
To carry the note
That never was wrote.

This is the Maiden all for Lorn
Who now by her friends is tattered and torn ;
But chief by Ma'am Bowen
To whom it is owing
That Minifie Gunning
Has used all her cunning
The groom to prevent
That never was sent
To carry the note
That never was wrote.

These are the Marquises shy of the horn
Who flew from the Maiden all for Lorn,
Who now by her friends is tattered and torn ;
But chief by Ma'am Bowen
To whom it is owing
That Minifie Gunning
Has used all her cunning
The groom to prevent
That never was sent
To carry the note
That never was wrote.

---

written to Lord Blandford in her own name, begging his pardon for promising herself marriage in his name, but imputing the first thought to his grandmother. This letter the Duchess of Marlborough carried to the Duchess of Bedford to open her eyes, but with no success ; she only said, ' You may be easy, for both mother and daughter are gone to France.'—Walpole to Miss Berry.

And these are two Dukes,
Whose serious rebukes
Frightened the Marquises shy of the horn
Who flew from the Maiden all for Lorn,
Who now by her friends is tattered and torn ;
But chief by Ma'am Bowen
To whom it is owing
That Minifie Gunning
Has used all her cunning
The groom to prevent
That never was sent
To carry the note
That never was wrote.

This is the General somewhat too bold
Whose head was too hot, though his heart was too cold ;
Who made himself single before it was meet
And his wife and his daughter turned into the street
To please the two Dukes,
Whose serious rebukes
Frightened the Marquises shy of the horn
Who flew from the Maiden all for Lorn,
Who now by her friends is tattered and torn ;
But chief by Ma'am Bowen
To whom it is owing
That Minifie Gunning
Has used all her cunning
The groom to prevent
That never was sent
To carry the note
That nobody wrote.

In the same year, September, 1791, Lord Blandford married
a daughter of Lord Galloway, and soon the whole story was
forgotten. Mrs. and Miss Gunning reappeared in London
under the ægis of the old Duchess of Bedford, "as bold as
ever," Walpole says ; "but their place in town talk is occupied
by Lady Mary Duncan."

So ended this extraordinary society scandal, which was due
to the mad ambition of mother and daughter. The amazing
folly of the whole adventure, and the manner in which the
young lady and her parents acted, can only be accounted for
by what Walpole called "the amazing folly of the race of
Gunning." "So," he says, "is their whole story ; the two
beautiful sisters were exalted almost as high as they could go.
Countessed and double duchessed, and now the family have
dragged themselves down into the very dirt."

The General was to have his share of obloquy. Left to

himself, for the Duchess of Argyll had died this same year, he fell into evil courses, got into debts and difficulties—it was said, ran away with the wife of his tailor—finally an action was brought against him for an intrigue with a Mrs. Duberly; a jury, swayed by Erskine's eloquence, awarded the injured husband 5000*l.* The General, accompanied by Mrs. Duberly, went to Italy, and lived at Naples, where he died.[1] The day before his death he altered his will, and left his wife 8000*l.*, and to his daughter his estate in Ireland. This seems as if it were a tardy act of justice, and gives an idea that *reparation* was needed; this, however, may not have been so, but that a sense of what was due to his wife and daughter influenced General Gunning to make a just disposition at the last.

Mrs. Gunning did not long survive her husband. She died in Deen Street in 1800, and was buried in Westminster Abbey. Three years after her mother's death the once famous Gunilda married Major Plunkett, of Kinnaird, in Roscommon. He was a gentleman of good family and a Catholic; having taken a prominent part in the Irish rebellion of 1798, he had been sentenced to death; he managed to effect his escape to France, and was excepted from the act of indemnity. After his marriage the influence of his wife's relations procured him liberty to reside quietly in England for many years; he and his wife lived at Long Melford, Suffolk, his presence being winked at by the government. Here Gunilda seems to have re-established friendly relations with her family; she was very popular in the county, and the father of a gentleman still residing at Long Melford was well acquainted with her, and considered her a very charming woman.[2] She occupied herself writing books; one of these, entitled "The Man of Fashion," was published in 1815 and inscribed to the Princess Charlotte, by the daughter of the late Lieut.-General Gunning, and the niece of the late Duchess of Argyll and the Countess of Coventry. Mrs. Plunkett died in 1823, and is buried at Long Melford, where a handsome monument was erected to

---

[1] Before his death he contributed to the Gunning annals "An Apology for his life"—a most unreadable biography.
[2] Mr. Almack, of Long Melford.

her memory by her husband. After her death Major Plunkett received a full pardon, and returned to his own country with his two daughters.

There are Gunnings still living in the County Roscommon,[1] but they do not descend from either Bryan or John Gunning. There was a Lieutenant George Gunning, of the 1st Dragoon Guards, who was at the battle of Waterloo; this gentleman wrote a book about his own branch of the Gunnings, and the strategic position of the troops at Waterloo.

[1] Mr. Alexander, of St. John's, Roscommon, is a grandson of the Rev. Alexander Gunning.

THE story of this beautiful and gifted woman is well known. The incidents of her career have furnished the subject of memoir, novel, and play. All the elements of romance are, indeed, to be met with in her strangely eventful life, which began in extreme poverty, turned to brilliant success, and ended tragically.

All the world is acquainted with the incidents of her childhood; how she went barefoot through the streets of Dublin, calling out "all this fine salad for a halfpenny." Her mother, who was a hawker of fruit and vegetables, carried on her head a basket of these commodities placed, as was the custom, upon a wisp of hay, and bore in her arms an infant, Peggy's sister. Mrs. Murphy (for Woffington was a name adopted much later for stage purposes) was a most respectable woman of her class. Her husband, who was a bricklayer, had been killed by a fall from a ladder, leaving his widow and two children with no means of support, save what could be earned by the basket. Later on, however, some Trinity College students, who knew the little family, subscribed to buy the poor widow a sitting in College Green, where she set up a stall for fruit, etc., and carried on a brisk business, helped by little Peggy, who was a general favourite. Their home was a miserable garret in George's Court, an ill-smelling, wretched alley close to Fownes Court, and abutting on the narrow, picturesque quay which borders the Liffey.

"There is a tide in the affairs of men which taken at the flood leads " we know where. This, which is meant metaphorically, had actual shape with Peggy, for it was by the river's side that fortune found her out. Some distance from Fownes Court and close to St. Patrick's Cathedral, there was

a stream called the Poddle, which was tributary to the river,
and where the poorer women of the Liberties, as this portion
of the city was called, washed their clothes.

A certain Madame Violante,[1] who had lately come to Dublin
as a tight-rope dancer, one morning passing through this
quarter, was attracted by the beauty of the child, who was helping her mother with the family washing, and stopped to speak
to her. This lady was manageress of a dancing booth in Fownes
Court, and was on the look-out for juvenile performers. She
soon arranged matters with Mrs. Murphy, Peggy was transferred to her care, and began her theatrical education in the
year 1727. " Woffington," says Mr. Tom Taylor, " was actually
one of the children who were appended to the feet of Madame
Violante, a famous dancer on the tight rope in Dublin." This
exhibition, however, did not draw, and Madame Violante
turned her thoughts to a novelty. Gay's *Beggar's Opera* was
just then the rage in London. All the more so because it
had been the cause of the quarrel between the author and his
patroness, the Duchess of Queensberry. Madame Violante
conceived the idea of training children to sing and act the
opera ; her dancing booth was turned into a stage, and the
venture was a signal success, Margaret's first mark being
made as Polly Peachum. All Dublin went to see the juvenile
actors. Mrs. Delany, who was then on her first visit to the
capital, where she was destined to spend so much of her life,
records going to Madame Violante's booth, when the Duke
of Dorset, then occupying the post of Viceroy, patronized the
show in Fownes Court.

Madame Violante, after a time, disappears from the story,
and we find the young girl, now fourteen, engaged at Aungier
Street Theatre, then under the management of Elrington. He

---

[1] Madame Violante was an Italian rope-dancer, famed for her feats of
strength and agility. During the years 1726 and 1727 she had exhibited
her extraordinary performances in London, meeting with great success.
In 1728 or so she opened a booth in Dublin. Her achievements were
not wholly pleasing; she made forcible appeals to the lovers of the
dreadful and the dangerous. She danced upon the high rope with
children in some way appended to her feet, by way of enhancing the
difficulties of her task, and affording the public the prized spectacle of
imperilled life. As Madame Violante's apprentice, Mistress Margaret
Woffington first appeared in public tied to the feet of her mistress.

had taken her at the request of Coffey, a playwright of some merit, who, having discovered the talent of the uneducated girl, took great pains to teach her several parts. At first, however, she merely danced, and sometimes sang between the acts. Opportunities are never wanting where there is real merit, and Margaret's chance came much in the manner we are accustomed to read of in a three volume novel.

It was in the winter of 1737, and the play of *Hamlet* was announced, with a lady of well-known reputation and mature years in the part of Ophelia. A day or so before the date fixed sudden illness seized upon the actress, and the piece was about to be postponed, when Margaret, taking courage, implored the manager to let her fill the part. Managers were then not so flinty-hearted as they are now : they were romantic beings, and must have been somewhat easy-going. There remained the difficulty that the house had been commanded for the benefit of the sick lady. Margaret, however, had troops of friends, all the students of Trinity College were her devoted slaves—they packed the house from floor to ceiling ; they applauded every word said by their favourite. Her youth and beauty did the rest—her success was triumphant. The morning paper predicted a career for the débutante, and Elrington at once gave her a tangible proof of what success meant by taking her at a regular salary to play such parts as Nell in the *Devil to Pay*, Sylvia in the *Conscious Lovers*, and *The Recruiting Officer*.

Margaret, however, had a restless disposition, and panted for further distinction, her ambition leading her to try her strength on the larger field of the London stage. Gossip said she went there in company with Mr. Taaffe,[1] one of her many admirers ; this was not indeed unlikely—poor Margaret's morals being of an easy kind. It was also said that this gentleman, in order to marry a rich heiress, deserted

---

[1] There is no certainty as to this story of Mr. Taaffe ; a gentleman of the name is mentioned as belonging to White's club about this date, and at this time Horace Walpole writes of " Mr. Taaffe having behaved disgracefully," but he does not say in what manner. In 1751, a Mr. Taaffe was concerned in an escapade of robbing a Jew in Paris in company with Edward Wortley Montague, Lady Mary Wortley Montague's son.

her after a few weeks. . . In the summer of 1739 we find her seeking an engagement with Rich, or, at least, a trial previous to a settled agreement. It was a bold venture for the half-educated pupil of Madame Violante to measure swords with such actresses as then held the stage. Mrs. Pritchard, Clive, Cibber, Hunter, were all established favourites, and there seemed no place for her.

Margaret had the grand assurance of youth, and the conviction that once she had the opportunity, she would make her mark. She managed to persuade Rich, the manager, to give her a chance at Covent Garden, or, in all probability, she found some patron who did her this service. What lends colour to this supposition is that her first appearance took place upon a night when the Prince and Princess of Wales honoured the theatre with their presence.

This was on November 6th, 1740, just thirteen years after Margaret had commenced her theatrical career, projected from Madame Violante's feet. The play was *The Recruiting Officer*, with a variety of other entertainments, dancing between the acts, and the farce of *What D'ye Call it.*

Prince Fred and his hard shrewish wife, later on to become the most unpopular woman in England, had a grand box with a canopy of scarlet silk, adorned with gold tissue. They were a most unhappy pair, crushed and mortified by their unnatural parents, and presenting a spectacle very unlike that of the existing royal family. When we look through old memoirs and histories of this embroidered, befrilled, wicked, and delightful 18th century, there is nothing strikes us more than the undignified squabbles between the royal Georges and their heirs ; the nation took part in these domestic quarrels, now siding with the father, now with the son. George II., who was of a small mind and given to spiteful revenge, was wont to make his resentment felt by those who took the young prince's part, or showed him any respect. He carried this feeling so far as to refuse his patronage to the tradesmen who supplied his son, or to the managers of public entertainments, who, like Rich, gave the prince a royal reception.[1]

The Recruiting Officer reads now as a dull play ; one cannot

In the quarrels between George III. and his son we have a repeti-

imagine how it could have been made so delightful as it seems
to have been to our great grandfathers; it has none of the
fun of *The Country Girl.* Nevertheless, Miss Woffington
scored a great success, probably because she appeared for the
first time in man's clothes. All through her theatrical career
Peg fancied the wearing of masculine attire; her fine
figure and beautiful feet and ankles showed to more advantage than in the singularly voluminous and unbecoming attire
then worn by actresses. We must also remember that in the
eighteenth century there were "no burlesques" or leg pieces.
Actresses, although by no means either modest or moral,
would have been hooted off the stage had they appeared in
the light garments in which our favourites often show themselves. Those, and they were very few, who wished to exhibit
such good points as they possessed, did so by playing men's
parts. We are told that Woffington was a wonderfully good
imitation of a man—her *air*, graceful, yet rakish, was in-
imitably gallant, and provoked applause before she opened her
mouth. When she spoke her delivery was pert and pointed,
and her witchery of eye fascinating. Her *Sir Harry Wildair*
in Farquhar's comedy, which she revived, was simply
irresistible. The part was supposed to be so difficult that
since the death of Wilkes, who had created it, the piece
had not been put on the stage. Now it produced a perfect
"furore;" the whole town went to see the new actress; "the
men were in love with her, the women envied her;" her tall,
elegant figure was seen to the utmost advantage in the rich
dress; she handled her sword with an elegant nonchalance,
and played the rake with such infinite spirit, as to give a flat
contradiction to what Farquhar had said, that when Wilkes
died Sir Harry might go to Jubilee. And yet this representing of men's parts by the weaker sex is open to much question from an artistic point of view. That Shakespeare set the
example in many of his plays does not make the precedent
applicable, as that great master of all dramatic propriety never

tion of the same story. In both cases the mothers of the princes did
nothing towards softening, but everything to increase, the animosity
between father and son.

allowed the woman's nature to be obscured. In "Rosalind" her womanly weakness of body and mind shows transparently through her disguise. Garrick always maintained that it was impossible for a woman to usurp a man's character; although she might adopt his dress, it was a mere *pro tempore* personation, and never deceived anyone. Just in the same way a man dressed in woman's clothes is easily detected. Ill-natured persons affirmed that Garrick's opinion on this subject was dictated altogether by jealousy of Mrs. Woffington's success in a part which, in his hands, was a complete failure; he never played it more than twice, whereas Mrs. Woffington's *undramatic* rendering had a run of twenty nights, which was then considered a triumph.

Her engagement with Rich was now signed and sealed, and her salary raised to nine pounds a week. This would be considered poor pay for a star in our theatres, but in the last century the star system was not known, and where there were several leading ladies the profits had to be more evenly divided. A curious, but rather significant, change took place after Margaret Woffington had made her hit in *Sir Harry*. Up to this, she had been set down in the bills as *Miss* Woffington, but from this time she appears with the prefix of Mrs.

This was Garrick's first season in London; his fame was only beginning, and he fell frantically in love with the new actress. There was everything to attract them together —the same age, the same profession, the same struggle to win a place for themselves. Garrick, whose taste was refined, was more taken by the tender, pensive mood Margaret could assume at will, than by her bold and reckless gaiety. He addressed her in refined verses that show, at this time at all events, he was serious in his wish to make her his wife; and yet had a little doubt that she was worthy of the honour.

SONG TO SYLVIA.

If truth can fix thy wavering heart
    Let Damon urge his claim.
He feels the passion void of art,
    The pure, the constant flame.

Though sighing swains their torments tell.
　　Their sensual love contemn,
They only prize the beauteous shell
　　But slight the inward gem.

By age your beauty will decay.
　　Your mind improve with years
As when the blossoms fade away
　　The ripening fruit appears.

May Heaven and Sylvia grant my suit
　　And bless the future hour.
That Damon who can taste the fruit
　　May gather every flower.

For three years Garrick was her devoted lover; in 1742 they went to Dublin, both engaged to play at the new theatre in Smoke Alley. Both were sure of a brilliant reception. Margaret was, indeed, an old favourite, and had been, as we know, the child of the town; she now returned with the cachet of London favour upon her performance. Garrick's success on this occasion has been chronicled by the historians of the Irish stage. "The theatre was not unworthy of the actor; it was built upon the best principles, was spacious, and remarkable for the excellent opportunities it afforded for seeing and hearing; it was, besides, the largest theatre in Dublin; the stage was, however, cramped and small. Only the year before, all the new improvements had been introduced; there was a spacious crush room or saloon, where the company waited after the play was over, chatting loudly until the carriages or chairs came." This was always a matter of difficulty, for Smoke, or Smock Alley, as it was afterwards called, was a miserable lane close to the river side, but wide enough for only one carriage to pass at a time. Placards were issued begging ladies not to wear hoops, as without them it would be easier for the carriage or chair to make its way, to say nothing of giving more room in the boxes. The noise made by the block in the alley, the shouting of the torch-bearers, the swearing of the coachmen, and the quarrels of the footmen, made sleep impossible for the inhabitants of the miserable houses in the narrow lane; many of them had their heads out of the windows, making choice observations on the ladies coming out of the theatre and their cavaliers. Hardly a night passed without a quarrel between some of the fashionable "bucks," and a duel would be the consequence.[1] During this engagement Margaret played constantly with Garrick as Ophelia to his Hamlet, while he was Plume to her Sylvia.

On their return to London they set up a joint establishment at 6, Bow Street, with Macklin to act as chaperone; this curious arrangement must have caused some surprise, but it does not seem that it offended in any way against the ideas of propriety or evoked any censure. The financial arrangements were carefully looked into, the lady paying her share, and the accounts were audited by Garrick. The trio lived comfortably, but it was remarked that in Garrick's months of housekeeping everything was conducted parsimoniously.

"I remember," says Dr. Johnson, "drinking tea with him long ago, when Peg Woffington made it, and he grumbled at her for making it too strong."

This household arrangement was dissolved by mutual consent as such arrangements generally are ; either in consequence of the heavy debts the actress had contracted, or that her inconstancy disgusted her lover, who of all men was the least likely to condone her irregularities.

He was jealous of the actress's many admirers, and indeed was growing weary of his fickle mistress. Still, the engagement was not broken off, their relations continuing in a fitful manner, but with little love on his side. There was no doubt he had every reason to complain, and that he did right in finally breaking with her. No power on earth could have made her loyal to her lover, but that he had all the love her capricious nature was capable of is equally certain. Their final parting was, however, delayed. She went to live at Teddington, where she amused herself making fools of old men like Cibber and M'Swiney. There was a curious circle at her villa, made up principally of jovial students and professors ; here, too, came that strange heroine of the drama,

---

[1] The overcrowding of the theatre in the very height of a hot summer produced an epidemic from which the city suffered severely ; it was called the Garrick fever.

George Anne Bellamy, then in her early youth, and sighing
to be an actress ; also Mrs. Woffington's sister, she who had,
as we know, shared with the fruit and vegetables the privilege of being hawked about the streets of Dublin. Margaret's
first care on realizing a certain income was to send her young
sister to a convent in France ; and now Miss Polly had come
home, and was an exceedingly pretty, sweet-looking girl, with
gentle, captivating ways. She showed some gifts for the
stage, and this summer it was proposed to make a trial of her
abilities in private theatricals. The play was chosen and the
parts cast in a moment. Garrick, *Orestes ;* Miss Bellamy,
Andromache ; Polly, *Hermione ;* and Mr. Sullivan, a fellow of
Trinity College, Dublin, *Pyrrhus.* All the neighbourhood were
invited, and came, but the honours fell to Miss Bellamy, with
whose acting Garrick and Sheridan, who were amongst the
spectators, were much pleased. This ended in her going on
the stage where her mother had been many years.

Polly, however, did far better on the wider stage of the
world. Her beauty and sweetness captivated a young clergyman who was present on the night of the theatricals. This
was the Honble. and Rev. Robert Cholmondeley, third son to
the Earl of Cholmondeley. The Earl was a man much distinguished for his merits ; he held many high appointments, being
Master of the Horse to Frederick, Prince of Wales, Chancellor
of the Duchy of Roxburghe, member of the Privy Council.
His wife was the only daughter of Sir Robert Walpole, Earl of
Orford. It will be imagined how a family of such position
should view the introduction of a sister of the celebrated Peg
Woffington into their domestic circle. The girl might have
been as good as she was pretty, still, they may be pardoned for
doubting it, and for objecting very strongly to a connection
which they considered a degradation to one of their son's
rank and calling. The young people had determined to marry,
and the Rev. Robert snapped his fingers at parental opposition, especially as Mrs. Woffington had undertaken to provide
for his increased expenses. Whether this fact had any effect
upon softening the Earl's prejudice, or whether Mrs. Woffington's fascinations did the work, it is impossible to say. Lord

Cholmondeley travelled to Teddington to fulminate his decree of separation between his son and Polly, but after an hour's conversation with his beautiful hostess, he withdrew all his objections, and received his future daughter-in-law with kindness. When, however, he began to assure Mrs. Woffington that her influence had reconciled him to the match, she answered him with some spirit, " My lord, I have more reason to be offended with it than you have, for before I had only one beggar to support, now I have two."[1]

All this time the actress was working hard. She was the mainstay of Rich's theatre, showing a sense of duty towards the public and loyalty to the manager which, unfortunately, she lacked in other relations. Admirers crowded round her, men of indifferent character, as Lord Darnley, Hanbury

---

[1] This was hardly true. The Rev. Robert had two livings, one at St. Andrew's, the other at Huntingdon, so that he could not have been such a pauper. After her marriage, Mrs. Cholmondeley became a well-known character in society, both in London and Bath. She was of the blue-stocking coterie, and considered a witty, vivacious, rattling woman, whose parties were more relished by Sir Joshua than those of either Mrs. Vesey or Mrs. Montagu. She is constantly mentioned in Miss Burney's memoirs as an authority. " Mrs. Cholmondeley has been reading and praising *Evelina*, and my father is quite delighted at her approbation, and told Susan I could not have a greater compliment than making two such women my friends as Mrs. Thrale and Mrs. Cholmondeley." On another occasion she gives a lively sketch of the whole family in that graphic style which places before the reader the scene and the actors in it. " Mr. Cholmondeley is a clergyman, nothing shining either in person or manners, but rather grim in the first and glum in the last. Yet he appears to have humour himself and to enjoy it in others. Miss Fanny Cholmondeley is a rather pretty pale girl; very young and inartificial, and though tall and grown up, treated by her family as a child, and seemingly well content to really think herself such." The narrative then goes on to describe the entrance of Mrs. Cholmondeley, and to retail with the writer's usual wearisome exactness all she said in praise of the most wonderful book that ever was wrote. She seems on this occasion to have acted with the vulgarity with which Mr. Taylor charges her. " I was once," he says, "in company with Mrs. Cholmondeley, who seemed to think herself a wit, endeavoured to monopolize the conversation, and evidently betrayed the vulgarity of her origin." Her daughters married into good families. Miss Fanny became, in 1788, the wife of an Irish baronet, Sir William Bellingham, then one of Pitt's secretaries. There is at Castle Bellingham a portrait of Mrs. Cholmondeley by Cotes, a sweet, gentle face with a charming expression. The family have also a fine picture of Peg Woffington. Lady Bellingham, when a child, sat for Sir Joshua's well-known picture *Crossing the Brook.*

Williams, and others of the same class, who brought her
name into disrepute. Such was the levity of her character,
that she encouraged them at the very moment that the
marriage with Garrick seemed possible. He had actually
bought the wedding ring, and she told Murphy he tried it on
her finger, and yet, with the very goal in sight for which she
had been for so many years sighing, she could not remain
steadfast to her lover. But although her conduct was such
as to merit the blame of all virtuous persons, those who throw
stones at her should remember her early training before condemning her. From the streets of Dublin to Madam Violante's booth, from thence to a still worse school of vice, the
green room, crowded as it then was with all the fashionable
roués of the day, surrounded by men who made a jest of all
virtue ; without a good woman to hold out a hand to save her,
was it any wonder that she should have thought but little of
even outward morality ? Nor is Garrick free altogether from
blame ; his delay in the first instance was not so much caused
by his scruples as by his parsimony, and when he was rising
to a position of wealth and honour he did not care to have the
drag of so doubtful a wife. His friends, too, persuaded him
that such a marriage would be injurious to him.

The whole matter worried him, and it was doubtless true
what he one day told her, "that he had lain tossing all the
night thinking of this wretched marriage, that it was a foolish
thing for both, who might do better in separate lines, and
that in short he had worn the shirt of ' Dejanira.' "

" 'Then throw it off at once, sir," said she in her shrill in-
harmonious voice. " From this moment I decline to speak to
you, unless in the course of our professional business." And
so ended their love idyll, begun in sunshine, finishing in
storm.

Their quarrel soon became known, and the public interested
itself in the separation between their favourites. Most people
sided with Mrs. Woffington, and caricatures bearing very
hard upon the actor appeared in the shop windows. There
was no doubt he deserved it. He had asked her to be his
wife with the full knowledge of the life she was leading, and

MRS. WOFFINGTON

[To face page 128.

he only awoke to the fact when his fancy had passed away. In
the ardour of his passion he had written

> " Once more I'll tune my vocal shell,
> To hills and dales my passion tell
> A flame which *Time* can never quell
> Which burns for thee, ' my Peggy.' "

And now, when it suited him to throw her aside, he reviled
her coarsely. These are the bitter lines in which he took
leave of her :—

> " I know your Sophistry, I know your Art
> Which all your dupes and fools cajole.
> Yourself you give without your heart,
> All may share that but not your soul."

This ungentlemanly attack upon the woman he had once
loved to infatuation did not improve Garrick's position ;
there was a strong feeling against him when the actress
gave her version of the affair. Altogether the actor suffered
in popular feeling more than she did—nor did her spirits
sink under his desertion. However, it is not always the
wounds that bleed outwardly that are the most dangerous, and
it may be safely affirmed that long after she had passed from
Garrick's memory, his conduct rankled in her mind. She
became from that time less womanly, harder, and more recklessly pursued the downward path.[1] After the final rupture, the
quondam lovers only met on the stage, where they had occasionally to appear *as lovers*, which must have been embarrassing.
Time, however, which softens most things, accustomed both to
the situation, but worse was to come. Tate Wilkinson, one of
the most entertaining of theatrical *raconteurs*, gives an amusing account of the change in her demeanour after Garrick
became joint patentee of Drury Lane with Lacy. No longer
having the manager to support her in her haughty and some-

---

[1] After her engagement with Garrick was broken off, she was seen
by Tate Wilkinson at the theatre in Paris, attended by Owen M'Swiney,
her ex-manager. She was quite captivated by Angelo, the well-known
fencing master, and made no secret of her admiration for him. When he
appeared at a public fencing match in Paris she presented him with a
bunch of roses which he pinned on his breast and defended against all
efforts to dislodge it. She returned to London with this gentleman.

what tyrannical dismissal of anyone who offended her, she had to keep her easily excited anger within due bounds.

Neither could she queen it over her rivals, Mrs. Clive and Mrs. Cibber, both ladies, especially the latter, being very much in the managers' good graces. No two leaders of fashion ever hated one another more unreservedly than did these great dames of the theatre, Mrs. Clive and Mrs. Woffington; in the green-room their bitter conflicts, their frequent interchange of angry looks, words, and gestures occasioned much diversion. Mrs. Clive was coarse, violent and very rude: Mrs. Woffington was well bred and seemingly very calm; she often threw Clive off her guard by an arch severity which the warmth of the other could not parry.

Margaret's proud nature must have keenly felt the sting of seeing others preferred to her, and, as soon as she could, she quitted Drury Lane and returned to her first manager, Rich, at Covent Garden. There she remained for three years, playing the best parts. She spared no pains nor trouble to learn the drudgery of her profession, and in some characters she has never been excelled, her *Rosalind* was perfect, so too *Beatrice* in *Much Ado about Nothing;* her greatest triumphs were always in comedy. Nature had, indeed, given her many qualities for tragic parts, but the harshness of her voice marred her success in pathetic situations. One of her critics said "she *barked* out her sentences with dissonant notes of voice as ever offended a critical ear;" another, that the violent as well as the tender passions grated on the audience when delivered in her dissonant voice. This defective intonation exposed her many times to the ridicule of the gallery; she never was able to overcome it, and no doubt, like her other and more serious failings, had its origin in the streets of Dublin, where in her childhood she injured her throat by crying, "Salad a halfpenny a bunch."

Mrs. Delany, writing in 1752, says: "Mrs. Woffington did the part of Lady Towneley better than I have seen it done since Mrs. Oldfield's time. Her person is fine, her arms a little ungainly, and her voice disagreeable, but she pronounces her words perfectly and she speaks sensibly. . . ."

Victor, the manager of the Smock Alley Theatre in Dublin, used almost the same words in speaking of Peg Woffington's "Lady Towneley."

It must have been in Dublin that Mrs. Delany saw Mrs. Woffington play the part. She went there in 1751 in consequence of a serious quarrel with both manager and public. "I remember," says Tate Wilkinson, "when Barry, the divine Barry, either had, or pretended to have, frequent sore throats. On these occasions the comedies in which Mrs. Woffington played principal were brought forward," and at the bottom of the bill were generally announced, in letters of unusual size, the names of Quin, Barry, and Mrs. Cibber—this where she alone should have stood capital. Mrs. Woffington was not one who would tamely submit to be so placed before the public in a subordinate position, neither would she consent to be thrust forward as a stop gap. Of this she constantly complained, and at last declared that the next time it happened she would not play. The next day *Jane Shore* was announced, with Mrs. Cibber on the title-rôle, but immediately after was withdrawn and *The Constant Couple*, with Mrs. Woffington as *Sir Harry Wildair*, substituted. Mrs. Woffington sent word *she* was ill, and positively refused to play. Rich was forced to substitute *The Misers*. Unfortunately she chose a bad moment. The public were beginning to tire of these continual disappointments, and on her next appearance, as *Lady Jane Grey*, the whole weight of their resentment fell on her.

"Whoever is living," goes on the narrator, "and saw her that night, will own they never beheld any figure half so beautiful since. Her anger gave a glow to her complexion, and even added lustre to her charming eyes. She behaved with great resolution, and treated their rudeness with glorious contempt. She left the stage, was called for, and with infinite persuasion was prevailed upon to return. However she did, walked forward, and told them she was there ready and willing to perform her character if they chose to permit her, that the decision was theirs, on or off, just as they pleased; it was a matter of indifference to her." The "ons"

had it, and all went smoothly afterwards, but she always per-
sisted that the row was got up by Rich. The two principal
houses in London being now closed against her, she returned
to Dublin, and was engaged by Sheridan for the season at a
salary of 400*l.*, which he gave her reluctantly enough and
only on the pressure of friends; but she made such a furore
that the manager netted 4000*l.*, and gladly engaged her for
the next season at double the price. In the city of her birth
every honour was paid to her. All the public prints were full
of her praises. She was compared to Julius Cæsar, as having
come, seen, and conquered.

Miss Bellamy, who was also in the company, relates, in
her curious memoirs, several amusing scenes, as when Mrs.
Furnival stole the dress she was to wear as *Cleopatra*, and
another time how she and Mrs. Woffington had a battle royal
over a yellow satin dress with a purple robe. The ladies of
the company often used language only fitted for fish-wives.
Here, too, report had it, the beautiful Miss Gunnings came to
inspect the stage wardrobe, and were helped by Mrs. Woffington
to choose the dresses they wore at Lord Harrington's ball;
but this was merely a story of the hour.

Mrs. Woffington always loved the little Irish capital—her
native place—and was at her best when under the influence
of old associations, full of heart and spirit and carrying her
 audience (who were critical judges) by an effervescence of
gaiety which, without being vulgar, had an infectious buoyancy
that delighted all who witnessed the performance. An old
playgoer, writing to Lady Orrery, tells her that "the acting
of the brilliant Mrs. Woffington is, in general, admirable. In
Andromache she is dignified and her deportment elegant; in
Hermione she discovered talents as have not been displayed
since the celebrated Mrs. Porter."

This year, 1752, was a most brilliant season in Dublin. The
Duke of Dorset had just replaced good-natured Lord
Harrington. The new Viceroy had everything to make him
popular with a gay people like the Irish. He had governed
them before with singular success, and his munificent
hospitality at the Castle, which equalled, if it did not surpass

that of the Duke of Devonshire, was still fresh in the memory of many, and doubtless proved a powerful factor in gaining him popularity. He was also a patron of the drama, and constantly visited the theatre, especially after the arrival of Mrs. Woffington, whom he remembered as the little Polly Peachem of Madame Violante's company, and who was, moreover, a more recent friend. He gave her what was called "a command night," a function which still holds its place amongst viceregal festivities, and which is always considered a mark of particular favour. In those days, when there was a goodly gathering of rank to be found in the little city, and an unusual amount of beauty, the scene must have been brilliant; the Lord Mayor and his aldermen attending in their robes, and all officers being in uniform.[1]

This year, too, the Beef-Steak Club had been established by Sheridan, with the view of "allowing the followers of the Sock and Buskin to have some hours of social mirth and relaxation;" the club met on Saturday in accordance with the custom then prevailing at most theatres for the actors to dine together on that day; a very large room in Sheridan's house adjoining the theatre was given up for the purpose of the entertainment, and furnished with considerable taste, and even elegance. By degrees, however, the original idea was totally subverted. No performers, save one female, were admitted, and although it was still called a club, the manager alone defrayed the expenses. This year, when Mrs. Woffington allowed her name to be associated with it, it opened with a list of from fifty to sixty persons, chiefly Lords and Members of Parliament. About thirty of these sat down to dinner in the large room, the only Thespian admitted being Mrs. Woffington, who was placed in a great chair at the head of the table,

---

[1] This little show was up to quite lately highly popular in Dublin. A retinue of some seven or eight carriages starts from the Castle, each proceeding according to the rank of the parties. Soldiers and a band receive them at the colonnade of the theatre. The house is crowded to the roof, the state boxes thrown into one, and set off with mirrors, chandeliers, draperies. The manager, habited in a court suit and holding a pair of wax candles, leads the way, and the Viceroy, surrounded by a brilliant staff and a blaze of scarlet and gold, enters, the whole house standing while the National Anthem is sung.—From *All the Year Round.*

and was, by acclamation, elected President. "It is easy to believe that a club instituted on such lines, with a lovely President animated by wit and spirit, soon grew into the favour of fashionable men, who were all *friends* of 'the Presidente,'" and "as not a glass of wine was then drunk without giving a toast, we can imagine," says Victor, "the strain of the toasts given at that club." This and the whole style of the conversation and proceedings soon became a matter of general talk and scandal, and rendered Sheridan exceedingly unpopular. "The gay, the lovely, the volatile Woffington," says Hitchcock, "frankly avowed she preferred men to women (as the latter only talked of silks and scandal). She invited *all* the guests; and the members who paid *nothing* were allowed to bring honorary members, by her permission." He adds that "she filled her office to admiration, and with the utmost propriety."

We may credit the admiration, but can hardly believe in the propriety of the actress's conduct. As a proof of her total want of such a quality, she put her name to some bold lines addressed to the Viceroy, of which those here quoted will give an idea of their tenour :—

> May it please your Grace, with all submission,
> I humbly offer you my petition.
> Let others with as small pretensions,
> Tease you for places or for pensions ;
> *I* scorn a pension or a place,
> My sole design's upon Your Grace,
> The sum of my petition *this*—
> I claim, my lord, an annual kiss.

The impudent familiarity of these verses did not improve Peg's position with the respectable portion of the community ; at the same time it was well known she had never written them. "Peg Woffington's verses," writes Mrs. Delany, "are decidedly suited to the character of the woman, but not made by her." The author was known to be Dr. Andrews, the Provost of Trinity College, LL.D., and guardian of the youth of Dublin University, who was on terms of the greatest intimacy with Mrs. Woffington.[1] The ladies of Dublin very properly showed

[1] The Provost's House in College Green was filled with portraits of

their disapproval of the popular favourite's unwomanly boldness, by withdrawing their patronage from her, and bestowing it
on Miss Bellamy, who had just come to Dublin, and was playing
minor parts at Sheridan's theatre. *Her* benefit was patronized
by Lady Gormanston, Lady Kerry, Mrs. Butler, and Mrs.
O'Hara, all leaders of fashion.

So long, however, as Woffington was the "popular idol,"
she cared very little for what was said of her, but pursued her
reckless course unheeding. The people delighted in seeing
their old favourite, who many of them remembered running
barefoot through the very streets in which she now drove in
a grand coach, with a footman in livery on the footboard.
She showed the mob her lovely face with its glorious smile, and
they cheered her to the echo. On these occasions she generally
had her mother with her, to whom, to her credit, she always
behaved as an affectionate and generous daughter. The old
lady had every comfort,[1] and was to be seen at Adam and Eve,
or Clarendon Street Church, in a velvet cloak trimmed with
fringe, with a diamond ring on her finger, and an agate snuff-
box in her pocket. She was much considered in her own
circles.

Mrs. Murphy's ardent Catholicism must have received a
shock from a curious incident which occurred during Mrs.
Woffington's engagement and which astonished the town, albeit
it took a good deal to astonish the world of a hundred years
ago. The manager and the actress set off together to Quilca,
a small place Sheridan rented in the County Cavan, about
fifty miles from Dublin. "I was not in the secret," says
Victor, "and I wondered all the more, as I knew the
manager's private sentiments of that lady, which tallied with
my own ; viz., that she had captivating charms as a jovial,
witty, bottle-companion, but very few remaining as a mere

the actress in every one of her characters. It was said Peg procured
him the appointment, and that he paid her 500*l.*

[1] Her filial duty to her old hawking mother was remarkable. When
a child she had always brought her every little present her talents
secured ; and when she came into the enjoyment of a regular salary she
settled 40*l.* a year on her and *two changes of apparel.*—FitzGerald's
"Kings and Queens of an Hour."

female." And now for the secret, which was presently, as Scout says, "no secret at all". . . Mrs. Woffington had been left an annuity of 200*l.* by her old admirer, Mr. Owen M'Swiney, on condition that she abjured "the Roman faith, and became a Protestant." That she should have gone to Quilca to pronounce her recantation before "the Primate of the Mountains," accompanied by Mr. Sheridan, has an air of improbability, unless it was that she was afraid of Mrs. Murphy's interposing her maternal authority. In any case, one may say without lack of charity, that poor Peg was not a desirable addition to either religion. Her sister, the lovely Mrs. Cholmondeley, had conformed many years previously. . .

Her engagement in Dublin was now fated to come to an end in rather a similar manner to that which marked the end of her engagement with Rich in London. In the days of which I am now writing the populace was as easily excited about political matters as they are in our more rational age; for in Ireland every man, whatever else he may not be, is sure to be a politician. The Duke of Dorset, who had begun his Viceroyalty with every promise of success, had suddenly become unpopular through the introduction of a bill for paying a portion of the English national debt out of the Irish revenue. This caused immense dissatisfaction; the bill was negatived by a small majority of eight, and the patriot members were borne to their homes on the shoulders of the triumphant mob. At this unfortunate moment Sheridan produced the play of *Mahomet*, in which there were some lines which the pit and gallery applied to the Court party. Sheridan refused to allow the offensive lines to be withdrawn or altered, on which a riot ensued, which wrecked his theatre and put an end for the time to all performances. Mrs. Woffington returned to the London stage, reappearing at Covent Garden in September, 1754. Her brilliant career was, however, near its close; her stock of health, upon which she had drawn too largely, began to fail her, and a great change was noticed in her glorious beauty. She struggled with gallant spirit against the inroads of disease, but the final scene came at last. It is dramatically told by Tate Wilkinson, who was standing in the wings as Mrs. Woffington, in Rosalind, and Mrs. Vincent, in Celia, were going on the stage in the first act :—

"She went through Rosalind for four acts without my perceiving that she was in the least disordered ; but in the fifth act she complained of great indisposition. I offered her my arm, the which she graciously accepted. I thought she looked softened in her manner, and had less of the ' hauteur.' When she came off at the quick change of dress, she again complained of being ill, but got accoutred, and returned to finish the part, and pronounced the epilogue speech : ' If it be true that good wine needs no bush,' etc. But, when arrived at, ' If I were a woman I would kiss as many of you as had beards,' etc., her voice broke—she faltered—endeavoured to go on, but could not proceed ; then, in a voice of tremor exclaimed, ' O God ! O God ! ' and tottered to the stage-door speechless, where she was caught. The audience of course applauded till she was out of sight, and then sunk into awful looks of astonishment, both young and old, before and behind the curtain, to see one of the most handsome women of the age, a favourite principal actress, and who had for several seasons given high entertainment, struck so suddenly by the hand of Death, in such a time and place, and in the prime of life."

It was thought that she could not survive many hours, but she lingered for three years in a miserable condition, unable to use her limbs, no longer recognizable as the lovely Peggy ; she had become a mere shadow of her former self. She died at the comparatively early age of forty, leaving the not inconsiderable sum of 5000*l.*, which she bequeathed to her sister, Mrs. Cholmondeley, much to the disappointment of Colonel Cæsar of the Guards, who had been one of her many friends, and who counted on inheriting what she had, with which view he had induced her to make a romantic promise that each should inherit from the other. The wills had been actually executed, and the gallant colonel was assiduous in his attentions, fearing that now her end was approaching natural affection might assert itself, and that a new will might be made in favour of Mrs. Cholmondeley. This is what actually happened. Her sister took advantage of the colonel's leaving the house one evening earlier than his usual hour, and sent for the lawyer, and the will was altered to suit her mind. One cannot but rejoice at the discomfiture of Colonel Cæsar.

The actress's charitable disposition had benefited the poor of her neighbourhood very substantially; she was lamented by them bitterly, and they cherished her memory for many years. She was buried in Teddington Churchyard, in a shady corner of which there is a tablet set up against the wall, with this inscription :—

" Near this monument lies the body of Margaret Woffington, spinster, born October, 1720, departed this life March 28, 1760, aged forty years."

Cold words enough, considering she had supplied a mother's place to the sister, whose very position in life was due to the actress's hard-earned money.

It was an autumn evening on which I visited Teddington Churchyard, and stood before this mean little tablet which roused my indignation. The wind sighed sadly, as it seemed to me, over this proof of human ingratitude, and the air was filled with profound sadness. But, after all, what does it matter? How can a few sculptured words, more or less, avail to those who are shut out by that black wall that divides them from us? They do not know of our neglect, nor of our sorrows; is it not, therefore, as a sort of satisfaction to our own grief that we raise these marble memorials to those, who in life " we could caress with every tenderness of speech and touch " ?

If, however, Mrs. Cholmondeley was not burdened with too much sentiment she had a keen sense of economy. We find that the same tablet did service for Master Horace Cholmondeley, aged six months !

And now, before taking leave of Peg, I should like to set before my readers an admirable summary of her character which appeared in the pages of *All the Year Round* many years ago.

" She was an actress, so far as her private life is concerned,
quite of the Restoration pattern ; and yet she was felt to have
well merited the terms of the monody written upon her death
by Hoole, the translator of Tasso. He recorded the excellence of her professional life, and continued :

> " Nor was thy worth to public scenes confined,
> Thou knew'st the noblest feelings of the mind ;
> Thy ears were ever open to distress,
> Thy ready hand was ever stretched to bless,
> Thy breast humane for each unhappy felt,
> Thy heart for others' sorrows prone to melt, etc."

It is to be remembered of her that to the public and to
her art she had been faithful ever. She is thus described by
Murphy, who knew her well : " Forgive her one female error,
and it might fairly be said of her that she was adorned with
every virtue ; honour, truth, benevolence, and charity were
her distinguishing qualities. Her understanding was superior
to that of the generality of her sex. Her conversation was
in a style of elegance, always pleasing and often instructive.
She abounded in wit, but not of that wild sort which breaks
out in sudden flashes, often troublesome and impertinent :
her judgment restrained her within due bounds. On the
stage she displayed her talents in the brightest lustre.
Genteel comedy was her province. She possessed a fine
figure, great beauty, and every elegant accomplishment."
" She had ever her train of admirers," writes Wilkinson ;
" she possessed wit, vivacity, etc., but never permitted her
love of pleasure and conviviality to occasion the least defect
in her duty to the public as a performer. . . . She was ever
ready at the call of the audience, and, though in the possession
of all the first line of characters, yet she never thought it
improper or a degradation of her consequence to constantly
play the Queen in *Hamlet ;* Lady Anne in *Richard the
Third ;* and Lady Percy in *Henry the Fourth*—parts which are
mentioned as insults in the country if offered to a lady of consequence. She also cheerfully acted Hermione or Andromache ;
Lady Pliant or Lady Touchwood ; Lady Sadlife or Lady Dainty ;
Angelica or Mrs. Ford ; and several others alternately, as best
suited the interests of her manager." Victor writes of her :

" She never disappointed one audience in three winters, either
by real or affected illness ; and yet I have often seen her on the
stage when she ought to have been in her bed." While
Hitchcock, the historian of the Irish stage, contributes his
testimony in her favour: " To her honour be it ever remembered, that, whilst in the zenith of her glory, courted and
caressed by all ranks and degrees, it made no alteration in her
behaviour ; she remained the same gay, affable, obliging, good-
natured Woffington to everyone around her. . . . Not the lowest
performer in the theatre did she refuse to play for; out of
twenty-six benefits she acted in twenty-four. . . . Such traits
of character must endear the memory of Mrs. Woffington to
every lover of the drama."

TWENTY years had come and gone since Miss Ambrose and the beautiful Gunnings played their part on the stage of Dublin society. They were, however, not forgotten. Their stories were told to the rising generation, and their success held up to admiration and for imitation.

Over the capital itself these years had produced a complete revolution. The roughness which had marked the manner of life in Lord Chesterfield's day had now disappeared, and in its place an elegance and almost sumptuous magnificence in the mode of living prevailed. The mean houses occupied by the nobility were exchanged for fine mansions designed by eminent artists. The Earl of Kildare,[1] soon to be Ireland's only duke, set the example, which was quickly followed by others. Squares, streets, and stately mansions rose on all sides. Lord Charlemont *designed*[2] for himself Charlemont

[1] Thomas, Earl of Kildare, created marquis 1761, and Duke of Leinster 1773. This nobleman, the friend of the refined Charlemont, and the elegant Powerscourt (called the French lord), was in every respect one of the grand noblemen of the time. In 1745 he commenced building Leinster House, removing there from the old home of the FitzGeralds in the "Earl of Kildare's Liberty." His new residence commanded an extensive view over the Bay of Dublin, and from the top windows he could see the ships lying in Dunleary Harbour, seven miles away. Not a house then broke the view. Leinster House was designed by Cassels, a German architect, and was finished by Wyatt, who, amongst other improvements, added the picture gallery which contained many fine paintings. Lord Kildare was the most popular nobleman of his time ; he was apostrophized as "loved Kildare, of all our lords the chief and first."

[2] The propensity for building had become so great in Dublin that all professions embarked in it. Gentlemen were often their own architects, contracting with journeymen to finish the job at a low price. This would not have been the case with Lord Charlemont, who was a splendid and generous patron. He brought over artists and carvers from Italy and France to do the decorative work at Charlemont

House, which he filled with paintings, statues, and books. Lord Powerscourt had an Italian palace in William Street;[1] Lord Meath[2] had a beautifully decorated house in Stephen's Green, where also Lord Mountcashel, Lord Montalt, the millionaire, Buck Whaley,[3] and a score of other notables had stately mansions. One has only to look at these old-fashioned houses, many of them decayed and fast tumbling into ruins, to see the scale upon which they were built; the huge porticoes with fifteen or twenty steps leading up to them, the spacious halls (with capacity for holding half-a-dozen or more Sedan chairs), the broad stone staircases, the exquisite chimney-pieces, the elaborate ceilings, the friezes, the medallions, the panels wrought by the Italian artists, who were brought over at immense expense, all is in the best taste, and tells the sad story of the extravagance of these Irish noblemen and gentlemen of the last century.

To the reader of old memoirs what brilliant flashes come back of the days when the little Irish capital was more like a foreign city than a portion of sober Great Britain. There was plenty of money to be had, and living was cheap. The peasantry, it is true, were a miserable, ignorant horde of serfs, while the gentry and nobility were in their turn mere serfs of pleasure, dancing, fiddling, gambling, drinking, as gallant gentlemen in those days were bound to do. And the women! what lovely faces! what sparkling eyes and pouting lips! The Gunnings had many successors since their day, and now, in 1771, we see before us a dream of fair women. Pretty Letty Gore, the daughter of a Judge of the Exchequer and niece to Lord Arran, sweet Molly Henn of Paradise,[4] fair Kitty Tyrell, named by common consent the

---

House, which was crowded with *objets d'art*, paintings by Hogarth, busts by Nollekens, a fine library of the choicest books. All these, alas! are now dispersed. The house itself is a government office.

[1] Powerscourt House, now the counting-house of Messrs. Ferrier and Pollock, is a grand stately mansion, with a Venetian window of beautiful design.

[2] Now the Church Temporalities Office.

[3] Now the Catholic University.

[4] Miss Mary Henn, daughter to Richard Henn, Esq., of Paradise, Co. Cavan. She was a standard beauty and toast, and some pretty verses

Maid of Garnavilla, lovely Miss Hoey, the three beautiful
sisters Montgomery, Lord Carhampton's daughter and others.
The loveliest of all is the subject of our sketch. Her sweet
face looks at us from the title-page, as painted by Angelica
Kauffmann.[1] This is Dorothy Monroe, whose pitiful little
story we are going to follow. Nothing very tragic or new—
here are no triumphs to record, nor brilliant double duchessing;
it is an oft-told tale this, of disappointment and failure.

DOLLY MONROE.

It is said these things are predestined; no one can tell. At

were written in her praise. She was extremely beautiful, winning and
lovable. She married, early, Donagh O'Brien, second son of Sir Edward
O'Brien of Dromiland, Co. Cavan, and ancestor of the present Lord
Inchiquin. The Henns are a highly respected family, and have held
high legal appointments.

[1] Angelica Kauffmann, the female R.A., visited Dublin in 1771,
where she painted numerous portraits and decorated several houses.
Much of her work still remains, notably a good specimen can be seen
at Lord Meath's in Stephen's Green. Much of her decorative work has,
however, faded, and some is ascribed to her which was executed in all
probability by either Richardson or Waldire.

all events, no one's future can be forecast. Mr. Rogers was wont to say that "marrying was all luck; plain or pretty, clever or stupid, it was all the same; if it was to be, it would be." This is the only consolation that can be found for those who, like Dolly, fail to secure the plums that grow on the tree of good fortune.

We must, however, as in the case of Eleanor Ambrose, pause here to take a look back into the political situation of the country, this situation having, strange to say, a decided influence upon the future of the heroine of our story. The fair promise of her young life was, if not altogether blighted, most certainly shadowed by its evil effects.

To understand how this happened, we must turn to history. The twenty-one years that had passed since Lord Chesterfield's viceroyalty had brought no peace to Ireland, which was more harassed, perplexed, and distracted than ever. Viceroy succeeded viceroy, none remaining long enough to work any permanent good. Harrington, Dorset, Halifax, Northumberland, Bedford, Hardwicke, and Hertford had all tried the problem and failed. This failure was practically certain so long as the system of governing by means of the *undertakers* continued in force, a system which meant, in plain English, that government in Ireland was altogether in the hands of a few great personages : these men were possessed of large estates and considerable Parliamentary influence, and "undertook" to carry the king's business, whatever it might be, through Parliament, on condition of obtaining a large share in the disposal of patronage. The power of the "undertakers" was much increased by the fact that the Lord Lieutenant spent only six months in two years in the country he was supposed to rule over. This same system, as already pointed out,[1] was applied to the principal officials, who, being Englishmen, resided in their own country, devolving their duties to paid underlings, which gave rise to the saying that Ireland was always in deputation. George III. had it much at heart to put an end to this abuse. The difficulties, however, were almost insurmountable. No

---

[1] See Introduction.

English nobleman could be induced to remain permanently in what was considered an exile. The Earl of Bristol, who had accepted the post on the resignation of Lord Hertford, declined (although he was half-way to Ireland) when he heard what was expected of him. This was in 1767. The situation was most critical. Parliament was insubordinate. The country was seething with agitation; outrage and disorder were rampant and unchecked. White boys, steel boys, peep-o'-day boys, paraded the lonely villages and undefended towns, burning houses, maiming cattle, and murdering inoffensive persons. Trade was at a standstill, public works suspended. Parliament, occupied with its internal jealousies and dissensions, cared little for the general distress. The reckless extravagance of the upper class, the pervading dissipation and high play in which they indulged, the almost universal bankruptcy, made political corruption an easy task. It was said, and with truth, that an honest politician was hardly to be met with, and as the like immorality pervaded the Bench as well as the representative assembly, a fair trial for any criminal was doubtful.[1]

In such a situation of affairs much would depend upon the choice of a Viceroy. The last act of the administration of the brilliant, erratic Charles Townshend[2] was to appoint his elder brother, Lord Townshend, to the office. A more unfortunate election could hardly have been made. At the beginning he appeared in all sincerity to have the welfare of the country at heart, and there seemed every chance of his securing popu-

---

[1] See Chesterfield correspondence.

[2] The brilliance and the eccentricity were alike inherited from his mother, the beautiful crazy heiress, Audrey Ball Harrison. This extraordinary woman was notorious for the lawlessness she allowed her tongue and the want of decorum she displayed in her life and manners. After some ten years of marriage, she separated from her too-enduring husband, and ranged society, a sort of chartered freebooter. Her tongue made her the terror of her enemies, the delight of her friends. Horace Walpole, who was amongst the latter, gives us one of his word photographs of the lady, who was fond of visiting Strawberry Hill. We feel as if we knew her perfectly. We can see her rushing up the narrow staircase, brushing against the china monsters "all but sweeping them away," and crying out, "Lord God, what a house! It is just such a house as the parson's, where the children sleep at the foot of the bed."

larity, his personal gifts being of the kind likely to win the Irish people. His abilities, likewise, were undoubtedly superior to many of his predecessors' and successors'. He was unfortunately utterly destitute of tact and judgment, and as time went on (especially after his wife's death) he committed a fault which is peculiarly fatal to rulers of Ireland. He sought for popularity by sacrificing the dignity and decorum of his position, and thus he brought both himself and his office into contempt. Mr. Lecky has sketched his character in the following words:—

"His antecedents were wholly military. He had served at Dettingen, Fontenoy, Culloden, and at the siege of Quebec he had become Commander-in-Chief upon the death of Wolfe; but his conduct on this occasion had not raised his fame. He was by no means an unamiable man, he was brave, honest and frank; popular in his manners, witty, convivial, and with a great turn for caricature, violent and capricious in his temper, and exceedingly destitute of *tact, dignity*, and *decorum*. He drank hard, and he was accused of low vices and a great love of low companions. His military knowledge was of much use in some parts of the Irish Government, but he was totally inexperienced in civil administration. He made many mistakes from want of this knowledge, and acted with a total want of necessary diplomacy."

The first act of his unlucky administration was conclusive of his want of prudence. Hardly was the initial Session of Parliament inaugurated, when he brought forward two unpopular measures. Horace Walpole, writing to his constant correspondent, Sir Horace Mann, says, "The Irish began their Session with a complaisance *not expected* of them considering how *wrong-headed* they are. After voting the augmentation of 3000 men, they have thrown out a Money Bill, and it is a question whether their Parliament should not be prorogued with a high hand."

Prorogued accordingly it was—with a very high hand, the new Viceroy using the powers he possessed not to call together another assembly for fourteen months. Townshend made use of this interval to break down the power of the "Undertakers." [1] He had come as their secret enemy, and with his characteristic vehemence threw himself into the task.[2] He complained in his despatches that they had usurped the real authority and had reduced the Lord Lieutenant to be nothing more than a figure-head. His plan was to create, if possible, a *Majority*, this majority to *be his* by right of purchase, being therefore subordinate to his will, and to secure this end he spared neither money nor personal influence. His first step was to look about for men whose patriotism was most likely to yield to *some one* of the golden keys he had in his pocket. Foremost amongst those whom he desired to gain to his side was Henry, Viscount Loftus. This nobleman had this very year succeeded Nicholas, Earl of Ely, his nephew, who had likewise bequeathed to him, in addition to the family estates, the large fortune which had come to him through his mother, daughter and heiress to Sir Gustavus Hume.[3] The new Peer's inclinations, therefore, as well as his training, placed him on the opposition benches, in addition to which he had received his political education from his uncle, John Ponsonby, Speaker to the House of Commons, a man of singular uprightness, who earned for himself in this most corrupt age the reputation of being an honest friend to his country. From him Lord Loftus, in his early and poorer days had met help and kindness. He was bound by gratitude to support him, and to continue with the party to which he by right belonged, i.e. to the Patriot Lords [4]—so named because having everything they

[1] When Townshend's term of office had expired it was found he had spent a million of money on this work, besides scattering honours and titles broadcast.

[2] Lord Chesterfield disliked the Undertakers quite as much as did Townshend; he managed, however, to play his cards better.

[3] Nicholas, Earl of Ely, married 1736, Mary, daughter and heir to Sir Gustavus Hume, of Castle Hume, County Fermanagh. The only son of this marriage died in 1771, without issue, and was succeeded by Henry Loftus as Viscount Loftus, the Earldom being extinct. It was said that the last Earl, who was of weak intellect, was induced by Lord Loftus to leave the Hume estates away from those who should by right have inherited them, and that the disappointed heirs constantly threatened lawsuits.

[4] These were:

Leinster	Mount Cashell	Bellamount
Westmeath	Charlemont	Mornington
Shannon	Lisle	Wandesforde
Lanesborough	Longford	Mountmorris

could desire, they were naturally supposed to be incorruptible, and able by their firmness and rectitude to act as safeguards against the universal corruption and bribery. Unfortunately Lord Loftus was of a strangely weak and vacillating character; it was well known that he was altogether governed by his wife, a lady of singular spirit and determined will, haughty and aspiring to even higher rank than what she had unexpectedly attained. Her vaulting ambition would be likely to overstep any obstacle in the way of her wishes.

Townshend quickly grasped that here, ready to his hand, was the very instrument he wanted. To gain over Lord Loftus to his side, and to detach him from his friends, was a triumph all the sweeter, as thereby he could break up the caucus of Undertakers who made part of the Loftus following. Nothing was therefore left undone to secure the head of the clan. Townshend, being a kinsman in a distant degree, made this slender tie an excuse for affecting a cousinly intimacy with the family, and soon convinced himself that the popular rumour which gave to Lady Loftus certain masculine appendages was, as popular rumour generally is, correct. If anything was to be done with the husband, it would be by securing his wife's co-operation, nor was he long in finding out the lady's master passion, and with this knowledge victory was sure to be his. Not content with the good fortune that had come to her, Lady Loftus sighed for higher distinction—the two former Lords had held the rank of Earl, why should not the present enjoy the same honour? "Or even go a step farther," whispered Townshend's emissaries, "a Marchioness is a higher sounding name—oblige his Excellency and you shall see he can be grateful." It must be placed to Lady Loftus's credit that the possible gratification of her own personal ambition was not a sufficient bribe to induce her to use her influence with her husband to desert his old friends and join a new policy. Had not Lord Townshend at this very time become a widower, it is probable Lord Loftus's deser-

| Louth | Knapton | Molesworth |
| Moira | Powerscourt | |

Of these Lord Shannon broke away like Lord Loftus, and for a promise of place and power joined Lord Townshend's party.

tion would never have taken place, neither would poor Dolly's story have been written.[1] It does seem somewhat hard that a young girl's heart should have been made the shuttle-cock in this game between the wily politician and the ambitious lady, but so it was ; history repeats itself, and Dolly was not the first nor the last victim to a worldly woman's plots.

Lady Loftus was Dolly's aunt. It had been thought a good match for Frances Monroe when, seventeen years previously, she made the conquest of Henry Loftus, for although at that time he did not stand to succeed to the family honours, still he was a man of family, connected with men in high position. It was a decided rise in the social scale for the Monroes, who, it is said, were not *pur sang.* Monroe is not a Celtic name, therefore we may assume the family was a graft of James the First's setting. They dwelt in Down, at a place called Roe's Hall, where we find Dolly was living, one of a large family of children, when Lord and Lady Loftus succeeded to their new dignity and fortune. They were childless, and Dolly's beauty had made her a special favourite of both her aunt and uncle, who had treated her always as a daughter. What was more natural than that they should now wish her to share the advantages of their elevated position, and invite her to spend the season in town, and enjoy all the gaieties ? We may imagine how this offer was received at Roe's Hall ; how it was thought an unprecedented stroke of good luck, a step on the ladder of good fortune. We may be sure Dolly was sent off in all haste with a wallet full of good wishes and prophecies of greatness in store. These prophecies seemed from the first likely to come true. Dolly's beauty at once secured for her the first place amongst the Dublin belles, who had to acknowledge their rival's supremacy. She was barely seventeen, a sweet, simple, enchanting creature, who seems not so much to have commanded admiration as to have stolen into men's hearts and made them utterly captive. The old and the young, grave Provost Andrews of Trinity

---

[1] Charlotte, Lady Townshend, was the only surviving child of James, Earl of Northampton. She brought into the Townshend family upwards of 250 quarterings, besides the barony of Ferrars and that of Compton.

College, handsome Hercules Langrishe, Henry Grattan, then a
stripling, and a score of gallants were at her feet. She was so
besieged that she could not walk in the Mall, but had to rise
at six o'clock, and, under safe guardianship, make the round of
Stephen's Green. The pamphlets and papers of Dublin (a
veritable scourge they were) vied with one another in apostro-
phizing her beauty or addressing her admirers. A nobleman
who wished to have her portrait is told,—

> " Fond swain, I hear your wish is such
> Some painter should on canvas touch
> The beauties of Monroe ;
> But where's the adventurer will dare
> The happy mixture to prepare
> Her peerless charms to show ?."[1]

The poet then goes on to describe how such a picture should
be drawn.

> " First let the cheek with blushes glow
> Just as when damask roses blow,
> Glistening with morning dew.
> Contrasted with the virgin white[2]
> With which the lily glads the sight
> Blend them in lovely hue.

> " And truly then that cheek to grace,
> Upon her flowing tresses place
> The chestnut's auburn down.
> Her lips you may in sort depaint
> By cherries ripe, yet ah ! 'twere faint
> Should them with hers be shown," etc.

The acknowledged belles of Dublin, Miss Letty Gore, the
Misses Montgomerys, and others, must have passed a bad
quarter of an hour reading these praises of their rival. Dorothea's beauty was also the theme of her lover's pen in " Baratariana."[3] In the history of the Island of *Barataria* we have

---

[1] Epistle to George Howard, Esq., by George Faulkner.
[2] A couple of years later Goldsmith introduced her name into "The
Haunch of Venison."

> " Of the neck and the breast I had still to dispose,
> 'Twas a neck and a breast that might rival M–r–s."

Mr. Forster in his biography says, " M–r–s " was Lord Townshend's
Dorothy Monroe.
[3] *Baratariana*: a collection of curious letters published in Dublin
during the administration of Lord Townshend, and written in imitation
of the famous Junius Letters. They are now valuable as presenting a

Dolly's love story given under false names. We also learn that her stature was majestic, but air and demeanour nature itself. The peculiar splendour of her carriage was softened and subdued by the most affable condescension, and that the softest roses that ever youth and modesty poured out on beauty glowed on the lips of Dorothea, her checks were the bloom of Hebe, and the purity of Diana was in her heart.

Many years after Grattan declared that this "beautiful description of a young girl"[1] was written by Langrishe, and was worthy of the original. Meantime she had many suitable offers of marriage, to none of which her guardians would listen. Lady Loftus had high views for her niece. *She* had married well, why should not Dolly, with her beauty and opportunities, attain as high fortune as the Gunnings, whose rise was fresh in her ladyship's recollection? At all events there was no need for hurry. Provost Andrews could be kept dangling by

vivid picture of the country, the political corruption that prevailed, and the animosities between class and creed. The authors of these undoubtedly spirited letters managed to keep their secret as to their identity, but it was revealed in Grattan's Life by his Son, in which we learn that Grattan's letters were signed *Posthumus* and *Pericles* and that he also wrote the dedication. Flood's signature was Syndicombe. Langrishe's principal contribution was the History of the Island of Barataria. "Barataria," an island mentioned in "Don Quixote," is meant for Ireland. Everyone is spoken of under the name of a Spanish Don, but by the key we know that Sancho was Lord Townshend, his secretary, Don Georgio Buticarney, Sir George McCartney, Don John, the Right Honourable Hely Hutchinson, Don Philip, Tisdall the Chancellor, etc. The Commons goes by the name of "the Cortes." In this bitter satire Langrishe took ample revenge on the wicked uncle and aunt of Dorothea as also on his rivals Townshend and Provost Andrews. Grattan said before his death that the characters were just and admirably drawn, as that of Tisdall, who looked *dismal* but felt not the least concern. "Baratariana" has always possessed peculiar interest for students of Irish History in the last century.

[1] Dolly's portrait by Angelica Kauffmann, which is in the National Gallery, Dublin, does not convey the idea of so beautiful a creature. The face has a prim expression, and the features are formal; the larger canvas, a family group, also by Angelica, represents Lord and Lady Ely full length, Dolly seated at the harpsichord and Angelica Kauffmann standing; this gives a better impression of the beauty so much eulogized by her contemporaries, and presents a very charming young girl with radiant eyes, auburn hair, and sweet, innocent expression. Mr. Armstrong, the present director of the National Gallery, thinks this portrait is so much after the manner of Cotes that it would be more likely to be his work. This, however, cannot be the case, as Cotes died before 1771, when this picture was painted.

judicious management; Langrishe's love, which was content
with any treatment from the adored one, could be allowed to
drift on. It was a good enough match if no better turned up,
and therefore the intimacy between the lovers was allowed
under certain restrictions. All this time Lord Townshend had
not come on the scene. He was still supposed to be in grief
for the loss of his wife, an amiable, interesting, and rather
brilliant woman; although not possessed of beauty, she
managed to retain the affections of her erratic husband, who
truly lamented her, as he had reason to do, as with her he
lost his only hold on the Irish people, who had been quick to
recognize Lady Townshend's worth and the desire she had to
benefit them by every means in her power. The Viceroy
evinced his grief in an hysterical fashion, at one moment
weeping bitterly, the next indulging in the wildest excesses
with his boon companions. After a time he was sufficiently
recovered to solace his affliction by the charms of society, the
first house he visited being his kinsman's, Rathfarnham
Castle. There he saw Dorothea in all her charms of auburn
hair and radiant eyes. His evident admiration raised in Lady
Loftus's mind a picture of future greatness, in which her
favourite niece would play the principal, herself the secondary
rôle. No sooner did this ambition seize upon her than it
vaulted by leaps and bounds, until nothing could satisfy
her but the accomplishment of her desire. Townshend
watched with amusement the scheming chaperone play her
cards. He saw in this happy chance a means of obtaining
the end he had in view, and which he was almost hopeless of
attaining. With this view he enacted the part of an ardent
lover to perfection; three times a week his coach with six
running footmen was seen tearing along the road to
Rathfarnham Castle. Presently his visits became *daily*, for
he was superintending the painting of Dolly's portrait by
Angelica Kauffmann. "Sure there never was such devotion,"
my lady would say, as she watched with exultation the wooing of the noble suitor, translating according to her own
wishes the different signs of his love. "His incoherent
sentences and distracted manner were accepted by the

countess as confirmation of his intentions, a natural perplexity and embarrassment of elocution were the confusion of passion, and ambiguous inference, as it was unintelligible, was supposed to convey a solemn declaration."[1] The astute Viceroy, who saw, as if in a mirror, all that was passing in the lady's mind, and was highly diverted by it, was careful not to

LORD TOWNSHEND.

commit himself to anything definite. General admiration cannot be used in evidence, and of such he was most liberal. The situation, to one of his nature, was thoroughly humorous, the more so that he managed to obtain from the sanguine match-maker all that he required. How could she refuse anything to one who was about to confer such distinctions as she supposed upon her family? She saw Dolly figuring as the

[1] *Baratariana.*

vice-queen, herself second in command and adorned with the tiara of a countess, while the earl, her husband, had the dignity of Deputy Viceroy. Such a picture was surely worth a few votes, and as for the spoiling of two young lives, that did not count. It must be owned that in this important crisis of her life Dolly acted in a manner that deprives us of all pity for her subsequent mortification. She gave up with very little struggle the man she loved, for one old enough to be her father, and whose advantages of fortune and station were his sole claim to her regard. Townshend had no gifts which could attract a young and beautiful girl ; the good looks which had given him charm in his youth had long since vanished. He was a plump man with a merry, round, un-studious looking countenance, with jovial manners. He could be amorous, but never tender. What a contrast to the re-fined, handsome, persuasive and accomplished Langrishe,[1] whose picture has been drawn for us by Grattan, as a man born for society and endowed with qualities that would have charmed a court without the aid of flattery. His mind was a perpetual spring. His manner playful and irresistible. It must have been a sore trial to the poor girl to dismiss him at her aunt's bidding. It is an old story, however, and one that repeats itself many a time during a London season, with not perhaps quite so romantic a setting as the garden at Rath-farnham with its roses and quaint sun-dial, where tradition has it (rightly or wrongly who should say?) the lovers parted. But now comes the sad part of the story, one which illustrates in a strong light the wisdom of the old saying that " A bird in the hand is worth two in the bush."

Shortly after the dismissal of Langrishe (a fact of which Lady Loftus took care Townshend should be apprised) Lord Loftus took the final step which separated him from his old friends, and when Parliament met was found with his followers on the Ministerial benches. This defection, which was most gratifying to the Viceroy, was equally depressing to

---

[1] Langrishe was an accomplished musician and excellent amateur actor.

the Opposition;[1] Lord Charlemont, the old friend and political guide of Lord Loftus, made ineffectual efforts to prevent the catastrophe, the vigilance of Lady Loftus, however, presented an insuperable barrier, and her influence over her vacillating husband carried the day. When the triumph was secured she naturally looked for her reward. The first instalment was paid at once. Christmas, 1771, saw the announcement of Lord Loftus's new title as Earl of Ely. So far the coronet she had coveted was hers; as regarded the necessary words which were to make Dolly vice-queen, the Viceroy was silent. Having secured *all* he wanted, his attentions declined, his coach was no longer to be seen tearing along the roads to Rathfarnham. Soon report began to couple his name with that of Miss Montgomery, whose father, a Scotch baronet with Irish estates, was one of his set. Still the newly-made countess would not relinquish hope. With a fatal want of dignity she went on a visit to the castle, dragging with her the reluctant Dolly; this in the vain expectation of rekindling the wandering fancy of the fickle nobleman. She even tried the very stale device of whetting his ardour by circulating in the papers a report " that the Right Honourable Francis Andrews, Provost of Trinity College, Dublin, was about to lead to the Hymeneal altar the beautiful Miss Monroe." Townshend, whose keen sense of the ridiculous made him destitute of all self-restraint, and who, like his brilliant mother, gave way to every humour of his lively imagination, amused himself by addressing a satirical ballad to the antiquated Provost,[2] as if approving of the projected union.

> " Blush not, dear Andrews, nor disdain
> A passion for that matchless dame,
> Who kindles in all hearts a flame
> By Beauty's magic force.

---

[1] The ballads of the day satirized this defection in scathing terms:—

> " Those nicknamed Marquis, Lord and Earl,
> That set the crowd a-gazing,
> We prize as hogs esteem a pearl;
> Their patents set a-blazing.

[2] Provost Andrews, it will be remembered, was a lover of Peg Woffington.

What though o'er Dolly's lovely head
Summers twice ten are scarcely shed?
Is it on that account decreed
    She must refuse—' of course' ?

Miltown,[1] coeval with thy sire,
Durst to a blooming maid aspire
And feel, or feign, a lover's fire
    At seventy-five or more.

Nor think, my friend, because I prize
Her auburn hair and radiant eyes,
    I envy *your* espousal.

No rival passion fills my breast,
Long since from amorous pains at rest,
Nay more—to prove what I've professed
    I'll carry *your proposal.*"

Bligh,[2] who in Churchill's battles bled,
A fascinating virgin wed.
No jealous dreams disturbed his head
    Though sinking at four score.

Intrepid Lucas,[3] lame and old,
Bereft of eye-sight, teeth, and gold,
To a green girl his passion told
    And woo'd the yielding bride.

Then prithee leave that face of care,
Let not your looks presage despair,
Be jovial, brisk and debonnair.
    My life, you're not denied !

[1] The Earl of Miltown.
[2] General Bligh, ancestor to the Earl of Derby.
[3] Lucas was the first publisher of the *Freeman's Journal.*

As an instance of bad taste amounting to brutal insolence these verses are unsurpassed. It is difficult to believe that any man could have so wantonly insulted a young creature, to whom he had so recently been making even false professions of attachment. One would rather incline to the supposition (judging from the bitter tone underlying the unnecessary declaration of his own indifference) that in some way, unknown perhaps to her watchful aunt, Dolly had rejected his lordship's advances. One would be glad to think such was the case, that the girl's better nature asserted itself, and that she set herself free from the worldly machinations of her matchmaking aunt. Her family maintained that this was the fact; the universal testimony, however, of the world in which she lived, has handed down the tradition that Dolly was left to wear the willow; and that Langrishe never renewed his proposals, leads to the presumption that such was the case.

Meantime the unpopular Viceroy was growing more and more hateful to the people. "His temper," says Mr. Lecky, "had grown savage by opposition, and he cast every vestige of decorum to the winds, constantly disappearing from public life to low haunts of dissipation, ridiculing all parties even at his own or their table. He scattered broadcast satirical ballads on friends and foes,[1] and on one occasion interrupted the sitting of the privy council by introducing two beagles,[2] whom he had christened Progress and Prorogation. These jokes were not taken in good part, while even the most corrupt of those he had subsidized winced under his thinly veiled contempt."

"Townshend has occasioned all the troubles," writes Walpole to Sir Horace Mann. "He lives with a carpenter, and drinks with two low fellows, and has written a satirical

---

[1] One of these ballads was "The Cotillon," in which Townshend makes a bitter attack on the public men in Ireland.

[2] In "Baratariana" a very lively account of the introduction of the dogs is given, and the manner in which the obsequious councillors received the new members—"Billy Hutchinson was distressed and looked lively—Tisdall looked dismal but felt not the least concern—Malone did not observe the joke—" etc.—See illustration on preceding page.

ballad on the chief men there, a mark of contempt that even money will not wipe out."

In making this last observation the student of Strawberry Hill shows his profound knowledge of human nature. You may rob a man of his purse with greater impunity than level a sarcasm at any of his peculiarities. Irishmen especially are sensitive to ridicule in an extraordinary degree, and there is little doubt that it was his sarcastic turn more than his bad government that drew down upon Townshend such envenomed attacks as those that appeared in the squibs and prints of the day. The animosity against him having at last risen to fever heat, the situation was no longer tenable. In the March of 1772, sixteen peers drew up a protest against him. A powerful party in the House of Commons led by Flood supported this motion of the Upper House, and made it their object to procure his recall, which the Home Ministers, thinking it was time to put an end to his disgraceful government, agreed to, sending Lord Harcourt in his place. No previous administration had done so much to lower political life in Ireland, and Townshend was one of the few Viceroys who earned for themselves personal dislike. "The people of Ireland," says Sir John Davies, "did ever love and desire to be governed by great personages." Anyone who has lived long enough in the country to study the character of the nation will endorse this opinion, and agree with Mr. Lecky when he adds that the Queen's representative has always been, except in a few cases, "the most popular man in Ireland," for the reason that Irishmen are peculiarly susceptible to personal influence. Up to the last Townshend continued his dissipated habits. When his successor arrived at the Castle he found him drinking and playing cards at three o'clock in the morning. "At all events you have not found me napping," said the witty Townshend, who remained for another fortnight as Lord Harcourt's guest, ostensibly for the purpose of giving satisfaction, now that he was a private gentleman, to those who resented any part of his behaviour and wished to call him out. He received challenges from no less than eight; the duels, however, did not take place on the Irish side of the

Channel; his enemies declaring that Townshend sheltered
himself behind the Vice-regal protection. This was a calumny,
as no one could deny his claim to courage. The day of his
departure was the occasion of a hostile display. It had been
supposed that he would go away quietly under cover of
night, but he somewhat foolishly hired a mob who surrounded
his carriage, cheering him as he went in procession through
the streets to Bullock Harbour.

> " To Bullock the mock monarch flees,
> In every bush a dagger sees ;
> But, safe beneath thy auspices [1]
> Escapes the indignant rabble."

While the vessel lay in the harbour, he had the pleasure of
seeing his effigy burned on the shore, and the next day the
Freeman's Journal and other papers were full of all manner of
squibs and indecent attacks upon his character. Even after
he had reached the other side his troubles were not over. At
Holyhead he found one of his challengers, Captain Montgomery, waiting for him. This quarrel was however adjusted.
Lord Bellamont, a young Irish Peer whom Townshend had
refused to see in Dublin, followed him to London, where Lord
Charlemont carried the challenge and insisted on Lord
Bellamont's right to satisfaction, or in lieu thereof a formal
denial from the late Viceroy of having wished to offend the
challenger. This Lord Townshend refusing, the two noblemen met at Chalk Farm, where the duel took place. Lord
Townshend wounded his adversary rather severely, and here
the matter ended.

We now return to Dorothea, who was enduring what,
to a proud nature, is intolerably painful, the mortification of
being not alone deserted, but that another should have
succeeded where she failed. Lord Townshend's marriage to
Miss Montgomery was announced shortly after the Viceroy's
departure, and as if this were not enough, she had the additional
sting of seeing the man whose true heart she had cast aside
for the *ignis fatuus* of rank and ambition, suddenly rise to

---

[1] This alludes to the shelter given to him by the new Viceroy
Harcourt.

distinction. The talents which Langrishe possessed received due recognition. He was liberal in his sentiments and politics. He became a leading member of the House of Commons, and was an excellent speaker, his style being full of pleasantries and lightness, and his wit was sharp and pungent. He was a lover to be proud of, but it does not appear that he renewed his suit, perhaps it was as well that he did not. Anyhow, in a few years he married one Miss Myhill, niece, strangely enough, to another Lady Ely, and was made a baronet in 1777.

In 1773 the aunt [1] who had done so much to blight Dolly's young life died—it was said her illness was induced by the pain and mortification she had suffered at the failure of all her plans for the advancement of her husband and niece. It was reported that the disconsolate widower, six months after his lady's decease, offered Dorothea his hand and title, but she would not listen to such an outrage to her aunt's memory. Two years later, in 1775, she married Mr. Richardson of Rich Hill, member for the County of Armagh. Let us hope she was happy. We know little more of her except glimpses here and there. She is said to have taken a keen interest in politics, and to have made a figure in political circles. She lived to see the Union passed, and outlived both her husband and the lover of her youth. Sir Hercules Langrishe died in 1810 at the age of seventy-eight, and in his old age he loved to recall the past and to dwell upon the charms of Miss Monroe. Grattan, in his beautiful elegy upon his dead friend, alludes to their love. The lines which, for their rhythm and tenderness have been compared to Mason's Monody on Lady Coventry, had best be given in their entirety :—

---

[1] Lord Ely had only just completed the fine mansion he had built in Ely Place, and for which reason he changed the original name of the street, Hume's Row, to Ely Place, by which it has been known from the beginning of this century. Ely House, which was sold soon after his lordship's death, was then divided into two houses. It is remarkable for a wrought iron staircase of great elegance, for its panelled hall, and for the chimney pieces, which are of great beauty, and are considered heirlooms ; and to insure their not being tampered with, they were constantly examined by skilled workmen, in the interest of the family. They have by this time probably been sold.

" Oh. friend ! and while with death-like step thy hearse
Goes to the grave, may I, in weeping verse,
By love, by duty, and by sorrow led,
Attend the bier, and there review the dead.
Departed friend, oh ! thou wert born to please,
And live with mirth, serenity and ease.
Thine was the ready turn, the pleasant hit,
Thou soul of sunshine, and thou god of wit.'
For ever gentle and for ever gay
Thy life a philosophic comedy.
Alas ! thy humour and thy wit are gone,
And the gay colours of thy life are flown.
Sunk in the grave what varied powers we see !
How many pleasant thoughts have died with thee.
He loved his country, and he loved her laws,
He drew his pen in Freedom's sacred cause.
He sung the country's graces, as her wrongs ;
Love reached his heart, and Love improved his songs.
See Barataria comes his death to mourn,
And Dorothea weeping o'er his urn."

Poor Dorothea, who was at this time much stricken in
years, soon followed Sir Hercules to the grave. She died in
the following year, 1811. Her husband had been dead some
years previously, she had no children, her links with the past
were shattered and gone, and the generation growing up
around her cared nothing for her or her story. So it is, or
will be, with each one of us. Time is a grand destroyer,
and in his hands our day dreams lie crushed into ruins.

---

[1] Several instances of Langrishe's wit are told in Grattan's Life and
times. On one occasion he was riding with one of the numerous Viceroys
whose name has not transpired; his Excellency complained that his
predecessors had left the Park in such a condition as to be almost a
swamp. "They were too much 'occupied *draining* the rest of the kingdom," replied Langrishe. Another time he was asked where was to be
found the best history of Ireland, he answered, promptly, "In the
continuation of Rapin." For all this apparent patriotism the secret
service of Pitt reveals the unpleasant fact that this patriot received
£15,000 from the hated Saxon, for surrendering his right to vote against
the Union.

I.—ANNE, MARCHIONESS OF TOWNSHEND.

THE story of Dorothea would be incomplete, unless it were
followed by that of her successful rival, Anne Montgomery,
and therefore, although she was the second, some say the
youngest of the sisters, first place is due to her. It was
indeed no small tribute to her charms that she should have
succeeded where Dolly had failed. Her success was, however,
not achieved without recourse to an expedient which, although
it is not without precedent, can never be acceptable to a
woman's vanity.

The *nationality* of this fair trio of sisters is somewhat
questionable; that Scotland may claim them as well as Ireland
is undoubted, still a good case can be made out for Ireland,
for although Sir William Montgomery came from Peeble-
shire, where his place, Magbie Hill, was situated, he had
married Miss Tomkyns, an Irish lady of large property near
Londonderry: she died when the children were young, and
Sir William marrying again, and having a second family,
the daughters of the first wife were brought up principally
by their mother's relatives, and seem to have adopted her
country as their own, while their beauty and charm was a
matter of national pride, and the poets, who expressed their
admiration in lines of much elegance, invariably claim them as
"Hibernian belles." Elizabeth was the eldest, Barbara the
youngest, Anne [1] came in the middle. She was in her girl-

---

[1] Anne was the most beautiful of the sisters; she was tall, fair, and of
a most enchanting countenance. Elizabeth was shorter, but exceedingly
animated; this is alluded to in an ode addressed to Miss Montgomery by
one of her admirers,—

> Sylvia has spirit, sparkling eyes, and wit;
> Nor let her want of stature raise a strife,
> In less of matter there is more of *Life*.

hood when we first hear of her as attracting Lord Townshend's notice, shortly after his arrival in Ireland as Viceroy.

There is some uncertainty as to where this first meeting took place, whether at Carton, where Anne had a trifling part in the *Beggar's Opera*, played by amateurs, or at Rathfarnham Castle, when the *Masque of Comus* was given by children. This was soon after Lord Townshend's arrival. There was, as already stated, a connection between the Townshends and the Earl of Ely. Nicholas, the predecessor of Henry, Viscount Loftus, was then the head of the family, and no doubt the Viceroy had laid his plan to detach *him* and his followers from the patriot lords, for Nicholas was weak of intellect, and a ready prey to any stronger mind. So the entertainment was graciously accepted, and Townshend and his Countess came in great state to do all honour to their dear kinsman.

The masque was given with the most picturesque setting, the woods of Rathfarnham Castle lending it a peculiar charm. It was played by children, the eldest not more than thirteen, so Elizabeth and Anne must have been there as spectators, though their younger sister Barbara was one of the performers. The beauty of Anne attracted the attention of the Viceroy, who was of a singularly susceptible nature. He paid her the most extravagant compliments. The Countess, who, poor lady, was well accustomed to her lord's erratic fancies, treated the young girl with much kindness, and the sisters soon became the acknowledged belles of Dublin, where they were well known from childhood, and favourites with high and low.

The habit of versifying which distinguished the last century prevailed to an alarming extent in Ireland. Every man who could put two lines of doggrel together considered himself a poet, and wrote effusively: prologues, epilogues, fulsome addresses to public persons, sonnets in praise of the standard beauties, or satirical attacks upon political enemies. This rhyming mania was much cultivated by the *beaux esprits*. Mrs. Pilkington made Dean Swift's acquaintance by sending him "verses," while there was constant rhyming going on between the "Saturnine" Dean and his friend Dr. Delany; one almost wonders how, with their graver pursuits, they found time for this perpetual fire of birthday and other odes. The same fashion was cultivated by lovers, every compliment being expressed in the less convincing form of rhyme. Howard[1] who was an inveterate scribbler, wrote tragedies and verses by the yard, which were handed about, shown to particular friends at the club, or given to some fair lady to amuse her dressing-room coterie. Some of these were satirical in their nature, generally biting attacks on the Government, or an obnoxious person, sometimes extravagant praises of a fashionable beauty. It was in this way the three sisters received the appellation of "The Graces," by which they were known all over the country. The verses were addressed,

"*To the three favourite sisters on the occasion of their return after an absence,*" and set forth in some pretty lines Love's Mistake and the Jealousy of Venus.

Of late Love's Queen, all in despair
Fled through each region of the air,
   Her Graces were astray.
To seek them, Maia's winged son
From Pole to Pole with speed had run,
   It was a bustling day.

Cupid, who had to earth been sent,
Returned with haste and toil near spent,
   And vowed he saw them there.
That 'twas on famed Ierne's shore
Than which with beauties none shines more
   On the terrestrial sphere.

Straightway a troop of little Loves
Who tend their Queen where'er she moves
   And bask in her sweet eyes,
Flew for the nymphs, whom when they brought
Alack! 'twas found the urchins caught
   The three Montgomeries.

Soon as their charms shone full in view
The Paphian Goddess jealous grew,
   She feared her future reign.
Her boy she chid for his mistake,
Nor could forgive 'till he took back
   The three to Earth again.

---

[1] George Edmund Howard was, on his father's side, connected with the ducal house of Norfolk, by his mother with the Loftuses. He was educated at Sheridan's school, bound to an attorney called Nixon, and spent his time rhyming.

Another admirer addressed some verses on seeing them at a fancy ball, which were not quite so satisfactory. After comparing them to the three beautiful forms which appeared to Paris on Mount Ida, and the difficulty in their case of making a choice, he adds,—

> Yet Truth to speak had I the fruit
> Lest rage in sister hearts should glow,
> I'd end at once the whole dispute
> And give the apple to *Mauro.*

The writer must have been very simple to suppose *this* would be acceptable.

Unlike Dolly, however, the trio of Graces had other and more substantial charms than their lovely faces. They were co-heiresses to the large estates of their mother; not that I would insinuate that the vulgar accident of fortune had aught to do with the admiration the beautiful sisters excited. In the days in which they lived, men were more easily impressed by the power of beauty than in this mercenary age. As we have seen in the case of the Gunnings, a really beautiful woman could aspire to the highest position. Love will not be easily dethroned, and in the present day we have many refreshing instances that his reign is by no means at an end. There is, however, sufficient justification for the conclusion that romance is somewhat " gone by."

Very different to the Gunnings, the Miss Montgomerys were well educated; they had studied much, and had the advantage of an excellent training from the hands of Samuel Whyte,[1] who was a well-known schoolmaster of the

---

[1] Samuel Whyte was the natural son of Captain Johnson Whyte, Deputy Governor of the Tower; his sister married Dr. Philip Chamberlayne, Archdeacon of Glendalough, and through this marriage he was connected with the Sheridans, Mrs. Thomas Sheridan being a Miss Chamberlayne. After the death of Whyte's father, the estate going to the legitimate heir, Samuel was badly off, and by the advice of Tom Sheridan opened a school at 75, Grafton Street, Dublin. His first pupils were the Sheridan children. His school flourished, all the best families sending their sons to be educated by Sam Whyte. He had classes for young ladies, or visited them at their own houses, his terms being three guineas for eight visits. His lessons in elocution were highly considered, although Moore says his known partiality for the stage was not in his favour.

time. The blue-stocking mania, which possessed fashionable women of the last century, had its followers in Dublin, where Mrs. Pilkington, Constantia Grierson, Mrs. Brooke, and many others emulated Mrs. Montagu, Mrs. Vesey, and Lady Lucan. Arthur Young and Mrs. Delany were both struck by the wit and cleverness of Irishwomen of the upper class; "their education is careful and their reading, especially in classical history, extensive . . . the conversation (even of the young girls) is marked by much intelligence, this however is somewhat marred by extraordinary coarseness; they use expressions, which coming from such fresh and lovely lips, have a startling and unpleasing effect." This coarseness was, however, a marked feature of the last century; those sweet-looking creatures before alluded to who walked in the walled-in garden with the mulberry trees, so charmingly described by Mrs. Lynn Linton, were given to calling "a spade a spade." In the intervals of washing the china and getting up "the fine linen" they improved their minds with the reading of *Tristram Shandy* [1] and *Clarissa Harlowe* . . . The Miss Montgomerys were otherwise employed, their studies occupying most of their time. We hear of them attending lectures upon the optic nerve, which were crowded by ladies of rank and fashion, most of them pupils of Mr. Whyte, who immediately wrote an ode (versifying was of course *his* passion) describing the charms of each lady :—

> "In Anna's [2] sparkling eyes we find
> Each calm perfection of the mind." [3]

---

[1] Goldsmith, in the Chinese Citizen, dwells upon the toleration with which *Tristram Shandy* was received by the female portion of the community. He wonders at their applauding it, and, what was worse, introducing this free tone into their conversation. "Yet so it is, the pretty innocents now carry these books openly in their hands which formerly were hid under the sofa cushion."

[2] Anna was, of course, Anne Montgomery. Of the three sisters, Barbara seems to have been his favourite, although indeed the good Dominie had as many favourite pupils as Mr. Bentley has favourite novels; he was fond of them all, especially those who were raised to the peerage.

[3] This ode, called "The Lyceum," is to be found in *Hibernian Cresses*, published by Mr. Whyte. In it he passes in review all the ladies who were present on the occasion of the lecture. Anne Montgomery sat near

Since 1759, a special feature of Irish society had been private theatricals, which had seized upon the upper classes as a passion. Excellent performances had taken place at Lurgan, Castletown, and Carton. The Honourable Luke Gardiner built a theatre at his lodge in the Phœnix Park, where, assisted by his friends, Mr. and Mrs. Jephson, he gave constant entertainments. Most of these were under the superintendence of Mr. Whyte, who shared the prevailing taste, rather to the detriment of his more responsible and lucrative employment. He was never so happy as when getting up a play, superintending rehearsals, writing prologues, and instructing the fair performers.

The first appearance of the Miss Montgomerys on the amateur stage was at Leixlip Castle, the summer residence of the Irish Viceroys. The pieces were somewhat ambitious, *Tamerlane* and *The Fair Penitent*; the performers, Lords Kildare and Mountmorres, Messrs. Brownlow and Jephson, and the three sisters. This would seem to have been a private affair, and probably only the friends of the Viceroy were invited. Later there was a public performance in Dublin for the benefit of the prisoners in the Marshalsea.[1]

A check, however, was put to gaiety of any kind by Lady Townshend's death in 1770, after which, as we know, for a short period, the Viceroy transferred his attentions to Dorothea. It seems probable, however, that all through his real admiration was for Anne. Her portraits represent her as a beautiful young woman, and her mental qualifications were more likely to hold the affections of a man like Lord Towns-

---

him, and induced him to write the poem, which he did then and there; she furnishing him, as he sat on a bench at her feet, with a pencil and cards for the purpose, which she took from him as they were filled, and afterwards transcribed with her own hand for the *Shamrock*, in which they were published.—*Hibernian Cresses.*

[1] Grattan, writing on 13th February, 1770, to his friend Day, says:—
"I was so stupid as to refuse a ticket, and lost a most magnificent spectacle, and in the instance of *Miss Montgomery* and Jephson, a fine performance; the former an accomplished actress, the latter a formed actor." Several ladies, he adds, *dressed* for different characters, amongst them two of my sisters were numbered, but *none* spoke. In fact, the Miss Montgomerys refused to be the only women who would act, and therefore required *the appearance* of female society."

hend, who, with all his faults of judgment, was possessed of undoubted ability. His attentions were of a most decided character, and made the object of them the mark for all the usual gossip; Anne's name was in everyone's mouth, and her chances of being Lady Townshend was the subject of jests and wagers. This unpleasant position does not seem to have ruffled Miss Montgomery's composure. She was quite able to lend her help to Mr. Whyte, whose prize day was alway distinguished by an excellent dramatic performance given by his pupils. In 1772, *Cato* [1] had been chosen, and so much satisfaction had it given, that it was repeated on a larger scale at Crow Street Theatre " for the relief of the confined debtors in the different Marshalseas."

Whyte's popularity was made evident by the assistance he received on all sides; the Earls of Kildare, Bellamont and Dunluce were stewards; Lord Mornington [2] conducted his amateur band, while Mr. Whyte's fair pupils rallied round him, lending every assistance in their power. Foremost were the Montgomerys, whose charge it was to decorate the theatre, which they transformed into a bower of roses. Anne did more: she used her influence with her noble admirer to give his patronage to the performance. All these attractions contrived to make the performance fashionable, and, as everyone knows, fashion means success; the house could have been filled three

---

[1] The cast for *Cato* was altogether by boys. In the prologue, which was written by Mr. Whyte, occurs the following lines :—

> We plead our years. I am, sirs, only seven,
> Our Marcia's nine, her father scarce eleven.
> But with great Cato's sentiments impressed
> Honour and filial reverence fill our breasts.

An amusing story was told of the boy who performed Portius; he distinguished himself by an easy deportment which would have done credit to a veteran of the stage. In the love-scenes, however, there was a singular lack of the same fire, and his instructors took him to task for this coldness and languor. He gave as a reason that he could never forget it was a boy who acted the part, but if, said he, you will prevail on your pupil little Miss N— (a rising beauty of eight years old) to play the character, you shall see, sir, with what spirit I will go through the scene.—*Hibernian Magazine.*

[2] Mornington, a dilettante nobleman whose compositions still command favour, had founded a musical academy, altogether supported by amateur talent.

times over. Lord Townshend came in state, his box was crowded with officials in splendid uniforms. In the box next to him sat the three beautiful sisters; the Viceroy paid Anne the most devoted attention, and all the world said they were engaged. But in this the world, as it often is, was wrong.

This was Lord Townshend's last public appearance in Dublin. To the joy of his enemies, and their name was legion, his recall had come. The Government, yielding to the pressure put upon them by the Irish members, and finding it impossible to countenance Townshend's outrageous impropriety of conduct, appointed as his successor Lord Harcourt. Under these circumstances it is usual for the holder of office to at once vacate his appointment. Townshend, with a strange lack of dignity, lingered on in Dublin, although no shadow of power remained in his hands. Why he did so remained a mystery— unless it was that he could not tear himself away from Anne's sweet presence. This is what he, no doubt, told her. A writer in Baratariana alludes to this in plain language. " In what manner soever he spent his nights, his days were undoubtedly passed at her uncle's house, enjoying his gratuitous hospitality; and yet the charms of the fair Montgomery, which might have attracted the most elegant nature, could not fix his capricious mind." In other words, he once more played the part of a recreant knight, and took himself off without making the young lady any definite offer. That he should trifle in such a discreditable manner with a girl of Anne's position was not to be borne, especially as, unlike Dolly, she had a brother who would not allow his sister's name to be made a by-word for idle gossips to chatter over. Captain Montgomery lost no time in following the escaping lover, caught him at Holyhead, and, under pretext of a political quarrel, gave him the option of a duel or a proposal.

Lord Townshend—who had already as we know six duels on his hands—imitated the plan adopted under similar circumstances by the Duc de Grammont, and made the messenger the bearer of his declaration, giving some explanation of its tardy avowal which satisfied the injured feelings of the young lady. The marriage, however, did not take place for some

mouths, and in the interval Elizabeth, the eldest, got engaged
to the popular Amphitryon, Luke Gardiner ; and Barbara, the
youngest, to the Honourable John Beresford, the second son
of Lord Tyrone. Both marriages were all that could be
desired.

In Sir Joshua Reynolds' very delightful diary we find
this triple event noted :—

" Monday, March 1st, 1773.

" At 11 o'clock arrives an Irish gentleman, the Right
Honourable Luke Gardiner, now in London for his marriage
with Miss Elizabeth Montgomery, one of the three beautiful
daughters of Sir William Montgomery, of whom another is
engaged to Viscount Townshend, lately succeeded in the Lord
Lieutenancy of Ireland by Lord Harcourt, and the third to
the Honourable John Beresford ; all three marriages are to
come off this year or next at latest."

The outcome of Mr. Gardiner's sittings for his own portrait
(now at Petworth) was a commission from him to Sir
Joshua to paint the three beautiful sisters in a group. Accordingly the sittings began in May. Those who visit the
National Gallery can there see the result. Mr. Gardiner, who
paid the bill, naturally had the right to have his wishes con-
sulted. He desired, as he said in the letter he wrote introducing the Miss Montgomerys to Sir Joshua, to have their portraits " as representing some allegorical or historical subject."
This rather absurd notion was then in fashion, every artist had
to pander more or less to the fashionable craze which possessed
the lady of quality to hand herself down to posterity disguised
as one of the very immoral goddesses of Olympus ; although
as Alan Cunningham says, " What claim a Duchess of Man-
chester with a babe on her knee could have to the distinction
of Diana, it is difficult to guess."

The picture of the " Graces," as painted by Sir Joshua,
is fortunately only mildly allegorical. If allegory was to
be employed—and as his biographer remarks, it was not
the painter's suggestion, but the patron's—there could
be nothing more appropriate to these beautiful girls,

standing hand in hand on the threshold of Hymen, than to represent them as wreathing with flowers a statue raised to the God of Marriage. Before, however, the picture was finished, Lady Townshend had been married. Sir Joshua has therefore imparted to her a more dignified air. She stands next to the statue of the god (who is represented as *blind*); she is tall and stately, robed in white, and her face has a sweet and lovely expression. There is a wealth of beauty, so to speak, in the luxuriant colouring, golden hair, and most bewitching smile.

Charming as is my Lady Townshend, yet I like almost better Barbara, who kneels on the right hand, gathering flowers for the wreath. There is thoughtfulness in her young face, depth in the dark lustrous eyes, and a tender sweetness about the mouth, very captivating. Elizabeth, in the middle, has quite a sprightly air; pretty more than beautiful, with a certain spring and joyousness in the whole figure, as if well satisfied with what fortune has in store *for her*. Both these sisters (as yet unmarried) wear brown, of the peculiar hue affected by the painter, which makes a strong contrast with the white dress of the bride; the flowers look as if just gathered. Much interest attaches to this picture . . . not the least part of which being that it was bequeathed to the nation by the son of Elizabeth, the well-known dilettante Earl of Blessington, who made such a shipwreck of the good gifts of life.

Lady Townshend's appearance in the great world of London was duly heralded; she was presented at Court, and Mrs. Foley tells Mrs. Delany how she was surrounded by a posse of Montgomerys, and Mrs. Delany writes to Miss Dewar " that the men think the new beauty very handsome, but the women won't allow her a shred of good looks." From this we can gather that she was thought to be a dangerous rival.

Lady Townshend, however, did not long enjoy the benefits of her high position. Lord Townshend's affairs, which had been in a disastrous condition before he had accepted the Vice-royalty, were irretrievably ruined by the extravagance he had practised in Ireland, and his creditors upon both sides of the channel became so troublesome, that he was forced to consider their claims, the upshot being that he had to resign his office and retire into the country, where, like Cincinnatus, he devoted himself to the cultivation of his garden.

"Lord Townshend is undone," writes Lady Gower ; "and from possessing an income of 18,000*l.* a year has scarce one thousand left. He has gone into retirement with the sting of having involved his family in distress, when, had he acted on right principles, he might have been an honour to them and his country."

The one most to be pitied was Anne, who had done so much to win not so much the man she loved, as the high position he occupied. She seems, however, to have accepted the inevitable with equanimity and to have spent her life peacefully, contributing largely to the future generation. For the rest, the erratic Townshend was an altered man, and she had, so far as we know, no reason to complain of him.

In 1786 his affairs grew more prosperous ; he was raised to the dignity of Marquis, and the lucrative post of Master of the Ordnance was bestowed upon him. Anne henceforth was much in evidence in society. When the Prince of Wales married the unfortunate Caroline of Brunswick, Lady Townshend was made one of the ladies-in-waiting, and received many marks of friendship from the Princess. She lived on well into this century, surviving both her sisters as well as her husband, who died in 1807. One of her daughters married the Duke of Leeds ;[1] another, Lord de Blaquière.

We have now to follow the fortunes of Elizabeth and Barbara Montgomery, both of whose marriages were exceptionally brilliant.

Elizabeth's husband, the Right Honourable Luke Gardiner, was member for the county of Dublin, member of the Privy Council, and Colonel of the Dublin Militia. He was the sole representative (through the female line) of his ancestors the Earls of Blessington and Viscounts Mountjoy, and in 1779 he was made Baron Mountjoy, and later Viscount. He also

---

[1] The portrait of this lady was exhibited this year in the Grafton Gallery ; there is a resemblance to her mother, but the air of distinction so remarkable in Anne Lady Townshend, is absent from Anne Townshend Duchess of Leeds, who is for the rest a gentle, unpretending type of beauty.

inherited the Mountjoy estates, situated in Tyrone, valued at thirty thousand a year,[1] in addition to the Gardiner property, in and about Dublin.[2] He had a lodge in the Phœnix Park, and the Manor House in Henrietta Street, built by his grandfather, is described as a magnificent residence.[3]

In addition to these good things, Mr. Gardiner had qualities

[1] He inherited the Mountjoy estates through Anne, the only daughter of the Hon. Alexander Stewart, second son of William, first Viscount Mountjoy, whose male issue terminated 1769, in the person of William, third Viscount Mountjoy and first Earl of Blessington.

[2] The names of the streets in the now unfashionable region on the north side of Dublin are suggestive of the Mountjoy and Gardiner families :— Mountjoy Square, Mountjoy Street, Blessington Street, Gardiner Street, Gardiner Place, Mountjoy Place. There are good houses in Mountjoy Square and its surroundings, but it is now comparatively deserted, and bears that sad aspect common to out-of-date localities. The auctioneers and house agents have it to themselves, and seem likely to be the sole lessees.

[3] Mountjoy House was built in 1725 by Luke Gardiner, who married in 1701 Anne, the only daughter and heiress of Alexander Stewart. The old house is still existent and is let to lawyers as "chambers." It is so accurately described in the *Irish Builder* of July, 1893, that I annex the following :—"This magnificent mansion was erected about the year 1725, by the Rt. Hon. Luke Gardiner, grandfather of the fourth Viscount Mountjoy, ancestor of the Earl of Blessington, and may be described as the Manor House of Henrietta Street. The reception-rooms are seven in number, and the cornices and ceilings are finished in a rich and antique style. The ball-room is a noble apartment; the architraves of the doors and windows are adorned with fluted Corinthian columns surmounted by pediments. The drawing-room, to the left of the ante-room on the first-floor, possesses a beautifully carved oak cornice, the effect of which is peculiarly striking. The front staircase is spacious and lofty; the walls are panelled, and the ceiling is handsomely ornamented. The principal dining-room, looking into the garden, is square, with fine stuccoed ceiling, and walls in square panels stuccoed, the squares broken off at the angles by curves. The architraves of the parlour doors are as rich as carving could make them. There is a mock keystone or block of wood that for elegant and elaborate carving in relief cannot be surpassed. The stuccoed ceilings are in panels with enriched fillets, quite palatial, and only in the ball-room are seen arabesques in the centre. The window of the ball-room, which is over the *porte-cochère*, has three opes, the centre ope being arched, and this is the only architectural adornment externally. Mountjoy House had originally a fine *porte-cochère*, or covered carriage entry, arched with cut stone, on the park side, next to the present King's Inn buildings. The park, or ornamental ground, attached to this mansion, was purchased by Luke Gardiner from the Dean and Chapter of Christ Church, and was known as the "Plover Park." The whole of the Mountjoy estate in Dublin was sold in the Encumbered Estate Court, 1874, to Charles Spencer Cowper for 120,000*l.*

both personal and mental, likely to win a woman's love. He was young and handsome, brave, chivalrous, and accomplished, a brilliant speaker, a rising politician, a good amateur actor, and a most popular man in society. This last quality has its disadvantages for those who care more for domestic happiness than the tinsel brilliancy of society. Luke Gardiner, however, seems to have made a good husband, Elizabeth sharing his taste for social amusements and gaiety of all sorts; they led a racketing, highly fashionable life.

At the period of which I am writing Dublin was a cheerful little capital. Its mimic court was far gayer than that over which excellent "Farmer George" and his good, but somewhat dowdy, Queen presided. There was plenty of fun and frolic, and a general spirit of hilarity. In all that was going on Luke Gardiner and his young wife took their share. We find their names constantly coming up, here, there, everywhere. Private theatricals had not lost their charm, and there was the new diversion of masquerades, or ridottos, as they were styled, which were much to the taste of Dublin society.

Masquerades had been favourite amusements in London society from the time of George II., who had revived the fashion of "disguisement," which during the strict rule of the Commonwealth had been rigidly proscribed.

Heidegger, the King's purveyor of pleasure, was eminently successful in the manner of his entertainments, and after his death his mantle fell upon a certain Mrs. or Madame Cornely, whose house in Soho Square was much frequented. Fashionable leaders of society likewise gave splendid masquerades; it will be remembered that Lady Coventry declared herself to be tired of them.

The fashion had now spread to Dublin, where the gay, versatile nature of the people lent itself more readily to the humours of the masquerade than did the gravity of the English, who were content with looking the character each had assumed, without any sustained effort in supporting it;[1]

[1] In proof of the manner in which English masks drop their assumed characters, a good story is told by Fuseli, who was induced by Mrs. Wollstonecraft to form one of a party visiting the Opera House when a

whereas it is in fact not so much the costume as the spirit of *masking* that is required to render the scene attractive and enjoyable, what in fact the French understand so thoroughly, the *intrigue*, that rare combination of witty repartee, sly fun, delicate banter, and thorough adoption of the character assumed. This it is gives such piquancy to the situation.

Masquerades were very welcome to a gay and volatile society like that of Dublin; they were supported by all the wit and fashion of the city, and soon became most popular with all classes. As no expense was spared in the matter of costume, trade profited by the new fashion; while there was great scope for the display of a ready wit in the delineation of the assumed characters; there were[1] also opportunities for malice to whisper into the ear of a jealous husband or wife the poison of suspicion, or to spread some of the ill-natured tittle-tattle which in a small circle is always passing round.

Leading members of society kept open house from seven to twelve o'clock to receive the masks, who made the round of certain fashionable houses. The Duke of Leinster's, in Merrion Square; Mrs. Kilpatrick's, 24, Merrion Street; Lady Arabella Denney's; Mr. La Touche's, 10, Merrion Square; Mr. Rowley's, and many others, where they were received with much hospitality, and greatly enjoyed this exhibition of themselves.

In 1778, on St. Patrick's Day, a masquerade was given at Fishamble Street rooms, which was attended by 700 people.

---

masquerade was given. He says, " We were endeavouring to be amused by the masks, when a devil came howling about us, and tormented some of the party to such a degree that I exclaimed in a loud voice, ' Go to hell; ' but the dull devil, instead of answering as became his character, ' then I will drag you down with me,' or some such bitter remark, put himself into a real passion and began to abuse me roundly, until to avoid him I left the place."—*Life of Fuseli.*

[1] Criticisms were freely made in the daily papers, and the masqueraders were taken very severely to task if they did not do justice to the character they assumed; they were expected to give even the nicer shades of character, as when "a Caliban" was reproached for only recollecting "the savage" traits of that individual. The critics were hard upon any one who did not come up to the standard, as when a Mr. Holmes represented a jockey with no knowledge of either Newmarket or the Curragh, and Mr. Burrows essayed to play the magician with no gifts for that or any part.

The Duke of Leinster altered his costume twice, appearing first as a fruit-woman, who changed her oranges for Shamrocks as St. Patrick's Day advanced; afterwards as a physician. At this entertainment Mr. Luke Gardiner is especially noticed as an old woman carrying her father in a basket and her child in her arms, one of the best and most laughable masks in the room. At supper Mr. Gardiner appeared in a black domino; Mrs. Gardiner is also named as most inimitable as Sestina the opera singer. She likewise sang one of Sestina's songs.

In 1780 the gentlemen of Daly's Club gave one of the most splendid masked balls in honour of the Countess of Buckingham, wife to the Viceroy, and here again we have Mr. and Mrs. Gardiner, he as a sixpenny doll, and his charming wife as a " Fille de Patmos." One feature of these masquerades was the ingenuity shown in the selection of the characters, which undoubtedly evinces an originality of mind and knowledge of historical and classical subjects far beyond that of our up-to-date maskers, who do not seem to get out of the stereotyped groove of Mary Stuart, Snow Maidens, Watteau Sacques, and Henry VIII. A glance at the characters who appeared a hundred and fourteen years ago, may suggest to the fin-de-siècle masqueraders a welcome variety.[1]

Two Spanish Slaves. Lord and Lady Antrim. (Elegantly dressed, and fettered in the chains of Hymen.)
A Whey Woman. Mr. Maguire. (Nature itself.)
A Sixpenny Doll. Lord Mountjoy.[2]
A Fille de Patmos. Lady Mountjoy. (Most beautiful Mask.)
A Tancred. Lord Stratheven. (Superb.)
A Beautiful Nun. Lady de Vesci. (Universally admired.)
A Patagonian Venus and her little Cupid. Mr. Cordot. (Enormously amusing.)
A Leaden Mercury. Mr. Hewit.
The Scrapers. Mr. Cole and Mr. Hall.

---

[1] Sometimes parts were assumed that would shock our British matron, as for instance that of a lady who was expecting a certain event; the case, too, must have been imminent as she was hunting everywhere for Dr. Jebb, the famous practitioner in that line. Dr. Slop was also present, handing about his cards. Very few ladies of this generation would know him to be " Mrs. Shandy's medical attendant," but our great-grandmothers read Mr. Sterne's books for all they were so demure.

[2] Mr. Gardiner had been created Baron Mountjoy in 1779.

An Innocent Pretty Quaker, "Moved by the Spirit." Lady Harriet
    Corry. (Who, accompanied by two curious fiddlers, formed an
    excellent group, and played their parts with entertaining humour.)
A Portrait Painter. Mr. Wilson. (Original and amusing, though very
    satirical on a certain celebrated President of the R.A., distributing
    the following card :—Sir Joshua Carmine, R.A., London.)
A Bayes. Mr. Quin. (Curiously decorated with all the ensigns of
    literature and the rates of authorship.)
A Double Face. Miss Cavendish. (Very good.)
The Fair Quaker of Deal. The beautiful Mrs. Mathews.

"Masqueing" was not the only accomplishment in which the
young couple displayed considerable talent. They were both
far above the ordinary amateur actors. Elizabeth had profited
by the training given to his pupils by Sam Whyte; her clear
delivery of her words and freedom from all "amateurishness"
being due to his instructions in the art of acting. Without some
such training, it is idle to think of making any real success
upon either a public or private stage; though the idea common
to amateurs is that they come forth as heaven-born actors and
actresses. This notion is fostered by the applause of friends,
who declare gravely that Dick Harrison and Lady May run
Wyndham and Mary Moore very close, and as for Giddens he
is not in it with Jim Louther as the funny man . . . but if,
listening to this pleasing flattery, Jim essays to make a living
out of his talents, he is soon brought face to face with the
unpleasant truth that he has yet to learn the drudgery of the
profession, before his *great gifts* will be appreciated.

In January, 1778, Mrs. Gardiner took rather a bold flight in
attempting the rôle of Lady Macbeth, the occasion being a
grand entertainment given at Mr. Gardiner's private theatre
in the Phœnix Park to the then Viceroy, the Duke of Rutland,
who with his beautiful Duchess honoured the first representation with his presence. It is interesting to read the caste of
this performance 116 years ago.

Macbeth	. .	Captain Jephson.
MacDuff	. .	Hon. Luke Gardiner.
Duncan	. .	Mr. Staples.
Banquo	. .	Sir Alexander Schomberg.[1]

---

[1] Sir Alexander Schomberg, who commanded the Lord Lieutenant's
yacht, was a great admirer of Mrs. Gardiner's. The lines he addressed

Donald Blain	Sir M. Crosbie.
Fleance	Mr. Barry St. Leger.
Seward .	Captain Ormsby.
	etc.
Lady Macbeth .	Mrs. Gardiner.
Gentlewoman .	Mrs. Jephson.
Hecate	Mr. Swan.

Speaking Witches: Mr. Toler, Mr. Knox, Mr. Prendergast.
Singing Witches: Miss Gardiner, Miss Norman, Mr. Waller.
Apparitions: The Masters Montgomery.

To be followed by the

CITIZEN.

Commence	Mrs. Gardiner.

From this bill, it is evident that Mrs. Gardiner secured for herself what is called in professional slang "all the fat." According to the papers of the day, she carried away her audience both by her acting and her extreme beauty. She presented Lady Macbeth, not as a harsh, unloving woman, but as a tempting, seducing syren who armed herself with every womanly attraction to win Macbeth to her ambitious purposes.

Her dresses were dreams of beauty, and in the second act her parure of diamonds was valued at a hundred thousand pounds. In the farce which followed she acted in the most sprightly manner; her dress was "white *sattin* puckered with feathers, and when she spoke the epilogue, which was written by Mr. Whyte, she appeared in a *pink sattin* venetian night-gown [1] with an elegant blossom-coloured petticoat wrought by herself."

to her explain the effect her, or more probably Mr. Whyte's, reading of the part of Lady Macbeth produced upon the audience :—

> "You looked so charming, that Macbeth,
> When urged by you to acts of death,
> Might for excuse your beauty plead
> And think to sanctify the deed
> By saying nothing could be wrong
> That fell from your enchanting tongue."

It is worthy of remark that when Sarah Bernhardt recited the sleep-walking scene she took this view, and by her superb declamation won more pity than horror for the murderess.

[1] In the latter part of the century it was the custom for ladies to wear what was called bed-gowns at small friendly parties. They were richly trimmed and made of handsome material, and probably resembled the present fashion of loose jackets which are superseding tea-gowns.

It had long been Mr. Gardiner's ambition to be the representative of the titles, as well as the landed interests, of his maternal ancestors, and he had already made many efforts, in which he was ably assisted by his brother-in-law, John Beresford, to induce the Government to accede to his wishes. It was, however, only in 1779, that the hon. member for Down succeeded in making the first step, which was gained after the usual custom then in force. "Mr. Gardiner, to induce the Government to revive the title of Mountjoy in his favour, promised to bring forward the Government measure of protecting duties." There was nothing very astonishing in this; bribery and corruption were the order of the day. Ponsonby, almost the only honest man in the Commons, declared with tears in his voice, that there were 110 placemen in the House. The Government trafficked in the purchase of Boroughs! the Radical or anti-government papers reviled the traffickers in strong language. Votes, it was said, could be had by the half-dozen, and one vote was purchasable for the price of a good dinner.[1] In this state of general corruption, there was no need to raise a howl against Luke Gardiner's laudable desire, to add the four magic letters to his honourable name; he was, however, already unpopular. The measure he had introduced into Parliament in 1778 for ameliorating the condition of the Catholics had pleased neither side; this is often the case of the intervener in domestic quarrels. The state of political parties in Ireland had come to such an *impasse* that there seemed no way out of the difficulties; every political man was the object of intense hatred to his opponents. "Take it where you will," says Lecky, "the history of Ireland is for ever and inalienably mixed up with the distinctions of race and creed."

[1] The Government price for a Borough was 14,000*l.*; at the time of the Union the scale of payment was much higher. The revelations made in the account of the secret service of Pitt (J. W. Fitzpatrick) are on this subject curious, and do not raise one's opinion of human nature. A short ballad of the time runs thus:—

Ye paltry underlings of state,
Ye senators who love to prate,
Ye rascals of inferior note
Who for a dinner sell a vote.

There were, however, different causes at work to add to Gardiner's unpopularity. Both he and his brother-in-law, the Hon. John Beresford, had held for years a multiplicity of lucrative appointments and enjoyed extensive patronage.

Place-hunting was the rock upon which the parliamentary party in Ireland foundered. Every man wanted not only place for himself, but provision to be found for "his sisters, his cousins and his aunts;" neither was his nepotism purely unselfish. The holder of the office obtained through friendly influence had to pay an annual sum to his generous benefactor. This, however, did not deter the hungry crowd who hung on to the skirts of every great man, from besetting him with applications. Those who did not succeed in gaining what they wanted, vented their disappointment in scurrilous attacks, lampoons and ballads directed against their enemy. Gardiner was handled very severely. The clever riddle " Why is a Gardiner the most extraordinary man in the world ? " was made in his honour, although few people were aware that it contained a political signification. It is now quite forgotten, but in its day and up to the early fifties had a reputation equal to Byron's riddle on the letter H, which is now equally consigned to oblivion. The Gardiner riddle, however, has a good deal of point, and is worth reviving here.

Q. Why is a Gardiner the most extraordinary man in the world ?

A. Because no man has more honours on *Earth*, and he chooses good *Grounds* for what he does.

He turns his *Thyme* to the best account.

He is master of the *Mint* and fingers *Penny Royal*.

He raises his celery (salary) every year, and it is a bad year indeed that does not bring him in a *plum*. He has more *loughs* than a Prime Minister, does not want *London Pride*. *Rakes* a little under the *rose*, but would be more *sage* to keep the fox from his enclosures, to destroy the rotten *Boroughs*, to avoid the blasts from the *north*, and not to foster corruption lest a *Flood* [1] should follow.

---

[1] An allusion to Flood, the popular orator.

Lord Mountjoy's peace of mind, which was not much affected by his unpopularity, was much troubled by his desire to have an heir to his title and large estates. But although Lady Mountjoy had presented him with six daughters, it was not until 1780 that she gave birth to a son; who, to the intense grief of his parents, died the following year. In the July of 1782 this loss was repaired, and the birth of Charles John, the future Earl of Blessinton,[1] was the occasion of the most extraordinary rejoicings, which lasted for four days. The whole country was ablaze with bonfires; casks of ale were broached, and the fatted ox consumed. It is well human beings have not the power of reading futurity; if they had, it is to be feared these inaugurative festivals would lose much of their gladness. That the career of this much-wished-for child did not fulfil its promise was due to the deteriorating influences which surrounded him from his very cradle. His parents made an idol of him; he was never denied any wish, and any servant or preceptor who contradicted him was dismissed. For this foolish indulgence his father alone was accountable; Lady Mountjoy's health, which had been seriously injured by her excessive grief for the death of the first son born to her, was utterly shattered by the birth of the second. She fell into decline and died in 1783, at the early age of thirty-two, thus paying the penalty which often accompanies the fulfilment of an inordinate longing for some good hitherto denied by Providence.

She left a family of six daughters and the aforesaid son. The years Mountjoy[2] survived his wife were years pregnant with disaster to the country. Years too of excitement, of a certain measure of patriotic spirit which, like most movements of the sort in Ireland, was strangled in its cradle by its own parents. It would take too long, and be out of keeping with the present subject, to enter upon the history of

---

[1] Charles John, Viscount Mountjoy, born 1782; advanced to the Earldom of Blessinton, 1816; married, 1812, Mary Campbell, widow of Major William Browne; secondly, 1818, Marguerite Farmer, widow of Captain St. Ledger Farmer. In all *old* peerages, Blessinton is spelt without *g*. For memoir of Lady Blessinton see second series.

[2] Lord Mountjoy married a second time, 1793; he was raised to the rank of Viscount, 1795, and killed at the battle of New Ross, 1798.

the volunteers when they first started under the auspices of Lord Charlemont, Grattan, Langrishe, and Napper Tandy. They bid fair to work a revolution in the political and social condition of Ireland that would have placed it in a foremost place amongst nations. We know how, and from what causes, this splendid combination failed to fulfil its promise; how the poison was disseminated by the crafty intriguer; how man was set against man, jealousy, self-assertion and self-aggrandisement were brought into play, with the result most desired of Ireland's enemies, that all those who were influenced by real patriotism withdrew, and the self-seeker, the place-hunter, and the wire-puller, remained to undo the work only half begun.

When the volunteers laid down their arms, the first step was made towards the rebellion of 1798. The hydra-headed monster Bigotry, at all times inclined to be rampant in Ireland, and which under Grattan's enlightened influence had begun to lower its crest, rose up again to oppress, irritate, and persecute the weaker party.[1]

Foremost among the dominant party were the Beresfords, a large and powerful clan, having ramifications and branches all over Ireland, together with influence and support from their English connections. The head of the house was the Earl of Tyrone, whose eldest son was created Marquis of Waterford in 1789 ; John Claudius, who married sweet Barbara Montgomery, being the second, and by far the most remarkable, of Lord Tyrone's numerous family. The Beresfords have ever been a fine race ; the men brave, the women fair. They cannot be claimed as Celts ; here again we have the fruits of the plantation made by James I., which has grafted, so to speak, so many Saxon shoots upon the original sap of the Celt. The Beresfords fought against James II., but the family did not attain hereditary honours until the marriage of Sir Marcus Beresford with Katherine de la Poer, the only daughter and heiress of the second Earl of Tyrone, when the title was revived in favour of her husband.

[1] This subject will be treated with fuller details in Sarah Curran's Memoir, second series.

This Katherine de la Poer had no less than fifteen children, eight sons and seven daughters. John Claudius was the second son; he had married, in 1760, a lovely French girl, daughter of General Ligondes. She was recently dead at the time he met his second wife.

The gossips of Dublin said he was an odd choice for so young a girl as Barbara Montgomery—a widower with seven children, and twice her age—but then, as Barbara was but seventeen, that did not make the Honourable John even elderly. He was in fact thirty-seven, barely in his prime, a handsome man with a fine presence, of high family, wealth, position, and with singular force of character. His ambition, or, as his enemies called it, his greed of place, was abnormal, even in a time when pluralism was the crying sin of the country. The list of the offices he held tells its own tale, and accounts for much of his unpopularity.

"Beresford," says Mr. Lecky, "was one of the most distinguished examples of a class of politicians who were a peculiar and characteristic product of the Irish political system. He belonged to a family which, although utterly undistinguished in Parliament and in responsible statesmanship, had secured so large a proportion of the minor offices in the administration, had employed its patronage so exclusively for the purpose of building up family influence, and had formed in this manner so extensive a system of political connections and alliances that it had become one of the most powerful controlling and directing influences in the government of Ireland. In a curious and valuable paper drawn up for or by Lord Abercorn in 1791, it is stated that in that year what was called the Beresford party was reckoned at only eight members;" but the Chancellor, Lord Clare (whose wife was a Beresford), together with the Attorney-General and the Chief Secretary were allied to it. John Beresford was the first Commissioner with an official house and salary of 2000*l.*; he was taster to the Port of Dublin, an office worth 1000*l.* for his own life and that of his eldest son, who likewise enjoyed the post of counsel to the Commissioner, with a salary of 2000*l.*, while his second son, John Claudius, had a very lucrative office in the revenue.

We can thus form an idea of the hatred Mr. Beresford's good fortune earned for him from those who, had the opportunity been afforded to them, would have acted in a similar manner, but who now took every opportunity of blackening his character by all the means in their power. When, by his persistent efforts, the Custom House, one of the most elegant of architectural structures, was built, no credit was given to him, although there is ample proof in his letters to Gandon, the architect, that he was actuated by an honest desire to beautify the city, and had no ulterior view of building himself, as his enemies maintained, a palace at the expense of the country.[1]

There is, however, no doubt that Beresford's restless nature, which was for ever weaving fresh schemes for his own aggrandizement, led him to make use of this opportunity to improve the neighbourhood, and add to his own fortune. With this view he undoubtedly spoiled the appearance of the building, by placing it too near the water; this enabled him to build a handsome crescent of large houses, which he hoped would be occupied by merchants, who would find the close neighbourhood of the docks convenient for their business. This crescent was called, in his honour, Beresford Place; the centre house was Beresford's Bank, a new speculation of his which at first was highly successful. The rebellion of 1798, and the Union following close upon it, ruined all commercial enterprise, and Beresford's plans suffered collapse. The trade of the docks fell to nothing; the Crescent was never occupied by merchants; the Bank failed; and the sere and yellow of decay, which creeps over bygone localities, is on Beresford Place.

We are, however, anticipating. In 1774 there was no sign of this great upheaval; all was mirth and extravagance. Lord Harcourt, who had imbibed all the elegant tastes of the Court at Versailles, was reckless in his magnificence,[2] and

[1] Beresford asked from the Exchequer 10,000*l.* for building the Custom House, but it ultimately cost 100,000*l.*, a large sum for so impoverished a treasury as that of Ireland.

[2] The Harcourt administration was unrivalled for its extravagance, and almost beggared the nation.—*Grattan's Life.*

to keep pace with him the nobility had to lay heavy burdens upon their already heavily burdened estates.

The entertainments given were of the most costly description;[1] the distress was every day increasing and the discontent growing, while the press was not slow in pointing out the rocks upon which the country was drifting, but the counsels given were altogether dictated by party exigencies; every man was for himself and his own advantages. "*Après moi le deluge,*" said they, and so the evil grew, there seeming to be no remedy.

Through all the gay doings of the time, we hear very little of Barbara. From a poem addressed to her by Mr. Whyte, it is evident she had grown very demure, as by contrast to her joyousness in youth.

> Prancing and proud, she danced into the world,
> She talked, she tittered, tossed her head and curled.
> By Nature lively; she grew wild by art,
> For sure it was so pretty to be smart.
> But soon recovering, flushed with mirth and youth,
> Contented she soon came home to sense and truth.

Although she had not much to say to the gay world, there is occasional mention, here and there, of the beautiful Mrs. Beresford.[2] The papers, too, duly record the recurrence of

---

[1] "Our ladies and gentlemen," writes the *Spy,* "are raking the marrow of our bowels to support their extravagance. More rent for houses, more rent for lands, corn dear, provisions dear, wool *exceedingly* dear, times precarious, counting-houses shut, few notes current. London, France, Spain, Germany, swarm with thy children, O Hibernia. Why? Because they cannot find employment at home. One suit of native poplin in the wardrobe, regiments of silk of English manufacture. Hibernian ladies dressed in silk of gold and silver embroidery, while even one loom cannot find encouragement at home.

> Alas, Hibernia, how silent thou sittest
> As a babe smiling at thy destiny.

Thou sittest like a child on the *brink of a precipice.* While thou seest, or at least regardest not, the imminent danger which threatens thee.

[2] She continued a kindly intimacy with her old master. No. 1 of his Peruvian Letters are inscribed to the Hon. Mrs. Beresford, and she and her husband, who likewise had been a scholar of old Sam's, took endless copies on royal paper of the old gentleman's books, published by subscription. Mrs. Beresford's portrait was hung in the place of honour in his drawing-room, where little Tommy Moore, who was at the grammar school in 1779, saw it. It was, however, customary for Mr.

annual additions to her family, for, like Lady Mountjoy, she had an ever-increasing nursery. The thoughtful expression which is noticeable on her young face in Sir Joshua's picture deepened as the years went by; and she saw less and less of her husband, occupied as he was by his many ambitious schemes. She must have felt, too, a dread of what might happen some day, surrounded as he was by men who hated him with that fierce hatred born of jealousy. At last it seemed as if they would have the opportunity of satisfying their rancour; the English Government had long been aware of Beresford's unpopularity, as well as the reason for it. Every Viceroy in turn had complained that there was no chance of content so long as the dominant party, at the head of which were the Beresfords, continued in power. The condition of Ireland was indeed critical, and the storm that had been so long brooding was now ready to burst. Still the upper classes seemed to have been struck, as were the French nobility in a similar crisis, with a moral cataract; they were utterly blind to the signs of distress, of deep discontent, that were seething below the surface; they ignored the warnings of better advised politicians, and went on building fine houses, spending the money that was wrung from miserable peasants in fiddling, gambling, drunkenness, and all the amusements in which fine gentlemen indulged. The Government, however, were becoming alarmed; they distrusted the men in power, and disapproved of the oppressive measures that were being pursued. The English cabinet decided for a policy of conciliation, and, as a first step, Beresford was to be sacrificed to the public hate.

The Viceroy chosen to succeed Lord Harcourt, and to carry the flag of conciliation, was Earl FitzWilliam. No better choice could have been made. The FitzWilliams had been, for more than two centuries, closely allied with Ireland, and unlike many of her step relations, their influence had ever been used for the good of the country with which they were connected. Under Elizabeth, Sir William Fitz-

Whyte's lady pupils to present him with a medallion or portrait, in return for which he addressed an ode.

William held the office of Lord Deputy for more than thirty years, and acquitted himself of his trust to the satisfaction of the Queen and the nation he had to govern. In another generation, another FitzWilliam was raised to the peerage of Ireland, with the title of Lord FitzWilliam of Lifford, Co. Donegal, and later on his descendant was made Earl Fitz-William of Tyrone. The Lord FitzWilliam with whom we have to do was the 4th Earl in succession. He had married an Irish lady, one of the popular family of Ponsonby, and was well acquainted with the intricacies of government, and the difficulty of steering between the complex shoals and rocks of party. He was one of the most amiable of men, full of sympathy and generosity, with an abhorrence of the system pursued by the dominant party, having the Beresfords at their head. He came resolved to put an end to all domination of one party or creed, and determined that all citizens should, so far as possible, have equal rights one with another. It is idle to speculate whether he would have succeeded, or whether, as is more than likely, the knife of the assassin would have cut short his days. Men's minds were hardly ripe enough to allow of any fairness or consideration towards those who practised a proscribed and hateful religion, while the battle of the Boyne was still too fresh in the memory of the conquered, to be forgotten or forgiven.

Lord FitzWilliam's first act of government was to dismiss Beresford from his office of Commissioner.[1] This was received with universal rejoicing, and was the first step towards the extraordinary popularity enjoyed by the new Viceroy. The rejoicing was, however, only short-lived. Beresford was not a man to bear defeat quietly. He wrote letter after letter to the Ministers, declaring himself to be an injured, persecuted man; he appealed passionately for support to Pitt, and finally went over to London to lay his grievance before the Cabinet. It is not likely that he would have been listened to were it not that he was backed by the powerful influence of his

[1] Lord FitzWilliam asserted that he had stated to Pitt before accepting office, that he was apprehensive Beresford should be removed, and that Pitt made no objection. This, however, Pitt strenuously denied.

brother, Lord Waterford,[1] and that of Lord Clare, the Chancellor, who forced Pitt to recall Lord FitzWilliam and to reinstate Beresford.

The Catholic Relief question was made the ostensible reason for the Viceroy's recall. Lord FitzWilliam, however, always maintained that it did not enter, in the most distant manner, into the cause of his dismissal. "Had Beresford never been dismissed, I should have remained Viceroy," he said.

Beresford returned triumphant, and in a few weeks Lord FitzWilliam was recalled, and Lord Camden was sent in his place. This most unpopular act caused deep and serious dissatisfaction. Never since Lord Chesterfield's period of office had any Viceroy won such golden opinions as Lord Fitz-William; whether either of the noblemen would have retained the affection they had so quickly gained, would be a matter of doubt; neither of them had been long enough to decide this.[2] The easily excited Irish people expressed their sorrow at their favourite's departure by appearing in mourning on the day he left; they gave every sign of grief, drawing his coach to the water-side, while the shadow of coming calamity cast its gloom on every countenance. This was but too well justified; from that time a sullen, virulent disloyalty overspread the land, creeping, in the words of Grattan, at the heels of the countryman.

Lord FitzWilliam was naturally indignant at being sacrificed to the power of a clique. He said openly, that unless the influence of the Beresfords was broken, there would be no chance of effecting any permanent good in Ireland. He employed his clerks to write out an indictment against Mr. Beresford,[3] which was privately distributed; in it he made some accusations against his conduct in the sale of a public lease. In consequence of this a duel was arranged, but although the

---

[1] George De la Poer, second Earl of Tyrone, was created Marquis of Waterford, 1789.

[2] Lord Chesterfield remained eight months, Lord FitzWilliam two!

[3] Beresford himself, in relating his interview (with Daly who came to inform him of the intention of the Government to remove him) reports that Daly told him "no Lord Lieutenant could exist with my power, that I had made a Lord Chancellor, a Primate, and certainly a Commander, and that I was considered King of Ireland."

combatants appeared on the field, they were interrupted, and it ended by Lord FitzWilliam making an apology.

The result of all the excitement showed itself in riots all over the city; these broke out the day Lord Camden was sworn in, and were doubtless meant to terrify the newly-arrived Viceroy. A brutal attack was made upon the Chancellor, Lord Clare; paving-stones were thrown at him as he drove back from the ceremony of swearing-in Lord Camden, and he would have been lynched at the lamp-post before his house in Ely Place, only for a clever device of his sister, Mrs. Jeffreys. The mob also attacked the Custom House, where John Beresford was then living, but he had provided a guard of soldiers, who speedily routed the attacking party.

From this time Mr. Beresford's temper seems to have grown more savage; perhaps he thought he might as well earn the hatred he had evoked, or it may have been that all softening influences had passed out of his life. Barbara's tender face was no longer there to restrain him with its quiet thoughtfulness. She died, like her sister, Lady Mountjoy, at an early age, leaving a family of seven children.[1] Providence, with loving kindness, oftentimes removes those who are ill-fitted to bear the turmoil and hard knocks of life. Barbara was spared the sad days of 1798, in which her brother-in-law, Mountjoy, lost his life fighting the insurgents at New Ross, in Wexford.[2] If

[1] One of her daughters married Charles Edward Count D'Albanie; he was one of the two brothers who set up a claim to be the legitimate grandsons of the Young Pretender. John Wilson Croker, however, demolished this story, and, according to him, "the Count" was the son of John Carter Allen, Admiral of the White.

[2] The accounts of Lord Mountjoy's death were at first somewhat different. It was stated that he was killed early in the day; Major Vesey, however, maintained that he had been wounded and taken prisoner. When the fort was stormed, this was found to be correct, and that, with the brutality which characterized this uprising, his body had been cruelly mangled and butchered. This caused a feeling of great bitterness amongst his friends, and of regret amongst those of the opposite party who were not biased by vindictive animosity; it was remembered how he had stood forward as the friend of the Catholics when the Catholic Relief Bill had been introduced into Parliament some twenty years previously. A writer in the *Irish Builder* of July, 1893, draws attention to the remarkable coincidence that Viscount Mountjoy and Viscount O'Neil, who had laboured in favour of a Catholic Relief Bill, the one moving, the other seconding the resolution, should have been both killed in the

all that is told of John Beresford be true as to his unnecessary cruelty to the miserable herd of prisoners who fell into his hands, and the plots he wove against his own countrymen, there can be no defence made for him. In these cases, however, one must make due allowance for the excitement of the time, and the exaggeration which would thus naturally arise. One of the many accusations against him was that he fomented the agitations of the country by coercive measures on purpose to stir up the rebellion, in order to prove to Pitt that it could be easily crushed. For this purpose he kept an army of spies, who are spoken of in the secret papers of the time as "Beresford's bloodhounds." His worst cruelties would appear to have been the flogging of the unfortunate prisoners in the riding-school in Marlborough Street; this would justify the hatred with which, it is said, the populace regarded him.

In curious contradiction to these accusations we have the opposing testimony that when this "abhorred tyrant" had completed his year of office as Lord Mayor of the city, his carriage was drawn through the streets of Dublin by the very same mob who, we are told, had execrated him; and even his enemies were forced to acknowledge his term of office had been marked by singular prosperity.

To the readers of the disastrous history of the time, Beresford stands out as a central figure. Now that the clouds of prejudice and party faction have cleared away, we can judge him by a fairer standard than did those who lived in his time and suffered from his iron rule. His letters to Gandon show him to have been a well informed, accomplished gentleman. Had he lived in a less difficult time it is likely that he would have been a different man; there is much truth in Rousseau's doctrine that the manner of one's life depends a good deal on the surroundings in which we are placed, at least this would hold good where there is no very high moral standard.

same month and year by the insurgents, Lord O'Neil at Antrim. Lord Mountjoy at Wexford. The writer forgets that twenty years is a generation, and that probably the slayer of both noblemen was an ignorant soldier who had never heard of relief bills, but was possessed with a thirst for blood. Luke Gardiner deserved a better fate; he had a fine nature, and a tinge of romance hangs about his life and death.

Mr. FitzPatrick, one of those who have written most severely of Beresford's cruelty, bears testimony to his abilities and fine character. In his old age he came upon bad times; the failure of his bank was a severe blow, other speculations were unfortunate, and he had no longer the energy of youth to carry on fresh ones.[1] He died in 1805 at his country seat near Londonderry.

Such is the story of the three sisters who look at us from Sir Joshua's canvas; a hundred and twenty years have passed since the joyous trio of brides strung their wreath to Hymen. It is to be feared the blind god was not as grateful as he should have been to his postulants. The three marriages, after all, did not fulfil their promise; a sort of blight seeming to fall upon each one. The picture, which for many years, hung at Rath, Lord Blessington's seat in Ireland, was by him bequeathed to the nation, and now fills almost one side of what is called the Sir Joshua Room in the National Gallery.

[1] Like his brother-in-law, Lord Townshend, Beresford solaced his last years by turning his energies to agriculture and the cultivation of roses.

ELIZABETH LA TOUCHE, COUNTESS OF LANES-BOROUGH.

The beautiful subject of this sketch cannot be said, with strict adherence to truth, to be of Irish descent; but as she was born in Ireland, we claim our charming countrywoman, and consider it quite fair to annex her to our gallery of Irish Beauties. In fact there are many families, who by long custom, and residence of more than two centuries, have come to be considered Irish, but who in reality date back to the influx of French Huguenots which followed on the famous Edict of Nantes.

Mr. Lecky says that the large body of refugees who came over in the early part of the eighteenth century to Ireland were of the utmost value, on account of the many influences that were at this time drawing native talent and energy to the Continent. These refugees were of two kinds, the French Huguenots and the German Palatines. These last, who were imported by a few wealthy landlords, belonged to the labouring classes, and do not come into our subject. The Huguenot refugees, exiled for their religious opinions, were either of the upper and mercantile class, or skilled artisans in all branches of industry. With a singular lack of prudence, the bigotry of Louis XIV. sent forth these men to teach other nations the arts formerly known only on the Continent. The Huguenots, like their countrymen who were driven out of France during the revolution of 1792, played a distinguished part in the country which many of them adopted, never returning to their own land to take their place as citizens. In this way we find in Ireland the naturalized names of Bussé, Des Vœux, Chaigneau, D'Olier, Le Fanu, L'Estrange,

Maturin, Saurin, Lefroy, Le Nauze, Perriu, Cromelin, Borough, derived from Boroher and La Touche.

These names for many years stood first in all the learned professions, and to the energy of these men was due much of

COUNTESS OF LANESBOROUGH.

the progress made in Ireland during the eighteenth century in intellectual as well as mercantile matters. To them Dublin owed her first literary journal and her first horticultural society; while the linen and silk manufactures were brought to the highest standard, and their products sought for in home and foreign markets.

o

The most prominent members of the Huguenot colony were undoubtedly to be found in the La Touche family. They were, according to Lodge and Whitelaw, of English descent, bearing originally the surname of Digges.[1] They, however, left their native country in the reign of Henry II., and settled themselves at Blois, where they had large possessions—amongst them the estate from which they took their name La Touche. In their adopted country they rose to high places, and were ennobled and distinguished by peculiar privileges. In the 17th century, the doctrines of Calvin induced the then head of the family to leave the old Catholic faith, and to bring up his eldest son, David, as a Huguenot. The boy, when only fifteen, became the heir to the estates of the La Touches, but on its being known that he remained firm to his father's new religion, he was proscribed and had to fly, and all the property that escaped the rapacity of the crown was transferred to his brother Paul, who remained a Catholic. This was in 1671.

Young La Touche, driven from his home, entered Colonel Le Caillemote's regiment of horse-dragoons, which was exclusively recruited from the ranks of men who like himself were proscribed for conscience sake. They were a fine, lion-hearted, well-disciplined regiment, comparing favourably with the Irish Brigade, recruited from the proscribed Irish Papists. There is all along the line a strange coincidence of resemblance between the proscribed Huguenot and the outlawed Catholic. Both sacrificed everything for principle, both made their homes in a foreign land, both fought in the ranks of an alien army, and to emphasize the resemblance, the Irish Brigade was opposed to Le Caillemote's horse, at the battle of the Boyne, and at the most critical moment.

To the lover of history, there is something wonderfully romantic in the story of this battle. The setting that nature gave to the spot where it took place lends it a peculiar interest. The river—which is wide enough to let large vessels

---

[1] Up to the present time the La Touche family add the not very euphonious name of Digges to their surname, and will probably continue to do so to the end of time.

come up to the port of Drogheda—runs through one of the sweetest, most peaceful valleys in Ireland. It is bordered on one side by the famous pasture-lands of Meath, the greenest of green meadows, smiling with the fulness of prosperity; this is the picture as presented to-day. Two hundred years ago this river was strewn with corpses, these green plains were watered with the blood of 7600 veteran French soldiers, most of them picked men sent by his Catholic Majesty of France, together with the fine body of Irish dragoons, who were nearly all cut to pieces. There is no more pitiful story on record than the sacrifice of these brave men for a worthless weak despot, half monk half libertine, as was James; a miserable, feeble coward into the bargain, who fled away when, by his own folly, he had lost the day.

On the 29th June James and his army had reached this point, on his march from Ardee, whither he had retreated on hearing that William had arrived at Carrickfergus. When he reached the Boyne, James halted, it seemed to him a strong station. On his right lay Drogheda, strongly garrisoned, on his left a bog difficult to pass; in front were the fords of the river, deep and dangerous, the banks rugged and bounded by old houses, the houses by rows of hedges, the hedges by a range of small hills, and behind, the village of Dunmore, available for retreat, for behind it was the pass of Duleek, where two men abreast could not march.

His generals, however, were not all of James's mind; the wiser and more experienced advising a still further retreat behind the Shannon. There the enemy could be more harassed than here in a comparatively open country. The younger and more blustering officers loudly murmured against any further truckling, and advised the king to give battle. James listened first to one, then to the other counsel, apparently eager to take the wisest course, while in his heart his only thought was *flight*. He was weary of marching and counter-marching, irritated at the influence possessed over the army by Tyrconnell and Sarsfield, and provoked by the independence shown by his generals. He resolved on having his own way; and—with a show of courage that surprised those

who knew his faint-heartedness, and imposed upon them for
the moment—announced his determination to have done with
truckling, and to bring matters to an issue. Again, however,
he vacillated, and it was only sheer shame that kept him
from escaping to join the French fleet, which was advancing to
his support. It is an undoubted fact that he sent a private
letter by a trusty messenger to Sir Patrick Grant, desiring him
to get a vessel ready at Waterford to transport him to France.
William's arrival sooner than was expected forced him to
remain with the army.

William was ill in body and mind; he had little hope of
success, and a foreboding of coming disaster; but he fought
his way with the courage of despair, and surmounted every
obstacle. At the same time, it is plain to us—who regard
the past through the magnifying-glass which time lends to
all events in life—that it was James's own indecision and
obstinacy that were the principal factors against him in the
final struggle. From the first, the latter's want of firmness
was made evident; he could not decide as to the disposition
of the army, and in the end made a fatal mistake.[1]

From the beginning there had been a fierce jealousy between
the French and Irish troops. The veterans, who were the flower
of the French army, naturally looked down upon the Irish troops
who had not seen so much service. This the others resented,
loudly declaring that the post of honour in the battle should be
theirs, and that they would fire upon anyone who attempted
to take it from them. The result of this dispute was most
unfortunate, for in the disposition of the troops the ones most
to be depended upon were placed amongst the hills at the back;

---

[1] Round the neighbourhood of the spot where the battle was fought
there linger still many traditions. In their fear of what might
happen, many families concealed their plate and valuables in the
caverns under the bridges, or in the bed of the river; some of these
it is said are still full of treasures, which the owners never removed.
At Athcarne Castle, the room is shown where James II. slept
the night before the battle. In the Bellingham family there are two
curious relics, one the diary kept by Colonel Bellingham, who was the
King's equerry, and the small *necessaire* containing the flask and wine-
glass out of which William drank. There is a curious feeling in handling these little bottles, in which a portion of the wine still remains—it
seems to bring one in touch with the scenes of two hundred years ago.

while the Irish regiments stood in the front rank, and defended the bank of the river. On the other hand, William's disposition of his army was admirable. The Dutch, the French protestants, and the Enniskillens were to cross the river first; he knew the attachment of the first to himself, and of the two last to their religion. "It was not," Macaulay says, "until they had waded to the middle of the river that these brave men became aware of the difficulty in which they were placed. The whole place was alive with defenders. General Hamilton, who commanded the Irish foot, made a splendid defence, and was ably supported by the Irish Brigade, who advanced from behind the hills with steadiness and prudence. The double attack threw William's centre into confusion, and the Dutch stopped. It was at this moment that Le Caillemote's men came forward, led by their Colonel. A hand-to-hand fight ensued between them, and the Irish Brigade, who fell upon them with fury, broke their ranks, and put many of them to the sword. Colonel Caillemote, who was leading on his men, received a mortal wound; four of his men carried him back across the ford to his tent. As he passed, he continued to urge forward the rear-rank, which was still up to the breast in water, "*A la gloire, mes enfants, à la gloire!*" he cried. Schomberg, who had been watching the struggle from the bank, rode into the river, and taking the command, rallied the refugees who had been dismayed by the fall of their commander. "Come on," he cried, and pointing to the French soldiers, "come on! there are your persecutors." Those were his last words; the Irish Brigade surrounded him, and when they retired, he was a corpse; the battle was, however, gained. James had fled away to Dublin. His saying that he would never again trust himself to an Irish army, was answered by the contemptuous remark, that if the English would change kings, the Irish would fight the battle over again.[2]

[1] Frederick Schomberg, or Schonberg, had served under William the Second of Orange; he had obtained several victories in the Spanish war, and had reinstated on the throne the house of Braganza; now he had defeated the last hope of the Stuarts. He was eighty-two years of age when his gallant career was ended at the battle of the Boyne. Walker, the defender of Derry, was killed almost at the same moment.
[2] The conquerors showed somewhat an ungenerous spirit in the

Le Caillemote's regiment had suffered severely. What remained was embodied with the Brandenburgers, and followed the remainder of the campaign. Colonel La Touche had escaped with a slight wound, and took part in the siege of Limerick, conducting himself all through with great gallantry. When the war was finally over, Le Caillemote's regiment, or at least what remained of it, was disbanded, and David had to turn his attention to his own affairs. He was tired of soldiering, and felt drawn to the country which was to become his by adoption. The number of his co-religionists, who had made Ireland, and especially Dublin, their home, decided him upon settling himself in that city, where he set about making his fortune.

Amongst the arts introduced by the Huguenots,[1] and in which they excelled, was the weaving of rich and delicate fabrics. The old brocades, with their delicious colouring and their splendid texture, were the work of these exiles, who, when they first arrived, had been allowed to set up their looms in the crypt of St. Patrick's Cathedral. David La Touche established a manufactory in High Street, and employed his countrymen. By dint of industry and perseverance, in forty years he had accumulated a vast fortune. He abandoned commerce and turned his attention to finance. Already he had made large loans to Government, and finally opened the bank in Castle Street in conjunction with Kane, Lord Mayor of Dublin.

moment of triumph. The literature of the day teems with songs and hymns, all in a spirit of crowing, which must have irritated the beaten party. These songs were sung through the streets of Dublin by the college boys, and in moments of popular excitement have been periodically revived. "The Battle of the Boyne," "The Relief of Derry," and "The Protestant Boys," were the favourites; one of the least offensive is Colonel Blacker's arrangement of "The Battle of the Boyne," which has a good deal of literary merit.

[1] The Huguenots made the linen manufacture flourish. Mr. Cromelin was the principal introducer of this branch of industry; he had carried it on in his own hereditary establishment in St. Quentin. The family of Cromelin settled, like the La Touches, in Ireland, and have property in the north. Unfortunately, in the later land troubles they experienced considerable loss. The Misses Cromelin have, however, shown the good old Huguenot spirit by setting to work to build their own fortunes, and so far seem to have realized the proverb of *aide toi le ciel t'aidera*. One is a rising novelist, the other is much considered as an elegant decorator; she has a large staff of workmen and assistants, and undertakes every species of decoration.

The following notice of Mr. La Touche is handed down by his countryman, Latocnaye :—

"*Quoique* Banquier c'etait un homme humain et charitable on rapporte sur ses vieux jours, il ne sortait jamais sans avoir ses poches pleines de schellings, qu'il donnait aux pauvres ; comme on lui répresentait que s'il donnait à tous ceux qui lui demanderaient il ferait la charité à bien de mauvais sujets. ' Oui,' repondait il, ' mais si mon schelling tombe à propos *une fois dans dix* c'est assez ! ' "

This truly excellent man could not, however, escape the venom of the political pamphleteer, then a veritable scourge to society. For taking the Government side in the famous dispute on Wood's halfpence,[1] the banker was made the subject of one of Swift's scurrilous ballads, in which the following verses occur :—

> Poor Monsieur his conscience preserved for a year
> Yet in one hour lost it 'tis known far and near.
> To whom did he lose it ? A Judge or a Peer ?
> > Which nobody can deny.

> This very same conscience was sold in a closet
> Not for a baked loaf or a loaf in a cosset
> But a sweet sugar-plum which you put in a posset
> > Which nobody can deny.

> But the slaves that would sell us, shall hear on't in time.
> Their names shall be branded in prose and in rhyme,
> We'll paint them in colours as black as their crime
> > Which nobody can deny.

> But Potter and copper La Touche we'll excuse,
> The commands of your betters you dare not refuse,
> Obey was the word when you wore wooden shoes,
> > Which nobody can deny.

It is not likely that the stout heart of the gallant old Huguenot would be troubled by this evidence of party feeling ; moreover he was now nearing a far greater assize than the tribunal of his fellow-citizens. When the last summons came

---

[1] About the year 1772, during the administration of the unpopular Duke of Grafton, one William Wood, a hardware man and also a bankrupt, by applying himself to someone in power, and alleging the great want of copper money in Ireland, procured a patent for coining 108,000*l.* in brass money to pass as current money, It was soon discovered to be a vile job. The Irish people were to be allowed no liberty to refuse the brass money.

he was found on his knees praying. It was on Sunday, while service was going on in the Castle Chapel, that he was seized with a fit of apoplexy and passed away. He was ninety years of age, but in those days men lived longer than they do in our days of express existence, and ninety was nothing out of the common. In the *Dublin Courier*, of October 15th, 1741, his death is mentioned with all honour. " He was a sincere friend, a very merciful landlord, and tender to his debtors, so that whatever could render a character truly amiable in public life was what he was possessed of." The same authority tells us that he left all his property to his eldest son, and a handsome legacy to the youngest.

Colonel La Touche, when he settled down, had taken to himself a wife. She was of his own religion, a rigid Calvinist of the Dutch pattern. To them were borne two sons, David and James. James married the daughter of David Chaigneau, of Corkayne, Co. Dublin—this lady, who was very beautiful, preferred the attentions of a certain Duke, and, for him, deserted her husband. Mrs. Delany, writing in 1739, says : " Madame La Touche has put out an apology for living with his Grace of Dorset, and declares that love was the predominant and hereditary passion of her family!" After this, it was easy for James La Touche to procure a divorce, and in 1743 he married again, and died, full of age and respectability, in 1763, leaving eleven stalwart sons to carry on the name of La Touche.

David, meantime, had not been idle ; he had married the only daughter of Dean Marlay, afterwards Bishop of Dromore. The Marlays are so often mentioned by Mrs. Delany that we feel them to be personal friends. She was " the sweetest woman," he a man of society, fond of the arts, and in much request. Like most of the dignitaries of the Church in the last century, his cloth did not interfere with his pleasures. We cannot take Swift, Sterne, or chaplain Warner, as bright examples of high-class clergymen, nor even accept Dr. Delany quite seriously ; the Bishop of Dromore was of the same pattern as his friends. He was a good preacher, with a mellifluous voice, but one could hardly imagine his administering consolation to the stricken peasants dying of typhus fever on the road-side. He was more fitted to take the part of "Locket" as he did in *The Beggar's Opera*, given by the Duke of Leinster at Carton, when Lady Lousia Conolly played Lucy and Lord Charlemont Peachum, the whole being under the superintendence of Mr. Whyte.[1] It seems strange that this somewhat unclerical conduct should have squared with the more rigid principles of the descendant of the man who had given up all worldly advantages for the sake of his conscience. There is no reason to suppose, however, that the sons were not quite as good Churchmen as their father had been. They were in every way excellent men, and highly thought of by their

[1] FROM THE ORIGINAL BILL OF
THE BEGGAR'S OPERA, PLAYED AT THE EARL OF
KILDARE'S, CARTON, 1761.

Cast of the Characters.

Macheath	. .	Captain Morris.
Peachum.	. .	Lord Charlemont.
Locket	. .	Rev. Dean Marlay.
Felch	. .	Mr. Thomas Conolly (of Castletown).
Polly	. .	Miss Martin
Lucy	. .	Lady Louisa Conolly (of Castletown).
Mrs. Peachum.	.	The Countess of Kildare.
Mrs. Slammerkin	.	Viscount Powerscourt.
Jenny Diver	.	Miss Vesey.
Cocker	. .	Miss Adderly.

The prologue, which was written by the universal provider of verses, Sam Whyte, had a modern ring; one could almost fancy a present-day performance opening with—

"Our play to-night wants novelty 'tis true;
That to atone, our actors all are new.
And sure, our stage than any stage is droller,
Lords act the rogue and ladies play the stroller."

After some compliments to the matchless charms of Peachum's wife,

"For spite of art and care
The Lords and Graces will attend Kildare,"

the poet ends with the doubtful compliment to the Dean—

"But when the mimic scene is o'er
All shall resume the worth they had before.
Locket himself his Knavery shall resign
And lose the Gaoler in the *dull divine*."

The Miss Martin, of the *dramatis personæ*, was one of the Dublin belles. She lived in Channel Row, and in *Hibernian Crosses* there are different verses addressed to her.

fellow-citizens. As time went on, their financial operations considerably increased. The well-known bank, with which their name was associated for many years, was built by David La Touche, in Castle Street, where for more than a hundred and fifty years a flourishing business was carried on, which included the commercial interests of nearly all Ireland.

In 1778, when the Irish exchequer had unexpectedly run dry, the then Lord Lieutenant, the Earl of Buckingham, applied to La Touche's bank for a loan of 20,000*l.*, which was immediately advanced on the credit of the Government. On another occasion one of those sudden panics, which are as dangerous to the financier as squalls are to the navigator, arose and threatened to shipwreck every commercial house in the city. The block in trade became so serious that the House of Commons ordered a special commission to examine into the solvency of the different bankers and men of business. The result was a declaration that the Houses of Glendowe, Finlay, and David La Touche and Sons were excepted from the general bankruptcy, and had more than sufficient funds to cover all demands. Meantime every proof of confidence was given to Mr. La Touche by his clients and friends. A certain Mr. Whaley, a wealthy but [1] eccentric man of the day, wrote to the banker the following laconic but satisfactory letter :—

[1] The people of Ireland are as remarkable for facility and point in the application of nicknames as were the people of ancient Rome. In our sister kingdom a personal defect, an accident in life, a good or a bad action, often attaches a characteristic or humorous epithet to a man, that remains with him during life. In the rebellion of 1745, the laws against persons professing the popish religion were revived in Ireland without cause, and pursued by a few weak bigots with avidity. Rewards were offered for apprehending priests, and the fellows who pursued this infamous avocation were termed priest-catchers. Mr. Whaley having accumulated a considerable fortune, was honoured with the commission of the peace, and in consequence of the proclamation became a furious persecutor of the popish ecclesiastics. In one of his priest-hunting excursions, it happened that by firing a fowling piece, he lodged the wadding in the thatch of a Romish Chapel, which, taking fire, was soon consumed, a circumstance which gained for him the hatred of the country people, who considered the offence to be a gross sacrilege, and his Christian name being Chappel, they annexed to it the epithet of *burn*, and he was notoriously known by the name of Burnchappel till the day of his death.—From the *Hibernian Magazine*, 1789.

"Mr. La Touche, hearing there is a run on your house, I send you one hundred thousand pounds." Another story was told of this erratic individual. Having married late in life, it was a joyful surprise to him to know that his wife was about to present him with what he fondly hoped would, and which did prove to be an heir to his immense wealth ; he gave her a cheque, couched in the following words :—

> My good Mr. La Touche,
> You must open your pouch,
> And pay my soul's darling
> One thousand pounds sterling.

David and James La Touche partook of the dilettantism then so much the fashion in Dublin. They were, moreover, not only gentlemen of fine tastes, but generous patrons of artists, many of whom visited Dublin at their instance ; amongst these may be named Marinari, a decorative artist in Pergolesi's style, and De Gree, who was starving in a garret at Antwerp when Mr. La Touche found him out and assisted him. Bartolozzi was another who owed great obligations to the La Touche family ; he executed a number of beautiful mezzotints for the brothers ; many of them are still at Belview.[1]

David La Touche resided for many years in Stephen's Green, and it was not till towards the end of the century[2] that he moved to a fine mansion in Merrion Square. In 1786, the tide of fashion had set in this direction, and we find that almost every house was built for a nobleman or person of distinction. La Touche's house, which in later years was divided,[3] stood in

[1] Belview, in the County Wicklow, the family seat of the La Touches.
[2] Many of the nobility built houses in Stephen's Green, which had a most extensive acreage. Gandon says it was finer than any square in London, and was a good deal larger than Lincoln's Inn Fields. There was a handsome gravel-walk called the Beaux Walk, and another of grass with a row of lime-trees which gave shade in summer, in the centre a statue of George the Second, cast by Vanhost.
[3] 10, Merrion Square was divided in 1820, and the larger portion bought by Sir Thomas Staples, a somewhat eminent lawyer, and a well-known figure in Dublin society. He lived to the ripe old age of ninety, and was a link with the previous century, coming in touch with the rebellion of '98, which he well remembered, the battle of Waterloo, in 1815, and the Crimean War, of our own times. He was of a spare figure, courteous in manner, with an old-world polite-

the centre of the block on the east side, and had a fine appearance, the style being so much after the Adam pattern as to give rise to the supposition that the celebrated architect had found his way to Dublin. This, however, was not the case; so far as can be ascertained, there is no work of Adam in Dublin. Merrion Square was altogether planned and most of the houses built by Eason, but Mr. La Touche's house may have been designed by Sir William Chambers, whose designs were used for Aldborough House, as well as for Marino.

The decorations of the interior of Mr. La Touche's house, which with commendable taste have remained unaltered, are worthy of notice. The chimney-pieces are in Wedgewood's unique style, the ceilings are elegant, and the walls are painted after the Etruscan pattern, so much used by Adam. It is a noble house. Unfortunately, like all old houses in Dublin, it has gone through a change of owners, and no longer belongs to the La Touche family. They still hold, however, Belview, Co. Wicklow, purchased by David La Touche, and one of the most lovely spots in what is called the Switzerland of Ireland. Like Powerscourt, it is surrounded with wooded glens through which runs the bright and ever shining Dargle on its way to the meeting of the waters. A Russian prince who made a tour through Ireland visited Belview in 1833, and is loud in praise of its beauties :—" Here is a summer-house," he says, " which seems to hang in the air, and overlooks the Glen of the Downs, a deep valley behind which two extinct volcanoes rear their conical heads. The summer-house had just been covered with purple heather; a less happy thought," he adds, " was a stuffed tiger lying as if alive in the ante-room."

---

ness but not much cordiality, except for his most intimate friends. His wife had been a beauty of the Regency days, and in her old age preserved the soft complexion, bright eyes, and thoroughly Irish manner which had caused George the Fourth to say she was " the handsomest woman he had seen in Ireland." Sir Thomas Staples was the son of Henrietta Molesworth, who escaped from the fire in which her mother, Lady Molesworth, and so many of the household perished. She was never able to walk, and the walks at Lissan, the Right Hon. John Staples' country place near Dungannon, had to be widened to allow her chair to pass. 10, Merrion Square is now occupied by Sir John Banks, K.C.B., a distinguished physician. Sir John is most popular with a numerous circle of friends both in London and Dublin.

David La Touche was Privy Councillor, and no event of any importance took place in the city in which he and his brother had not a part. When the fine body of volunteers was formed, he and his brother both were in command of a division.

The Right Honourable David left a family of one son and five daughters. Of the daughters, Elizabeth, the eldest, was the most beautiful, although all were handsome. There is great sweetness and tenderness in the portrait of Lady Lanesborough, a charm which would be likely to win many hearts, and all that is known of Elizabeth La Touche, which is not much, carries out what her face expresses. She was only thirteen years of age when she made her first appearance before the world of Dublin, taking the part of the Lady in the *Masque of Comus*, performed at Rathfarnham Castle before the Viceroy, Lord Townshend, of which mention has been already made. The stage was the green sward, the scenery the leafy woods. It must have been a charming sight; the performers were all children, but they were well trained by Mr. Whyte, and personated the nymphs and dryads with excellent effect, tripping their dainty measures to the sound of Lord Mornington's amateur band.

Years passed, and in 1774 we find Miss La Touche the recognized belle of Dublin, with a train of admirers. She is described by those who knew her as having a surprising elegance, which marked every movement, while her features had the most perfect symmetry. She danced divinely, and her mind was well cultivated, her good sense preventing her from indulging in any blue-stocking follies. She was, of course, a *favourite* pupil of Mr. Whyte's, who presented her, on her birthday, January, 1794, with a volume of selected poems from the best authors. She had just completed her eighteenth year, two years later, when a wonderful entertainment was given at Marlay; it was wonderful for the reason that twelve of the La Touche family took part in it, and that Henry Grattan wrote the epilogue. Here is the bill, where, of course, we find our friend Mr. Whyte and the young ladies who played as children in the same Masque at Rathfarnham Castle.

By Command of their Majesties,

OBERON AND TITANIA.

This present Monday, the 30th September, 1776, will be presented the MASQUE OF COMUS.

Comus .	. . .	Mr. Whyte.
Elder brother	. .	Miss Emilia La Touche.
Younger brother .	.	Miss Harriette La Touche.
First Spirit.	. .	Miss Marianna La Touche.
Second Spirit	. .	Miss Anne La Touche.

Bacchants and Bacchantes.

Master La Touche. Master John La Touche, Master Georges La Touche, Master Dunn, Miss White and Miss Maria La Touche.

Euphrosyne .	. .	Miss Dunn.
Patience Nymph .	.	Miss Maria Monroe.
Silence Nymph	.	Miss Gertrude La Touche.

and the Lady, MISS LA TOUCHE.

Sweet Echo. Mrs. La Touche, echoed by Mrs. Dunn.

In Act 1st, a glee by Mr. Dillon, Mrs. La Touche and Mrs. Dunn.
End of Act 1st, a Lesson on the Harpsichord, Mrs. John La Touche.
End of Act 2nd, Hornpipe, by Misses Harriette and Emilia La Touche.
In Act 3rd. A Double Minuet by Misses Harriette, Emilia, Marianna and Anne La Touche. With a reel by the same.

To conclude with a Country Dance by all the Characters.
An occasional Overture by Miss Quin.
Prologue by Mr. Whyte.
And the Epilogue written by Henry Grattan, Esq.,
and spoken by Miss La Touche.

It must be owned that this was rather a formidable programme to work through, but the beauty and grace of the performance, together with the sweetness of the ladies' voices, charmed the spectators. Grattan's epilogue is full of pretty fancies, as in the lines,—

" But why choose Comus ? Comus won't go down ;
Milton, good creature, never knew the town.
Better a sentimental comedy
That leads souls conscientiously astray ;
Whereabout good fond rakes are always ranting
And fond frail women so divinely canting
And sweet, sad dialogues with feeling nice
Gives flavour and variety to vice ! "

These two last lines might have been written by one of our own dramatists, so smart is their point.   In the lines beginning

"In all affairs of love and tender passion"

Grattan was supposed to have alluded to his own admiration, it did not amount to passion, for the beautiful speaker of his epilogue, who was not responsive to his suit. This, however, may have been mere idle gossip.   Miss La Touche, however, was in no hurry to leave the paternal roof.   She had a large circle of loving brothers and sisters, and adoring parents.   She turned a deaf ear to all her admirers until she had reached the advanced age of twenty-six, considered, in those days of early marriages, almost verging on old maidenism.   Good advice, and the prophecy that she would have to pick up the crooked stick was constantly dinned into the beauty's ears, until she justified herself by carrying off, in 1781, the *parti* of the season, the Earl of Lanesborough,[1] and so silenced the cackling of malicious chaperones.

Her day of triumph was not a long one; she was enjoying all the good gifts of life when the end came.   While on a visit to London, she caught the putrid fever, then raging, and died at the early age of thirty-two.

Her sisters Harriet and Anne were by this time married. Harriet, who was a beautiful brunette, to Sir Nicholas Cole-hurst, Anne to Mr. Vesey of Lucan House.   The names of the two remaining Miss La Touches figure in the list of the gaieties of Dublin, which waxed more and more furious as the final crash approached.   It was "a lightening before death sort of business."   These days bore fruit later on, in the

---

[1] Robert Herbert, Earl of Lanesborough, was the grandson of Lady Belvedere (see page 6). The family mansion was in Kildare Place, and was decorated by Richardson, who likewise decorated Lord Hawarden's house in Stephen's Green, now occupied by Mr. Digges La Touche. There was also a family mansion in London, situated where St. George's Hospital now stands. Here lived the eccentric Lord Lanesborough, whose passion was dancing; he gave up his time to the pursuit, and considered it a panacea for all the ills of life; so much so, that when Queen Anne lost her consort, Prince George, he advised her to dispel her grief by dancing. Pope has immortalized his Lordship's terpsichorean fancy in the lines:—

" Sober Lanesborough dancing
With the gout—"

melancholy history of the encumbered estates court. Putting aside the disastrous issue, the jinks and jousts of the Irish capital make pleasant reading, as when the Marchioness of Antrim gave a superb ball to the then Viceroy, Lord Westmoreland, the Grand Scots Ballet was danced by a number of ladies of rank; amongst these we notice the name of Miss La Touche; this was probably the youngest of the La Touche group of five, who later on married the Knight of Kerry, and was " lovely and beloved."

Mr. La Touche's son, Peter La Touche, married Charlotte, daughter of Lord Hawarden, who was likewise one of the many beauties of the day, and who retained to the great age of ninety-one her beauty and her charm. The writer remembers, some years ago, seeing the daughters of this lady. Although they were then in middle life, they were still lovely women, with a queenly presence unknown in the present generation. Sir Joshua would have loved to paint them.

The La Touche beauty has been handed down through several channels, Mrs. Ponsonby, the Hon. Mrs. Yorke and Lady Molyneux being the most well-known beauties.

Before closing this record of a very interesting family, I should mention another beauty who is in connection with the La Touches. Miss Molly Henn, who has been already named, was of the date of Dolly Monroe. Like Miss Martin, of Channel Row, she was a favourite with the versifiers of the day, and there is something very fresh and charming in the following :—

THE BIRD OF PARADISE.

So called from Mr. Henn's country seat in Clare, still in possession of the family.[1]

> While hungry bards from garret high
> To Myra's cheek or Stella's eye,
> Their amorous sonnets pen—
> Unpractised in the arts of verse,
> In simple strain let me rehearse
> The praise of Molly Henn.

[1] There have been intermarriages between the La Touche and the Henn families.

The present Lord Hawarden was created Earl of Montalt a few years ago.

It was, alas, the first of May,
I never shall forget the day
I saw her first—and then
Such modest worth, such winning een,
I could do nothing else but gaze
    On lovely Molly Henn.

Whiling away an idle hour the other day in Mr. Graves'
delightful gallery in Pall Mall, I came upon the portrait of a
lady whose queenly grace, majestic presence and splendid
attire showed her to be of the hightest distinction. I never
saw a lovelier face ; the eyes long and languishing, the mouth
bewitching, the whole air alluring, and withal, a commanding,
haughty dame. As I looked and admired, I fell to thinking
of all the stir and the scandal this lady's beauty had
caused, the trouble and confusion, the family quarrels she
had occasioned; for this lady of exceeding beauty became
Duchess of Cumberland, and to her was due the Royal
Marriage Act of 1772.

The Luttrells, or Lottrells, or Lutterells, date back to the
time of the Crusaders ; there was a Lord Chancellor Lutterell
in 1236, and Sir Andrew Lutterelle in 1259. When James I.
visited Ireland, the Lutterell of the day accompanied him.
The King was full of his scheme for planting the country with
loyal English subjects, as a sort of defence against the disloyalty of the natives. To Luttrell he gave a large grant of
land, four miles from Dublin, which was called Luttrellstown,
in return for which Luttrell was to give military service.

Like all settlers, Luttrell became *ipso facto* an Irishman,
intermarried with some of the best families, and attained
high distinction. In James II.'s reign, we find Simon Luttrell governor of Dublin, at the time of the battle of the
Boyne. An unswerving adherent of the Stuarts whether in
weal or woe, Simon retreated to Limerick with the remnant of
the Jacobite army, and managed to effect his escape to France,
and in 1688 he was attainted of high treason. Later, however, when the Treaty of Limerick was concluded, it was pro-

vided that if he returned in eight months, the attainder should be reversed, and his estates restored to him. A secret agreement was, however, entered into between his brother Henry [1] and General Ginkle, in consequence of which Simon was never allowed to return, and the estates were given to his disloyal brother. Henry's treachery had a bad end, for he was murdered by a band of ruffians in 1717. Neither was he, nor the brother who succeeded him, popular. O'Callaghan, the historian of the Irish Brigade, calls Henry Luttrell a *bad* man, who was father to a bad man and grandfather to a bad man. The second in this order of *demerit* was Simon Luttrell, created Baron Irnham in 1768, Viscount Carhampton in 1771, and Earl Carhampton in 1773. This favourite of fortune married the daughter and heiress of Sir Nicholas Lawes, Governor of Jamaica, and had a family of five sons and three daughters. These Luttrells were a wild, extravagant, dissipated race; handsome of person, charming of manner, brilliant and reckless. The Earl too had a high spirit, a mind cast in an original mould, and was an indefatigable votary of pleasure.

Strange stories were told of the revels at Luttrellstown, of extraordinary wagers, reckless gambling, and fierce quarrels between father and sons. The eldest, Colonel Luttrell, a distinguished officer, was of even a more combative temperament than his father.[2] He was of wild habits, with a reckless

---

[1] Henry Luttrell was suspected of having carried on secret negotiations with an agent of General Ginkle's concerning the surrender of Limerick, as he belonged to the party who were for coming to terms with the besiegers. Some of the correspondence fell into Tyrconnell's hands; the result was Luttrell's arrest and trial by court-martial. He would have been executed, but the surrender of Limerick saved his life. He was always looked upon by the Catholics as having betrayed the King, and being rewarded for the service by the grant of his brother's lands.

[2] The Earl, who had a fierce temper, quarrelled with his eldest son, and the quarrel had to be settled by a lawsuit. Both parties conducted each his own suit in a manner remarkable for its ability. The son, however, lost. Wraxall knew the first Earl, and describes him in his old age as active, and of a pleasing figure and high spirit, with an uncultivated, albeit powerful, mind, and an indefatigable thirst for pleasure. He relates a humorous trait of him. When he was dangerously ill in Bruton Street, Berkeley Square, the report that he was actually dead was

nature, to which fear was unknown. He was put forward by the Court party to contest Middlesex against Wilkes: this being considered so rash and dangerous an act, that policies of insurance on his life were opened at Lloyd's Coffee House, but he escaped uninjured. He was a first-rate shot, and to fight a duel with him was to court death, while his reputation, as regards honour, was of the worst possible. Junius, in his famous letters, draws his picture. "There is in this young man," he writes, "a strain which for its singularity I cannot but admire; he has discovered a new line in human character, and has disgraced *even* the name of Luttrell."

Of the daughters, Elizabeth, Anne, and Lucy, Elizabeth was in character akin to her brother. Not that she possessed his handsome person or attractive manners. Coarse and plain was Elizabeth, unprincipled and unladylike, with a habit of swearing, and a passion for cards and gambling of all kinds. Lucy was pretty, and nothing much is said of her but that she married Captain Moriarty. Anne was cast in a different mould from her sisters; nature being given to these freaks now and again. No doubt she had a touch of the high spirit of the Luttrells, or else she would not have played her part in life as she did, but it was tempered by other qualities. Her beauty was unsurpassed, in an age when beauty was of its highest order. It was of a refined type, and was joined to a rare gift of fascination impossible to resist, old and young falling within its spell. These good gifts were in company with an excellent understanding, which never allowed her to lose sight of prudence, or to venture beyond the limits of propriety. It does not seem that she was of a nature likely to be carried

---

carried to Carlton House. The Prince of Wales, who was then Regent, 1812, was at table with some boon companions, and being in a generous mood, gave way the Earl's regiment to one of the company, a general officer. When the news reached Lord Carhampton, he sent a friend, who was empowered to tell the Prince that so far from being a dead man, his Lordship hoped to recover his present illness, and therefore humbly entreated he might be allowed to retain command of his regiment; humorously adding, that His Royal Highness might be assured he would give special directions to his attendants, not to lose a moment, after it was ascertained that he was really dead, in conveying the news to Carlton House.

away by any whirlwind of passion, ambition rather than love being the master passion of her soul.

She had married, when a mere girl, Mr. Christopher Horton, a sporting squire of whom little has been said beyond that he was owner of Catton Park, Derbyshire. After a few years of marriage he died, leaving his widow a moderate provision. She was twenty-four, extremely pretty, with bewitching eyes, which she could animate to enchantment if she pleased; her coquetry was so active, so varied, and yet so habitual, that it was difficult not to see through it, and yet as difficult to resist it. She had likewise her accomplishments, dancing divinely being one of them. Since the days of Herod downwards, there is no art which more completely subjugates the masculine mind than the beautiful art of dancing. In the time of our great grandmothers, there was ample opportunity for displaying any proficiency a lady might have attained. The minuet with its many steps, its graceful curtseys, œillades and promenades, was a history of courtship, from the first attack to the final surrender. In the hands of a past mistress in the fine art of coquetry like Mrs. Horton, it could be made an instrument for completing her conquest over any individual of sufficient importance to meet her ambitious views.

Chance, the godfather of those who know how to make use of an opportunity, threw in Mrs. Horton's way the Duke of Cumberland, the king's brother. The Duke was the dullest of the royal brothers, none of them being remarkable for brilliancy. He was of a weak, unstable character, and Wraxall says, "limited as his faculties were, his manners rendered them apparently meaner than they would otherwise have been esteemed." This was no doubt due to the education the royal princes had received, which unfitted them for the positions they were destined to fill. The King suffered likewise from this want of proper training, which placed him always at a disadvantage. "If he had possessed the graces of the Prince of Wales, he would have impressed all who approached him with a conviction of the ability which he was really possessed of; *his* character, however, always commanded respect, whereas the Duke of Cumberland's feeble nature led him to become the prey of all manner of designing persons, while the unfortunate connections he formed, and the scandal consequent upon such proceedings as Lord Grosvenor's action for divorce, seriously injured the Duke's reputation with the nation; for although in general tolerant to youthful follies, the English people expect royalty to set an example of public morality."[1]

The Duke met Mrs. Horton while under the cloud of this late scandal. He was well pleased to distract his mind from the consequent annoyance by the pursuit of a new object of admiration. He was now, however, in the toils of a clever, ambitious woman, perfectly mistress of herself, and quick to seize every advantage a favourable chance presented. The young prince was easily captivated by the wily widow's fascinations, her divine dancing, her wit and Irish repartee, her quarter-of-a-yard eyelashes, her varied coquetries and ever-changing moods. She was everything by turns and nothing long. Through all this gamut of tricks she never for one moment lost sight of her end, and although it may be fairly doubted that the duke had ever intended to make her his wife, she so clearly proved to him that she would listen to no other proposals that, sooner than lose her, he eloped with her to Calais, where, on October 2nd, 1771, they were married, with all due legal forms carefully executed. No loophole was left through which the royal captive could wriggle, and so escape the responsibility of his action.[2] For a time the marriage was kept secret. After a proper interval,

[1] "I have been shocked," writes Mrs. Delany to Miss Dewes, "reading Lady Grosvenor and the Duke of Cumberland's letters. Such folly and wickedness, and withal so vulgar; and as to the sister at St. James's (Miss Vernon, one of the maids of honour) she makes a pitiable figure." There was also the other awkward affair of Olive Wilmot, whose daughter many years after produced certificates of a marriage between her mother and the Duke, four years before he married Mrs. Horton. These, however, were found to be forgeries, and the case collapsed. In addition to the vulgarity and wickedness of the correspondence of the Duke with Lady Grosvenor, there was also a total lack of even the commonest rudiments of education; they were ill-spelt and worse written.

[2] The witness to the marriage was Elizabeth Luttrell, the Duchess's elder sister.

given to the joys of happy love, the duchess began to tire of privacy, and to sigh for the regal state which was hers by right of her husband's rank. Like Elsa in " Lohengrin " she could not let well alone, and was for ever importuning the duke to set her right before the world. If all she was to have gained by the marriage was the Duke without the state, the bargain, from her point of view, would have been a poor one. For all his royal blood and coronet she must have had a bad time with her uncouth princeling, whose manners were akin to those of a rustic country squire. Those who knew him in the flesh have left many pictures of his far from regal habits. He was, however, submissive to his haughty wife's mandate, and, tired of her constant complainings that she was no better than " a virtuous mistress," he screwed up his courage to the sticking-point, and crossed over to England for the purpose of acquainting the king that he was married. The moment chosen for the confession was singularly inopportune. The Princess Dowager had been seized with her last illness ; although she had been anything but an affectionate mother the king was a most exemplary son. His feelings were excited, and he naturally felt disgusted when he found the errand upon which his brother had come. It was while they were walking together in the garden that the Duke awkwardly thrust a letter into the King's hand. It contained a notice of the wedding. The King quietly put it into his pocket, saying carelessly, " I suppose I need not read this now ? "

" Yes, sir," answered the Duke, " you must."

The King had no sooner done so than he burst into a rage : " You fool ! you blockhead ! you villain ! " and he then told him plainly, " That woman shall never be a royal duchess— she shall never be anything."

The poor Duke, abashed, asked humbly what he should do next.

" Go abroad," said the irate monarch, " until I can determine what to do."

The Duke therefore returned to Calais ; from which place he wrote, under his bride's direction, that she was expecting her confinement, and that no time was to be lost in estab-

lishing the marriage. The answer to this was the announcement of the King's intention to guard his own family from

H.R.H. THE DUCHESS OF CUMBERLAND AND STRATHERN.
(Anne Luttrell.)

similar alliances by introducing in the following session an
Act which would render them invalid. This foreshadowing
of the Royal Marriage Act of February, 1772, brought the
pair of culprits back to London, where they were objects of

much curiosity and interest. The floodgates of gossip were let loose ; on their first arrival they had the bad taste to instal themselves at Cumberland Lodge, while the Court was at Windsor, and were well snubbed for their indiscretion. " *He*," says Walpole, " is privately forbidden the Court— for of *she* there is no question ; Lord Hertford *is told* to tell *everybody* as a secret, which *they* are *desired* to tell *everybody*, that there is *no* road between Cumberland House and Windsor Castle." On the other hand, Mrs. Delany hears the *on dit* that the Duchess is to have four ladies-in-waiting (one of them being a cook's daughter), but she adds that for her part she thinks her royal highness has acted *most discreetly*, and has kept up a dignity equal to any princess of romance, for she has kept her lover an humble suppliant to the last moment. Horace Walpole writes more excitedly than is his wont to his crony at Florence, as to the madly absurd conduct of the Duke. He draws a comparison between this " mad boy " and the Duke of Gloucester, who was all prudence and amiability ; then he gives Sir Horace a portrait of the new " Princess of the blood—extremely pretty, although not handsome ; very well made, with the most amorous eyes in the world, and eyelashes a yard long. Coquette beyond measure, artful as Cleopatra, and completely mistress of her passions and projects—indeed, eyelashes three-quarters of a yard shorter would have served to conquer such a head as she has turned." This last remark would seem pointed by the jealousy that Walpole always entertained towards the Duchess of Cumberland for occupying a higher position than did his niece, who was *sub rosa* the wife of the Duke of Gloucester, and consequently implicated in the same disgrace. He alludes to this in this same letter: "I need not hint to you how unfortunate an event this is at the present moment, and how it clashes with the situation of another person." [1]

---

[1] Never imagining that this letter to his intimate friend would appear in evidence against his lack of truth, we find Walpole declaring to Lady Castletown, and all his friends, that he knew nothing of Lady Walde-grave's marriage until it became public. All through this curious history, what is most amusing is the trimming of Walpole — his fears and anxiety lest he should compromise himself in any way with

The Royal Marriage Bill came before the House of Commons on February 20th, 1772, when Lord Rochfort and Lord North delivered the following message from the King :—

"His Majesty, being desirous from paternal affection for his *own family*, and anxious concern for the future welfare of his people, and the honour and dignity of the Crown, that the right of approving all marriages in the royal family (which ever has belonged to the kings of this realm) as a matter of public concern, may be made effectual; recommends to both Houses of Parliament to take into serious consideration whether it may not be wise and expedient to supply the defect of the law now in being, and by some new provision more effectually to guard the descendants of his late Majesty, George II., from marrying without the approbation of his Majesty, his heirs and successors, first had and obtained."

The Bill, which was received with the utmost coldness by both Houses, raised a storm outside Parliament. The Church took umbrage at the power which would lie in the King's hands as to keeping his sons unmarried, this enforced celibacy possibly leading to scandals. On all sides it was unpopular in the highest degree. Ministers took alarm at the general excitement, and insisted upon modifying some of the provisions. They brought it in next day with a seeming softening but without any real difference. The Act was made binding only until the Princes had attained twenty-five years of age. This amendment did not serve any useful purpose. It was easy to see that it was pointed *at* the King's brothers, as none of his sons were marriageable.

The battle continued to rage furiously. The King, aided by the Queen, made the Bill a personal matter. It was given out by the Court circle that anyone who dissented from it would get a cold shoulder at Court. This was enough; "Adieu qualms, fears and care of posterity." Zeal, money, influence of all sorts went to work, with the result that the Royal Marriage Bill passed the Lords on the 3rd March,

the King, by his siding with the young couple, and yet his ill-concealed pleasure at having such an exalted person for a near relation.

1772, and was sent *down* to the Commons, where, after the most unseemly scenes, and some splendid oratory from Burke, Charles Fox, and Wedderburn, it finally passed into law.

The Duke of Cumberland was present the first day of the debate. Not a soul except the Duke of Richmond spoke to him. He had notes in his hand, which he seemed to con over as if intending to speak. The Duke of Richmond asked him if he had any objection to being named in the debate. He said " No," and added that he had come to satisfy himself whether there was any idea of setting aside his marriage ; if there were, he proposed to throw himself upon the justice of the House. But as there was no mention of this, he asked Richmond if he had not better retire, and so went away, and came no more to the discussion.

" The Royal Marriage Bill is at last finished," writes Walpole, on March the 27th, " after taking up nearly a hundred hours in the House of Commons : it was near being wrecked at last, being carried but by a majority of eighteen, while ten more who would have been against it were accidentally shut out, not expecting a division so soon. Never was a Bill that gave such deep offence, and from mere speculation. The people did not interfere, nor was it a matter of popularity to oppose it. Lord Mansfield bears all the odium, and deservedly, for no man else had a hand in drawing it. Lord North, though disliking it, supported it like a man, the rest treacherously condemning it, voting for it, and wishing it might miscarry."

" 'This measure, more than any other," says Mr. Lecky, " divided opinion in the country. The object was to prevent the great dangers which might arise from clandestine or improper marriages in the royal family ; it was possible in consequence of such alliances, that the title of successor to the throne might become a matter of dispute, and it was very possible that connections might be formed, and disgraceful elements introduced into the royal family, which would endanger the authority of the monarchy and lower its prestige." Its immediate result was to bring another offender on the scene. The Duke of Gloucester, who was abroad for his health, rushed home to acquaint the King with the fact of *his* marriage to Lady Waldegrave, which had taken place six years previously. The poor King was overwhelmed by this new blow, it was said that he cried all night. Still he refused to see the Duke or to make any difference in his case, although he was his favourite brother.

We have the whole scene laid before us by the graphic pen of Horace Walpole, in his letters to his confidential friend at Florence :—

"June, 1772.

" On the very evening of his return, the Duke of Gloucester allowed my niece to acquaint her father that they have been married since 1766. Lady Waldegrave does not take the royal title immediately, which I think very modest.[1] He adds,

---

[1] The following is Lady Waldegrave's letter to her father, Sir Edward Walpole :—

" MY DEAR AND EVER HONOURED SIR,

" You cannot easily imagine how every past affliction has been increased to me by not being at liberty to make you quite easy. The duty to a husband being superior to that we owe a father, I hope will plead my pardon ; and that instead of blaming my past reserve, you will think it commendable.

" When the Duke of Gloucester married me, which was in September, 1766, I promised him upon no consideration in the world to own it even to you without his permission, which permission I never had until yesterday, when he arrived here in much better health, and looked better than I ever saw him ; yet, as you may suppose, much hurt at all that has passed in his absence, so much so, that I have had great difficulty to prevail upon him to let things as much as possible remain as they are. To secure my character without injuring his is the utmost of my wishes, and I daresay that you and all my relations will agree with me that I shall be much happier to be called Lady Waldegrave, and respected as the Duchess of Gloucester, than to feel myself the cause of his leading such a life as his brother (the Duke of Cumberland) does, in order for me to be called Your Royal Highness. I am prepared for the sort of abuse the newspapers will be full of. Very few people will believe that a woman will refuse to be called Princess if it is in her power. *To have the power* is my pride, and using it in some measure pays the debt I owe the Duke for the honour he has done me. All I wish of my relations is that they will show the world they are satisfied with my conduct, yet seem to disguise their reasons. If ever I am fortunate enough to be called the Duchess of Gloucester, there is an end almost of all the comforts I now enjoy, which if things go on as they now do, *are many*."

To a close observer it would seem that towards the end of this otherwise delightful letter, the lady overshoots the mark a little. She protests, in fact, too much.

that it is a great satisfaction that her character is invulnerable, and it gives me much more pleasure that she has preserved her honour, than that she has obtained this great honour, which does not dazzle me. . ."

Again he writes :—

"There is an end of suppressing, palliating or disbelieving. *The* marriage—my niece's marriage—is formally notified to the King by the Duke of Gloucester. Last Wednesday I received a letter signed 'Maria Gloucester,' acquainting me that the declaration had been made and received by his Majesty with grief, tenderness and justice. I say justice, *tout oncle* as I am, for it would have been very unjust to the Duke of Cumberland to have made any other distinction between two brothers equally in fault, than what affection without *overt* acts cannot help making. This all implies that the Duke of Gloucester must undergo the same prohibition as his brother did, which I am told is to be the case, though the step is not yet taken."

The Duchess of Gloucester affected the most exaggerated humility, declaring that her only desire in marrying the Duke was to secure her character without injuring his, and that she would be much happier to be *called* Lady Waldegrave, and to be *respected* as the Duchess of Gloucester, than to feel herself the cause of his leading such a life as his brother (the Duke of Cumberland) "does, in order for her to be called Your Royal Highness."

All these protestations did not deceive the cynic of Strawberry Hill. He knew woman's nature too well to believe in this mock "self-denial." His opinion to his confidential friend is that the Duchess's prevailing passion, *ambition*, would not be long smothered ; nor was it.[1]

---

[1] "My niece the Duchess," he says, "has not written *in the same strain* of *self-denial* to her sister Dysart. To her she recounts the magnificence of the presents the Duke had given her ; and many other expressions show me that her ambition, which is her prevailing passion, would not be long smothered." Nor was it. She presently induced the Duke to hold a levee, which, to use her own expression, he had never practised. It was much crowded, and was ill-considered, as it irritated both the King and Queen, who were jealous of their own prerogatives.

Meantime our Luttrell Duchess was carrying things with her usual airy grace. Although under the ban of the royal displeasure, she went everywhere, and gave herself royal airs. Sir Joshua, who was painting her portrait, was mightily diverted by her condescension. The strangely-contrasted pair visited his studio in the April of this year. The painter's biographer records the manner in which the Duke behaved; like a big schoolboy, he grew weary of the interview, and took to knocking about the pictures that stood upon the easels and swearing to himself. The Duchess insisted he should say something to the painter about her portrait, which was begun; after staring for some time at the beautiful face just transferred to the canvas, he made the sapient remark, "What— eh!—so you begin with the head, do you?"[1] This was only a sample of his usual gaucherie.

The position of the royal pair was singularly unpleasant. "*He* was privately forbidden the Court, for of *she* there was no question. They were invited to none of the Court festivities, and when there was an installation of the Knights of the Bath, the Duke received a hint not to occupy his stall in St. George's Chapel." In all this we can trace the influence of Queen Charlotte. Excellent as she was, she had her womanly weaknesses, and would know how to wound her beautiful sister-in-law in her sorest point.

Not being recognized, nor allowed to enjoy any state or privilege of rank, must have been a cruel mortification to the haughty Luttrell. She thought it best to withdraw herself for a time from public notice, at least until the royal authentication had been given to the marriage, which was still delayed, on account of the imbroglio made by the Duke of Gloucester having concealed his for so many years. Bishop Norton, who had married him and Lady Waldegrave, was dead, and it now appeared there had been no witnesses,[2] which

---

[1] Another story told of the Duke was his meeting Gibbon the historian, and his accosting him with "How d'ye do, what, at the old trade? aye, always scribble, scribble!"

[2] Horace Walpole says :—" When I heard there were no witnesses I started with horror. It appears that the Duke was so afraid of her

raised a question of illegality. As all this would take time to examine, the Cumberlands went abroad. On their arrival at Calais, they were received, to her extreme pleasure, with regal honours, and went in state to the theatre. Next morning a deputation waited upon the royal pair with felicitations. The exchequer must have been low, for in return for these honours the deputation received only three guineas. In revenge for this shabby guerdon they despatched a dirty candle-snuffer with a bouquet to the Princess, and later sent another messenger to St. Omer to demand more money. After this rather unpleasant episode, the Duke and Duchess continued their journey to Italy. The different Courts were much embarrassed by their arrival, as the dilemma was how to receive them; everywhere the English ambassador having orders to allow them no royal precedence. This all seems like petty persecution, and it was no wonder the Duchess resented the treatment she received. Honours were later on paid to them, and according to Walpole the Duchess's visions of pride and folly touched upon madness. She came home, in May, 1774, resolved to assert her dignity. Both marriages had now been authenticated. There had been much question as to the legality of the Duke of Gloucester's, and some talk of his being married over again to Lady Waldegrave, which should be done speedily, as the Duchess was expecting her confinement.

The Duke of Gloucester's state of mind in regard to the whole affair brought on a fit of illness. He was harassed with anxiety, especially on account of the coming event. In presence of the Archbishop of Canterbury and the Bishop of Exeter he made a solemn declaration of his being " married to Lady Waldegrave, at her house in Pall Mall, on September 6th, 1776, by her own chaplain, Dr. Norton, now dead, but there were no witnesses present." He added, " Your lordships remember I was at the point of death in Florence. At that awful moment I called for Colonel Rainsford ; I told him I was married. I then enjoined him, on his duty to a dying

vanity that he would allow no witnesses who could prove to the marriage."

master, as soon as he should have closed my eyes, to hasten to England, and repair to the King, and declare my marriage, and say that my last request was that his Majesty would allow a small pittance to the widow of his favourite brother. My lords, Colonel Rainsford took notes of what I said: he has them in his pocket, and shall read them."

All this shows the Duke in a most favourable light as an honourable man; so, too, with his rushing off late at night to the Archbishop of Canterbury, who had the Bishop of London with him. Both were retiring when the excited Duke arrived, and insisted that both should hear him. He enjoined them by their duty to their country to go that moment to the King and tell him if he had still any doubts he should remove them. The two prelates pleaded that they would not intrude on his Majesty at that hour; " Ye shall not lay your heads on your pillows till ye have seen him," was the reply of the Prince.

The Bishops had to go, and soon returned with a reply that though satisfied, he would consent to the Duke's being married over again if he chose it. At last, however, he agreed to make no further difficulties, and his full consent was given just in time, for the Duchess was confined next day in presence of the officers of state and with all formalities due to her rank.

It seems truly absurd that, having accorded so much, their Majesties should have continued to treat the wives of the royal Dukes as if they were mistresses; but so it was, the gates of the Court circle were rigidly shut in their faces. The servile courtiers followed the lead of the Court, it being fully understood that those who were friends with the culprits were not *bien vue*. The Duchess of Cumberland fared no better, if anything worse, than her Highness of Gloucester. Her weekly receptions, like those given by the Duchess, were not attended. Fifty persons came to the first, but when it appeared that exclusion from St. James's was sure to follow those who visited either of the ostracized Duchesses, not a man or woman of position came either to Gloucester House or Pall Mall.[1]

The Duchess of Gloucester, who felt deeply the manner in which

The situation was accentuated by the quarrels between the two Duchesses. It would seem natural that being as it were in the same boat, they would have made common cause against the Court. The Duchess of Cumberland was well inclined, but her overtures were rejected by her sister Gloucester, who said, " No, I could not smell at the same nosegay with her in public." [1] Maria of Gloucester, although she could quote from the *Rehearsal*, was not remarkable for good sense. She would have acted more wisely in forming a defensive alliance. The Duke of Cumberland was altogether governed by his wife's family, of whom he stood much in awe. His love for his beautiful Duchess had changed into fear. The honeymoon which, Walpole said, had waned to half a moon before they left England, had not now a ray of warmth ; but he was too weak in mind to oppose her strong will, backed as she was by her own family. Elizabeth Luttrell, an incubus more terrible than any mother-in-law, made her home with her sister, and Temple Luttrell, a clever rising politician, was always at hand. The feeble Duke confided to Grenville that he heartily repented what he had done. It was too late, however. He was altogether governed by these *esprits forts*, and had to obey their orders in raising a standard of opposition against the King. Paragraphs appeared every day in the papers as if on behalf of the Duke of Gloucester, which greatly incensed the King against *him ;* this was the revenge taken by the Duchess for the rejection of her overtures.

Later she and her husband took a fiendish method of retaliating on the King and Queen. When the Prince of Wales had come almost to man's estate, the Duchess, who was then in the very zenith of a beauty which had increased by maturity, so wove her toils round the heir apparent, as to obtain a com-

society treated her, tried to disarm her enemies by a show of humility. She took no royal honours, and would not allow any one to kiss her hand.

[1] This referred to a proposal on the part of the Duchess of Cumberland that the four victims of royal persecution should appear at the opera in one box. Walpole, while praising the honesty of his niece's character, condemns her folly in quarrelling as she did with the Duchess of Cumberland.

plete influence over him.[1] He almost lived at Cumberland
House. Everything was done to attract him; to pander to
his taste for gambling, the Duke set up a faro table, and became
the prompter of his nephew's excesses, which he fostered and
encouraged. With the same object of annoying the King, his
brother, the Duke would insolently ignore him, and present
himself at the Court balls without invitation. The Duchess
gave a ball in the Prince's honour, which the King forbade the
Prince's household to attend. The Duke then invited them to
a dinner to indemnify them, but the King again interfered.
This was all petty tyranny, and very unwise on the part of the
King and Queen, as the Prince was too old to brook interference
with his pleasures. If Walpole is to be believed, the conduct
of the Duke was most indecent; he and the Prince would
spend nights in the most riotous manner, drinking until the
Prince was not able to stand.[2] There were also stories of the

---

[1] The intimacy first began at Brighthelmstone, in 1782. The Duke
then occupied a small old-fashioned house on the very edge of the sea,
belonging to Mr. Wyndham. The Prince went on a visit to him. The
first effect of this intimacy was a volte-face on the part of Society. The
Duchess's levées were crowded with all the rank, fashion and beauty of
London.

[2] An instance of this occurred within a few weeks after the Prince
was declared to have attained his majority. Lord Chesterfield invited his Royal Highness and the Duke to an entertainment at his
house on Blackheath. Several persons were there, and being all of
them *bon vivants*, the bottle circulated so rapidly as to produce
scenes of rather a tragi-comic character. Among other frolics, one
of the company, at breaking up, let loose a furious mastiff, which
was generally kept chained for fear of mischief. The dog, on gaining
his liberty, attacked one of the footmen, and tore his right arm in
a dreadful manner; then the animal sprang at a fine horse, which was
very nearly strangled; and now such an uproar arose as threw the
whole place into confusion. The gentlemen, being heightened by wine,
drew up in a circle, and commenced war upon the dog; but Towser kept
them at defiance, and made not a few of them repent their temerity. At
the close of the fray, the noble host slipped down a flight of steps, and
nearly fractured his skull. The contest then terminated, the young
Prince jumped into his phaeton, and, falling fast asleep, left the reins to
his uncle, who, as good luck would have it, brought him safe to town.
His Majesty was much concerned when he heard of this frolic; for,
as he was strictly temperate and regular in his own habits, he could not
endure the least deviation from sobriety and decorum in any of his
family. But though he reproved his brother for the indiscretion he
had committed, the remonstrance was thrown away upon the Duke, who
forgot his promises as soon as he had made them.

two insulting the King by talking within earshot of him in the grossest terms. One cannot but pity the poor harassed King, whose mind was growing feebler every day, and unable to deal with his heartless brother and son. When the Queen urged him to forbid their having such close intercourse, he said sadly, it was no use forbidding when he would not be obeyed. The Duke, on the other hand, made no secret that he should use his influence over the Prince to intimidate the Court into receiving the Duchess, and in this he succeeded. Although it was not a public recognition, the Duchess was constantly with the royal family ; it has been even whispered that her influence over the King grew to be equal to her power over the Prince. Few men could resist the spell of her fascinations. "Her personal charms," says Wraxall, "allowing for the injury they had sustained from time, justified the admiration they still excited. No woman of her time performed the honours of her drawing-room with such grace, affability, and dignity." *Tout vient à qui sait attendre*, but it must have been a triumph dear to the Duchess's heart to find herself admitted to the family circle from which she had been so rigorously excluded. In 1782 she formed one of a group, which included the Princess Royal and several duchesses, in a picture painted by Sherwin, representing the daughter of Pharaoh finding Moses amongst the bulrushes. To these violent delights succeeded violent endings. The capricious Prince took offence at his uncle's too great familiarity ; he did not care to be slapped on the back, and called "Taffy." A coolness ensued between the boon companions which induced the Cumberlands to go abroad ; they were in Rome in 1786,[1] but on their return, the breach between them and their royal nephew was made up, and the old terms of intimacy renewed. It was said that a private passage was constructed between Carlton House and the Duke's garden in Pall Mall, so that assistance could be given to the Prince in some of his not too creditable escapades. In 1788, when the king had his first serious attack, the Duke of Cumberland

[1] They visited Naples, and were entertained by Sir William Hamilton.

agitated that a regency should at once be established, and that the power should be in the Prince of Wales's hands. In all this we can trace the influence of his wife, who still desired to revenge the slights Queen Charlotte had inflicted. In 1790, however, much of her glory was shorn; the Duke, who, like his brother of Gloucester, had a weak habit of body, fell ill in the autumn and died, at the comparatively early age of forty-five. The Duchess—who survived him twenty years, dying in 1810—was not much more heard of in the world where she once made such a stir. The younger generation were grown up, and, as always, the elders had to give way. In 1796 she sold her house in Pall Mall and went to reside at Sheen.[1]

There are still a few words to be said about her family. Her sister Elizabeth (called in derision the Princess Elizabeth), a coarse, unprincipled woman, was devoured by a love of play, which brought her to a tragical end. Sir R. Heron, in his "Notes," says, "She played so high, and cheated so shamefully, that on the death of the Duchess, having no one to protect her, she was thrown into jail. Here she gave a hairdresser 50*l.* to marry her, and thus assume her debts; on which, according to the then state of the law, she obtained her discharge. She then went to Germany, where, being convicted of picking pockets at Ausbourg, she was sentenced and condemned to clean the streets chained to a wheel-barrow. To end such a state of misery the unhappy creature poisoned herself. This was indeed a curious finale for an earl's daughter, and the sister-in-law of a royal duke!"

Meantime Colonel Luttrell had been made Commander-in-Chief of the army in Ireland. He exercised immense influence during the troubles which overwhelmed that country in 1798. He was hand and glove with the Beresfords, and, it was said, practised great cruelties upon the rebels. When he succeeded

---

[1] In 1806 the Duchess was in Rome, where her position was a subject of perplexity to the authorities, to whom a rumour had filtered of the displeasure caused by her marriage. Lord Cloncurry, who was in Rome, seems to have acted a friendly part, and, owing to his intervention, a guard of honour was daily mounted at the Duchess's residence. In return for this she was sponsor to his son, who was given the name of Ann, after her Royal Highness.

his father as Lord Carhampton he showed an utter contempt for public opinion ; he was flippant and offensive in his language, arrogant and overbearing in his manner. He was the most unpopular man of his time, and on several occasions narrowly escaped the knife of the assassin. His great courage and indifference to danger got him the reputation of bearing a charmed life, and no further attempts were made upon him. Towards the close of his career he was implicated in a very unpleasant trial, and his accomplice, a certain woman called Llewellyn, was hung in Stephen's Green. A friend of his, Lord Boyton, fought a duel in his defence with Rowan Hamilton. Lord Carhampton sold Luttrellstown to Luke White, the fortunate winner of a lottery-ticket worth 20,000*l.*, which made the beginning of his colossal fortune. He changed the name of Luttrellstown to Woodlands, which is very appropriate to its finely-wooded and picturesque situation. It is still in the possession of his descendants.[1]

Lord Carhampton met his death, it was said by the superstitious, in consequence of a curse given to him by some woman upon whom his horse had trampled, as he rode away from his own door hale and hearty one summer's morning. He was brought back in an hour's time a corpse.[2]

He was succeeded by his brother John, as third Earl Carhampton, who had married the daughter and heiress of Lord Waltham. He had no sons, and his daughter, Lady Francis Luttrell, married Sir Simeon Stuart, equerry and aide-de-camp to the Prince Regent, and, after he became King, comptroller to the royal household. George IV. offered him a fresh patent for the Carhampton peerage, which Sir Simeon refused, saying he was better known by his own name ; which was undoubtedly the case, as being one of the *most extravagant* of an extravagant Court."

[1] Ancestor of the present Lord Annaly.
[2] The writer does not vouch for the truth of this story. There seems to have been a family curser kept on the premises in some Irish families. There is a curse in the Powerscourt family, in the Kavanaghs, of Borris, and many others. It is a sort of trade-mark of high birth.
[3] From a letter of the present Sir Simeon Stuart of Chattle, who is the representative of the extinct peerage of Carhampton.

Perched high upon one of the bleakest headlands of the
South of Ireland there stands a country house, consisting of
two wings, several round towers, and a square one, newly
added. A few trees, growing quite close to the house and
along the approach, were evidently objects of the most
tender solicitude to their first owners, who, to provide shelter
from the furious gales that raged along the heights, built
lofty protecting walls of solid masonry. These walls run in
and out in an utterly irregular fashion, irrespective of any
design except that of enclosing every scrap of growth that
might possibly develop into a tree. However incongruous
or inconvenient these rambling plans of house, towers, and
walls may have originally been, the lapse of time, and the
interest of the strange fortunes of past dwellers in the
mansion, make them appear now an interesting and picturesque
arrangement.

The carefully-cherished trees near the house have thick
trunks and stout limbs branching from them, as far and no
farther than the height of the protecting walls. Above these,
there is only a dense mass of matted and twisted small branches,
whipped north-eastward by the prevailing south-westerly
gales. There is something touching in this expenditure on
walls which bespeaks much love of trees and care for them
in the past, without which it would have been impossible for
them to exist in such a spot. A bird's-eye view of the
country from adjacent heights, shows how few and far between are even the stunted beeches, alders, or sycamores that
battle out their wind-distraught existence.

It must have been a resolute mind which first planned a

<hr>

[1] This memoir has been contributed by Miss F. W. Currey, of Lismore
whose sketch of the " Gallows of the Heir " will be found on page 233.

home on this exposed spot, only a little below the highest level for many a mile in every direction. From the house, seawards, the ground slopes rapidly down a field or two to the sea, where jagged cliffs and rocks of most forbidding aspect repel the attacks of the long Atlantic rollers, and there is always a sullen murmur of waters in the calmest weather. As Ardo stands to-day, the scrupulously white-washed walls gleaming brilliantly in the sun, the round towers, and curious high latticed wood-work wind-screens—all have a somewhat Moorish look. But no brightness of sun, or shining whiteness, can dissipate the ghostly and uncanny influence of the house, if one visits it when it is uncheered by the presence of its owners, and there is nothing of life or stir to divert the mind from the tales of tragedy and strange ups and downs of fortune of its former inhabitants. Still, it must be remembered that only a small portion of the old buildings, that occupied by servants, now remains, together with the long lines of masonry walls. The present house was built about 1833, before which time the place was fast falling into ruin. The old house must have been somewhat like the present one in design, as it had round towers and small iron-barred windows.

The earliest history of Ardo is vague, and recorded accounts of its traditions and inmates few. From these, and inquiries among the few living persons who can remember any of the family, together with some notes of conversations with a lady now many years deceased, who knew both Mrs. Coghlan and her daughters, this chapter is compiled.

The ancient name of the bluff headland was Ardigena, spelt much according to taste, after the manner of the olden time. It is believed to have been inhabited in the seventeenth century by persons of the name of Costen, and a gloomy tradition of treachery and violent death has been handed down in connection with the last member of the family. In and about Ardo, even twenty years ago, it was a tolerably complete narrative as told by cottage firesides. Now those who knew it in detail have passed away, and only one or two remain who recollect having "heard the old people talking about it." The dark story was one of the betrayal of a minor by his guardian. Young Costen, "the heir of Ardo," as he has been called since his tragic end, had for his guardian a villain named Fitzgerald, who, without much originality in wickedness, contrived to brand him as a thief by a stratagem similar to that which Joseph used against his brethren in Egypt long ago. After a friendly visit to his guardian, the unsuspecting youth departed on horseback with his valise, in which Fitzgerald had secreted a valuable silver tankard. The false guardian's next act was to hurry to a Justice of the Peace, and procure a search warrant to enable him to recover his stolen property. The justice, a harsh, insensible man, accepted Fitzgerald's story, and set off with him, accompanied by a body of troopers, in pursuit of young Costen, who found himself confronted by his accusers at his own hall-door, just as he reached home by a circuitous route. His innocence did not, of course, prevent his being thunderstruck at such a charge from such a quarter; but when the missing piece of plate was drawn forth from his valise, he apparently either lost his head, or realized that his persecutors were bent on his destruction, and that his only chance of safety lay in flight. His horse, one faithful friend, was still at his side; so, in his despair, he leaped into the saddle, and fled in the direction of Ardmore. To anyone who has traversed those rocky uneven heights, it is easy to picture the miserable chase—a wild affrighted youth hunted by the excited troopers, who were doubtless urged to the utmost exertions by Fitzgerald and his companion in authority. One version of the horrible end of the pursuit says that, his pursuers gaining on the fugitive, he leaped his horse across a dangerous chasm, and, gaining time by this desperate feat, doubled back on Ardigena, and urging his horse up a steep incline, was captured when the exhausted animal stumbled and fell. After that a rope was fastened around his neck, and he was dragged down to the rocks, and cruelly hung over a natural bridge, amid the taunts and execrations of his inhuman hunters. Another tradition says that he tried in desperation

to force his horse—when, literally, between the devil and
the deep sea—towards this same natural bridge, but the
animal missed its footing, and, rolling with its rider down the
cliff, he fell from the saddle, and, becoming entangled in the
reins, was accidentally hung at the spot called "Crook-an-

CROOK-AN-HEIRE (The Gallows of the Heir).

(Reproduced from original sketch by Miss F. W. Currey.)

heire," or "The Gallows of the Heir." This place of evil
memory is said to be haunted, and unearthly yells, wails, and
shrieks are heard above the noise of the ground-swell of the
sea, so that no one will pass the accursed spot after dark.
Other traditions respecting the tragedy assert that a cruel
stepmother was partly responsible for the crime. But most
accounts concur in attributing Fitzgerald's evil deed to his

betrayal of the monetary trust confided to him, and fear of discovery on the heir's approaching attainment of his majority.

After passing through several hands, the house and property were purchased by Sir Francis Prendergast. Another crime is said to have been committed during the ownership of the Prendergasts. A servant offended his hasty and arbitrary master, who, it was alleged, had him secretly hanged from a beam in the ceiling of a room in a part of the old house which still remains. Needless to say, such a crime produced supernatural sounds, and to get rid of the ghost and its noises structural alterations became necessary. When the old house was pulled down, a skeleton was found buried some feet below the dining-room floor, and was believed to have been that of the murdered servant.

The Coghlans obtained possession of Ardo early in the eighteenth century, and around their persons and fortunes its chief interest centres. The last male Coghlan who lived at Ardo was Jeremiah,[1] and his wife was said to have been a Miss Davis. The surviving children of his marriage were four in number, and surely never was there seen a greater inequality of natural gifts, as well as fortune and destiny, amongst the members of one family. The eldest daughter, Anne, married in 1795, at the age of eighteen, the last and one of the least reputable of the notorious Earls of Barrymore.[2] The second

---

[1] Jeremiah Coghlan ran away to sea when only a lad. He had a strange story, which is told in Gronow's memoirs.

[2] At the beginning of this century the Barrymores were conspicuous amongst the roués of the day. There were three brothers and one sister; they were known by the flattering sobriquets of *Hellgate, Cripplegate, Newgate,* and *Billingsgate.* The eldest was the most celebrated; he had a country house near Henley which was the scene of the wildest orgies; his career was short, and his death mysterious. His brother Cripplegate, so called from his lameness, indulged in all manner of excesses and extravagances; he was addicted to low company, and married the daughter of a sedan chairman. Newgate, the eighth and last Lord Barrymore, was not such a celebrated character as his brothers; he was, however, a famous whip, and his ambition was to be taken for a genuine hackney-coach driver. He was intimate with the Prince Regent, and indulged in all manner of extravagance; the final smash came after a splendid entertainment given to the Prince in Sackville Street, crowded with all the rank, beauty, and fashion of London. It was the expiring flame of the Barrymores. Wargrave was seized by

daughter, Eliza, married a widower, an *emigré* of exalted birth, one of the noblest dukes of France—the Duc de Castries. Both of these Miss Coghlans were of great beauty and charm. Lady Barrymore was small, but exquisitely formed ; the Duchesse de Castries was less lovely, but tall and dignified. Lady Barrymore had blue eyes and brown hair. The two younger members of the Coghlan family, Jeremiah and Thomasina—familiarly known as Jerry and Tamsin—were both idiots, and despite their sisters' grandeur, died in loneliness and poverty.

Frances, Lady Musgrave, widow of Sir Richard Musgrave, the second baronet, of Tourin, in the county of Waterford, who died at the advanced age of ninety in 1865, had often seen Mrs. Coghlan and her daughters, and visited at their house during her stay at Grange, the seaside residence of the Musgraves at Whiting Bay, near Ardo. Lady Musgrave said that Ardo House was full of interesting old furniture, of various styles and fashions ; there was also a spinet, and portraits of former residents at Ardo, including one said to be that of the unhappy "heir," young Costen, last of his race. There were also in existence at this time beautiful miniatures [1] of the celebrated sisters, in gold frames, one with a countess' the other with a duchess' coronet. There was also a portrait of the Duchesse de Castries, and her sons, Alix and Olonville de Castries. In those days, country visiting was attended with considerable difficulty, and Lady Musgrave used humorously to describe her *impressions de royage,* when as a young bride she set out to return complimentary visits paid to her by residents in the country around Whiting Bay. The roads were so rough as to be impassable for anything less strong than a springless farm-cart, and she found herself

the angry creditors, so was Castle Lyons and Buttevant. His estates in the north of Ireland followed, and were bought by John Anderson, of Armagh, with a reservation of four thousand a year for the Earl and four thousand for the Countess. This, however, was soon squandered, and the noble pair once more were paupers. Luckily for them the Duc de Castries, as stated in the text, came to the rescue.—[*Note by the Editor.*]

Every exertion has been made to trace these miniatures, so far ineffectually.—[Ed.]

obliged to pay her visits of ceremony in one of these carts, padded with straw, feather beds, and cushions to lessen the jolting. Lady Musgrave had many interesting recollections of scenes and persons besides those connected with Ardo. She knew the unfortunate Lord Edward Fitzgerald, and remembered him at Bath, where he turned many heads, her own included, so that she and other ladies used to ride out in green habits to please his patriotic humour.

To return to the Coghlans—gossip was often busy with regard to their way of living. Their means were known to be small, and the fine silks and laces and ribbons worn by the two elder and beautiful daughters of the house were accounted for, not unnaturally in those days, by a supposed traffic and friendship between Mrs. Coghlan, or " Madam," as she was called by her household and dependents, and the smugglers of the coast. She was said to befriend the latter by securing information as to the whereabouts of the revenue officers and their men, and by displaying signals from her windows at Ardo, which could be seen far out at sea, to inform the smugglers when it would be safe for them to land their dangerous cargoes in the neighbourhood. The Coghlans lived in a very expensive and reckless manner, and were fond of every sort of gaiety. A sister of " Madam " was Mrs. Connor, wife of Mr. Connor, who lived at that time at Lismore Castle as agent to the Duke of Devonshire. The society in which the Coghlans moved had the name of being a " rollicking set," and of course social display required supplies of all sorts, including smart clothes. Shops for ladies' fashions were few and far between in those days, and communication—even assisted by farm-carts and feather beds—slow and laborious ; and there appears to have been some considerable trafficking between Mrs. Coghlan and ladies who were her neighbours, in silks, tabinets, laces, and ribbons—especially whenever the wedding of a daughter or other festivity was impending, and had to be provided for. As her possession of these articles of supply was not very clearly accounted for, the smuggling theory became generally accepted. In those days smuggling was somewhat faintly reprobated, and the temptation to deal with smugglers often proved too much for the principles of people in a good position even. Two sons of a local clergyman, the Rev. Ponsonby Carew, who lived at Ardo for a short time after Mrs. Coghlan's death, were both reading for the Church, but were refused ordination by the then Bishop of Waterford on the grounds of their trial and conviction for buying smuggled goods.

In the Coghlans' time the kitchen was much the same as it is now; with a staircase in just the same position, leading upstairs to the servants' rooms, and divided from the rest of the house by a door. It used to be said that Mrs. Coghlan's custom was to leave the kitchen table well stocked with eatables and drink, and to open the postern door communicating between the kitchen and the out-door world, and then to retire upstairs, locking the connecting door. In the morning the table was clear of food, and in its place would be found silks and laces, and occasionally a keg of foreign wine or spirits.

The Coghlans were undoubtedly on good terms with their poor neighbours, for though Protestants, and living in an isolated place in turbulent times, they escaped without any injury. During the rebellion of '98 "Madam," then a widow, continued to reside at Ardo with her two idiot children. The only interference she suffered was the requisitioning of her hospitable kitchen as a meeting place for rebels. Probably the previous smuggling transactions suggested the later plan— but it was on a less profitable basis for Mrs. Coghlan. In such times, however, a lonely widow may well have thought she was buying safety cheaply enough, at the expense of potatoes, bacon, and drink. About 1817 the Caravats, a secret society of nocturnal habits and ill fame, used to come to her every Saturday night, and her already reduced circumstances were still further straitened by their exactions. A negro servant of the family, called "Gillick the Black," used to walk to the Blackwater, and cross the river to the town of Youghal every Saturday for marketing, and the "Caravats" were always well informed of what he brought out—meat, vegetables, fish, bread, everything, even to the gallon of whisky which their involuntary hostess was obliged to supply for them. There is an entry in Youghal parish church, St. Mary's, of the burial of this negro messenger. It runs thus: "1824. March 21. Gillick Coghlan. An 'African Black.'"

Ardo House was reputed to be both unlucky and haunted, and if it has a somewhat uncanny look even now, when so much restored and renovated, what must it not have seemed when falling into decay during the last years of Mrs. Coghlan's lonely life. Once when Lady Musgrave was being shown over the house in one of her visits to Mrs. Coghlan, she was cautioned against falling over a couple of loose steps in one of the staircases, which they had never, they assured her, been able to fasten down securely since a child's body had been found beneath them—a disagreeable discovery made just at the time of some wedding festivities. The crime of the child's death and concealment was traced to some unhappy servant's intrigue. Again and again, Lady Musgrave was assured, the steps had been mended, only to be found loose again; so at last their unsafe condition was acquiesced in—with no doubt the same resignation displayed in Ireland in more commonplace cases of ill-repair.

There was certainly no scarcity of supernatural phenomena at Ardo. In addition to the mysterious staircase, and the unaccountable noises on the spot where the Prendergast tyrant hanged his servant, and the wails and shrieks of the poor betrayed "heir of Ardo's" spirit haunting his lost heritage, the ghost of Jeremiah Coghlan, father of the two lovely and ambitious peeresses, cannot apparently rest at peace, but has been seen riding a ghostly steed about the roads of Ardo, where he once carried a crimson banner triumphantly in honour of the marriage day of one of his daughters. A gentleman now deceased, who formerly lived in the neighbourhood, and was much respected throughout the countryside, had the idea of purchasing Ardo some time after it had passed out of the Coghlan family's possession, but was deterred from doing so by the fatalities and superstitions with which the place was associated; and on one occasion he had a personal adventure which seemed to him to justify the common rumours. He was riding away from Ardo House by one of its approaches, which had formerly been lined by trees—these were felled, however, before the occurrence in question—when his horse, a well-bred, spirited beast, began to tremble violently, and at last stopped, and utterly refused to move on. His master could see or hear nothing to cause this fright, and tried to urge the animal forward ; he could not get it to stir, however, and it broke out into a violent lather of foam and sweat, so that at last he had to dismount and tie his silk handkerchief over its eyes. The horse then bounded forwards, and was almost uncontrollable during the rest of the ride home. This occurred at one of the places where Mr. Coghlan's ghost was said to wander.

Accounts differ as to the place where Anne Coghlan first met Lord Barrymore. A probable version is that which asserts that Miss Coghlan met her future husband at a military ball in Youghal—a town only a few miles from Ardo, though divided from it by the river Blackwater. It is also possible that they first met at Lismore Castle, where her relatives, the Connors, saw much company; or at Dromana, near Lismore, the seat of the Grandison family, and with which the name of Barrymore had tragic associations. Dromana is magnificently situated on a rock overhanging the Blackwater river, and commands a perfect view of the finest reach of the river, and of great stretches of wooded country, and the Knockmeldown mountains. One of the rooms facing the river, from the windows of which one can almost look down sheer into the dark water, is called the Balcony Room. It was in this room that Richard, the sixth Earl of Barrymore, shot himself in 1773, after a night of heavy losses at cards. He was the guest of the last Earl Grandison,[1] who died in 1800, and who was one of the chief figures of a very fast set when heavy stakes and high play were the fashion of the day. It is almost needless to say that Lord Barrymore's uneasy spirit cannot rest, but haunts the room where the tragedy occurred. The belief in this ghost, or ghosts rather

[1] For Lady Grandison, see page 49.

obtained curious confirmation some years ago, when, the room being used as an oratory, or private chapel, a lady sent her maid into it late at night to fetch a prayer-book which had been left there. The maid returned without the book, saying she had opened the door, but had not liked to go in, fearing to disturb the party of gentlemen who were in the room playing at cards. To this day noises and mysterious sounds disturb the silence of night at Dromana, and are laid to the accounts of the wild revellers and gamblers of this story. It is curious that the seventh Earl was shot accidentally in 1793, while escorting French prisoners between Folkestone and Dover, just twenty years after his father's suicide. The follies, vanities, and vices of Richard, the seventh Earl, are set forth in his obituary notice in the *Gentleman's Magazine* of May, 1793, with considerable frankness, by a candid biographer who, while entitling his subject " this popular, witty, and eminently gifted young nobleman," sandwiches flattering epithets with a record of profligacy, folly and stupid jesting, in a manner almost to suggest malice. " The Life of the late Earl of Barrymore," published by Symonds in 1793, will fill in the picture of this unedifying peer's life for those who care to know more of it, and contemporary books dealing with society gossip contain occasional references to him and his successor to the title. His only brother, Henry, the eighth and last Earl of Barrymore, married, two years after his brother's death, Anne, " eldest daughter of Jeremiah Coghlan, of Ardo."

After her brilliant marriage Lady Barrymore went the way of her husband, and found herself plunged into the vortex of dissipation of the fastest set in London, where her beauty and Irish charm found full appreciation, and she carried off with her from Ardo to town, Eliza, her almost equally beautiful sister. Among her sister's gay friends, and in the world of fashion, Eliza Coghlan won much admiration, but several proposed matches of an advantageous character failed to end satisfactorily through fear of the wild Barrymore connection. Subsequently she met and became the wife, as already stated, of the Duc de Castries, at that time an *emigré* living in London in comparative poverty. The children of this marriage were two sons, Alix,

Comte de Castries, and Olonville de Castries, who died young ; and one daughter, Adèle, whose life was cut short at the moment of its rarest promise. Through the De Castries family, Eliza Coghlan was grandmother of Marshal M'Mahon, Duc de Magenta. The Duc de Castries returned to France [1] with the Bourbons, and at the coronation of Louis XVIII., an Irish lady of rank, present at the ceremonies said she saw the Duchesse de Castries, *née* Coghlan of Ardo, seated before the assembled sovereigns, enjoying, by virtue of some De Castries privilege, the right to sit while others stood in the presence of royalty. It was also reported that when the Duc de Castries resumed possession of his *hotel* in Paris, abandoned in the "Terror," he found it unpillaged, and everything in order, just as he left it. Under the Bourbons he obtained full recovery of his estates and honours. The Duchess died at the height of her fortunes, and Lady Barrymore took her place with the children, and, childless herself, devoted the rest of her life to their care, taking up her permanent residence in France. The Duchesse de Castries, had had a great success as a beauty in Paris—crowds following her carriage to obtain a sight of " La Belle Anglaise." It is to the credit of Lady Barrymore and her sister that they never forgot their old mother in her loneliness among the wild stormy cliffs of Ardo, but sent her every day a minute account of their doings. It is to be feared that these letters, which would be such rich literary treasures in our day, were destroyed or lost in the condition of confusion into which Ardo fell, when the idiot children continued to live on there for a short time after their mother's death.

The contrasts of the family fortunes must have seemed vivid indeed to Mrs. Coghlan, ageing among her wild cliffs and rocks. For her, poverty, a crumbling, decaying mansion, the thundering of the surf, and the cry of the sea-birds, the foolish talk or foolish silence of the idiot children ; for her daughters, the

---

[1] The Duc de Castries, after his restoration to the family honours, was made governor of Rouen. Cyrus Redding mentions him as a polished man of the Bourbon school, who, as Demouriez says, would have thought all France ruined if an individual came to court with a ribbon in place of a buckle in his shoes. He was very unpopular.—[ED.]

gayest *salons* of Paris and London, the glitter of courts, the homage and flatteries to rank, and the apparent enjoyment of life and luxury to the uttermost. But while no shadow of unhappiness was ever believed to have fallen on the married life of the Duchesse de Castries, rumour credited the Countess of Barrymore with the reverse of her sister's experience. Stories were told of her husband's conduct towards her that were very miserable, and disgraceful to him. Possibly while outwardly gay, and seeming to enjoy a reckless, frivolous life, her thoughts went longingly homewards to her mother and the peace of Ardo.

After the death of their mother, somewhere about 1823, Jerry and Tamsin continued to reside at Ardo for a little time ; but the money matters of the family had become so involved that they were removed to Lismore, to live there under the care of a Mrs. Gurley, said to have been formerly in the service of the family. It was a cruel grief to poor little Miss Tamsin to leave her home, to which she was so devotedly attached, and her accustomed seat by the chimney corner, where she used to play with the dolls sent to her by those great ladies, her sisters, and prattle of everything under the sun, including the tragedy of the discovery beneath the stairs. She loved dolls, and a lady who often visited her at Lismore, described her thus :—

"She was very tiny and picturesque, always dressed in white, and she delighted in the engravings of the *Illustrated London News*, which we used to colour for her."

She liked attention, and being visited, and to receive presents of cake and pieces of silk and ribbon for her dolls. It must have been a strange, pathetic sight to see the little old lady—she lived to be eighty-five—dressed in childlike white, and with the expression and mind and language of a child, playing with her dolls. All those who knew her represent her as gentle and winning. A lady who knew her well wrote of her as follows, describing her rigid Protestantism : "I remember the old lady particularly telling me that the people she lived with, and who had the care of her, were earnestly endeavouring to induce her to become a

Romanist, but that she never would consent. She had been always in the habit of repeating the Lord's Prayer and Apostles' Creed morning and evening, and one evening they brought a priest, who tried to convince her that the creed was in favour of *his* religion, not *hers*, for she said, ' I believe in . . . . the Holy Catholic Church.' Now *his* was the Holy Catholic and *hers only* the Protestant, etc.; but she said, ' I never repeat those words now. I say, " I believe in the Holy Church of my own persuasion." ' This acuteness in getting out of the dilemma struck me as the only glimpse of brightness I ever remarked in her. Since then I have frequently known half-witted persons show understanding of a religious truth who were very obtuse about ordinary matters." Similar accounts of her strong religious feelings were given by other persons who knew her well and saw her often. She had pleasure in attending the church " of her own persuasion," and resented being taken by her guardians to a Roman Catholic one; and she would hide when a priest called, but was delighted to see a Protestant clergyman, saying, " Ah, this is one of my own persuasion." While at Lismore she had the miniature portrait of Lady Barrymore that Lady Musgrave saw at Ardo, and was very proud of it, liking to show it as the picture of her beautiful sister. She was very fond of birds, but always particular that they must be hens. Also of babies—she was devoted to them, and would examine every article of their clothing to see if it were clean and well made up. When Ardo House was about to be pulled down and rebuilt, poor little Miss Tamsin heard of it, and begged so piteously to be taken to her old home, that those in charge of her conveyed her there, where she wandered from room to room through the whole place, weeping bitterly, and sobbing that she was the last of the Coghlans.

Jerry, the idiot boy, was fond of kittens, and used to carry them about in his pockets in the happy days of his life when he lived in his mother's care at Ardo. The boys on the roads used to rouse his anger by calling him " Pussy Mi-aow." He was kindly indulged by Mrs. Coghlan's friends, and used to fall in love sometimes—but only with those of his own rank who came up to his ideal of "fine rollicksome girls." He was extremely attached to the mother of a lady still living in the neighbourhood of Ardo. He could only be taught to count as far as five, and thought he was doing real man's work when minding his mother's sheep along the cliffs, but they might all be stolen or strayed if only five were left for him to count and bring home.

Lady Musgrave met him after Mrs. Coghlan's death on the cliffs near Crook-an-heire, and he turned away from her, sobbing bitterly, after telling her in his imperfect fashion that his mother was dead. He was also said to have been found one night lying in a swoon on her grave. He had always loved her most passionately. His life at Lismore in the care of a stranger was apparently a change which told harmfully on his nature, if it was not the direct cause of his falling rapidly into a worse mental state. He grew depressed, and would not walk unless some one went out with him. Mrs. Gurley took him one day into the garden and made him hold on to a clothes-line, thinking he would let go when tired and walk about; after a time she came back and found him still in the same position. He is described as having been a well-developed, tolerably good-looking man. He used to be tied frequently by his caretaker to prevent him from climbing up the roof of the house—a poor substitute for the cliffs and rocks where he used to wander unrestrained. His sad life ended about thirteen years after the irreparable loss of his mother. The entry of his burial is contained in the registry of the Protestant cathedral at Lismore: "Jeremiah Coghlan, Esq., late of Ardo, September 4th, 1836."

Although the Duchesse de Castries and her sister cannot be charged with neglect of their mother, it is impossible to acquit Lady Barrymore of unconcern for her unhappy brother and sister's fate. Shortly before Jeremiah's death, the Comte de Castries, his nephew, came to visit a family of the name of Lalor, then residing at Ardo, to make arrangements about the head-rent due to his family, and a ball was given in his honour in the house, and the prettiest girls in the neighbourhood danced on the lawn before him. He also went to Lismore and found the condition of his idiot uncle and aunt and their way of living such as to cause him a considerable shock. The sum of 50*l.* was allowed for the keep of each, and this was not increased after his visit. Whatever were the young Frenchman's feelings, no action was taken in the matter, and nothing was done to improve the nature of their surroundings.

Little "Miss Ta," as she was sometimes called, lived to be eighty-five, preserving to the end her childish appearance and expression of countenance. The same registry that records her brother's burial gives hers also: "Thomasina Coghlan, January 24th, 1856; age, 85 years."

The sixth Duke of Devonshire hearing, during one of his visits to Lismore Castle, of the sad and lowly state of the brilliant Countess of Barrymore's sister, visited her, and was shown by poor little Tamsin all her store of dolls and their clothes, made from cast-off finery of ball-dresses that had been sent to her by her sisters. The duke said he remembered Lady Barrymore as the centre of the gayest society in London, and he was distressed at the pitiful fate of a sister of so renowned a leader of fashion. He sent her many presents, and showed her many thoughtful kindnesses, which even limited intellects can appreciate. One especially superb doll, a present from the duke from London, was one of poor little Miss Tamsin's most treasured possessions.

Through the De Castries family, the interest in Ardo passed to Marshal M'Mahon. Twenty years ago or so advertisements appeared in the pages of the Cork newspapers, having reference to the sale of this interest, inserted by authority of Marshal M'Mahon, and giving his name as owner of the interest for sale. Ardo, or Ardigena as it is still called, has passed into the hands of Sir Joseph Neale M'Kenna, who has made considerable additions and repairs to the buildings, and dissipated the eerie look that hung around the place, compelling the mind to dwell on its past tragedies and the strange fortunes of its former inmates.

It would be interesting to know if any of those precious letters from Lady Barrymore and the Duchesse de Castries to their mother are in the possession of the M'Mahon family, and also if they have any of the miniatures or portraits of the Duc de Magenta's grandmother.[1] These are well known to have been at Ardo towards the end of Mrs. Coghlan's life, and, with other family pictures, showed her lovely daughters in the perfection of their youth and beauty.

---

[1] Gainsborough painted two portraits of a Miss Coghlan who was a belle at Bath in 1772. This may have been either Lady Barrymore or her sister. The portrait was engraved by Raphael Smith, and published by Parker, 1772.—[ED.]

THE name of Farren would seem to be associated in an intimate manner with the stage. Nineteen years ago, old William Farren died. He had been in *his* day the best Lord Ogleby and Sir Peter Teazle, as is now his son, William Farren,[1] one of our soundest actors, equipped with all the point and finish which distinguished the comedians of the past, and which is only to be acquired by years of training such as never comes in the way of our up-to-date actor, who is nothing but an exotic grown under pressure, and forced into sudden prominence. He knows nothing of that delicate perception of humour which does not bear *too* much handling, but communicates its meaning to the audience by a glance, a smile, a motion of the head or hand, which is the real expression of comedy. In all this William Farren is admirable, his face, with the slightly Volterian mouth, lending itself to the sly humour of certain situations, as in the scene where he takes the spectator into the joke of Joseph Surface and the French milliner.

Another clever member of the family was the inimitable "Nelly Farren"[2] whose walk was not genteel comedy but the humour of burlesque in its early days, when it *did* possess some claim to be what it called itself. It has now blossomed into a bad attempt at opera comique.

[1] There have been three generations of William Farrens, all actors in the same line. The elder William was excellent as "Grandfather White-head," "Sir Harcourt Courtly," etc. Hazlitt said of him "he plays the old gentleman, the antiquated beau of the last age, very much after the fashion that we remember to have seen him in our younger days, and that is quite a singular coincidence in this."

[2] Nelly Farren, daughter to Henry Farren, William the elder's son: he too had the family passion for the stage, but made no mark.

I have not studied the genealogical tree of the Farrens, and therefore I am not in a position to state in what, if any, degree of relationship either of the above mentioned artists stand to the great actress Elizabeth Farren.

Elizabeth was the youngest child of a Surgeon Farren, who was blessed with a large family, but without adequate means to support his annual blessings, his practice being indifferent, and his habits too loose and extravagant to remedy the ill-effects of evil fortune. His wife who, we are told, was ladylike and of gentle blood, thought to mend matters by returning to the stage from whence the Surgeon had taken her. Unfortunately her talent was mediocre, and the small gifts nature originally bestowed upon her had diminished rather than increased by the cares of married life; this would go without saying. On the other hand, Mrs. Farren's two daughters and her husband threw themselves with ardour into the theatrical profession. It was the Crummles over again (that is if one can apply this expression to what went before, as it is likely that the Farrens furnished material for the Crummles); the entire family were stage-struck. Mr. Farren threw up the un-grateful office of ministering to the few pauper patients who employed him, and finally adopted the stage as a profession. His first venture was in Shepherd's company.[1] Not finding this engagement satisfactory, Farren resolved upon being manager of a company of his own.

A strolling or sharing company, as it was called, was not difficult to organize, no permanent theatre being required;

---

[1] Barnard in his "Retrospections," tells a story of Farren which proves that he was a man of far superior attainments to his brutal manager. While stopping at a country inn he wrote on the window-pane four lines :—

> How different David's fate from mine,
> His blessed, mine is evil ;
> His Shepherd was the Lord Divine,
> My Shepherd is the Devil.

With the true spirit of a courtier, Barnard tells us that he immediately thought that if he could induce the landlord to sell him the *pane*, it would be an agreeable souvenir for Farren's daughter, then Countess of Derby. The landlord, however, would not agree. "Mr. Barnard," said he, "ever since Mr. Farren wrote those lines I have never wanted a lodger."

and everyone having a share in the profits, with a like division of labour. The system was simple. The company generally consisted of sixteen persons; the profits were divided into twenty shares; the manager took to himself five—four for any risk incurred, one as a performer—the remaining fifteen were divided, each player having one share, without regard to individual merit. In Farren's company he and his family got the lion's share of profits, his wife and himself taking the chief parts, whilst the two children appeared as infant phenomena. Curiously enough there was a Mr. Snodgrass in the company, who figured in the bills as Osmond Brontes; another actor was christened FitzMontagu.

On Christmas Eve, 1769, we first get acquainted with the Farren company as it made its entrance into the town of Salisbury. Not being able, through want of means, to advertise their arrival, these sharing companies generally advertised *themselves* by a procession through the streets; in this way did Mr. Farren appear. First came *the drummer*,[1] then the weary troupe in their most decent apparel, then Mr. Farren with a stage walk, *à la* Crummles, leading by the hand his youngest child, Lizzie; a cart with the properties brought up the rear. The whole procession jarred upon the religious susceptibilities of the mayor of Salisbury, who was a god-fearing man, and strong in his denunciations against "players." On Christmas Eve too, disturbing the quiet of the town and obstructing the thoroughfare. He would see what right these strollers had to offend against his, the mayor's, principles. He at once made out an order for the manager of the troupe to appear before him, and demanded to see his license; this was not forthcoming, and although Farren pleaded that he had the money and was ready to pay, the mayor would not listen, and the luckless manager was clapped into Salisbury jail, there to spend his Christmas day. That he escaped this misadventure was due to the

---

[1] The drum was considered by some companies *infra dig.*, and at the bottom of the bills would be found—"This company does not *beat the drum*." Some companies could not afford a cart, and carried all their properties with them, which must have had a ragged, motley appearance.

quick wit of Mr. Snodgrass, alias Osmond Brontes, who assuming his own name and adding to it a clerical prefix, waited on the mayor disguised as a Church of England clergyman who happened to have just arrived in Salisbury and wished to give his worship some money towards the Christmas charities, if there was any prisoner in jail who for a certain sum might be liberated? In this way Mr. Farren was enabled to join his family, but the incident of his imprisonment is associated with a pretty touch of romance.

Early on this Christmas morning, while he was yet under lock and key, his little girl Lizzie made her way through the snow, which lay thick on the ground, to where her father was shut up; she carried carefully in her hand a bowl of bread-and-milk. The child would, however, have found it difficult to reach the window through which she was to pass her father's breakfast, if she had not met with kindly help from a boy a few years older than herself, who had seen her go by his father's shop and followed her to the prison. This boy was later on Chief Justice Boroughs.

For three years Mr. Farren continued his precarious calling of manager of a travelling company, the little Lizzie, like the infant phenomenon, being put up as an attraction, playing columbine in the Christmas entertainments, and dancing and singing between the parts. Farren, however, had fallen into intemperate habits; he constantly came on the stage too tipsy to play his part, and was quite unfit for the office of manager. This was a time of sore distress to the little family, from which, however, the death of Farren relieved them. Mrs. Farren was an energetic woman, and, free from the burden of a drunken husband, soon placed herself in comparative comfort. She removed to Liverpool, where her brother, a trader in good position, lived. Either he or Whitley, the manager of the Chester company, got her an introduction to Younger, the manager of the Liverpool theatre: she and her two daughters presented themselves to him. Younger was a humane man, as well as a prudent, far-seeing manager; he at once saw the merits of the two girls, and as salaries were in those days small in comparison to what they are now, he made no difficulty as to likewise engaging their mother. Margaret, afterwards Mrs. Knight, played chambermaids, and Lizzie the juvenile leads, varied by an occasional part, such as Edward the Fifth. It was to Younger she owed her first step in life. In 1777 he introduced her to Colman,[1] who engaged her for the Haymarket Theatre. The family therefore removed to London, taking lodgings in Suffolk Street, to be near the theatre, where the young actress appeared in minor characters; she did not, however, attract any attention until her constant friend Younger came to London as the stage manager of Drury Lane. Miss Farren was engaged permanently as an articled pupil, and during the winter of 1777-8 she played alternately at the two theatres, there being a coalition between the managers; her first part of any note was that of Miss Hardcastle, in which, however, she made little impression. Mrs. Clive, Mrs. Abingdon, Mrs. Baddeley, Mrs. Cibber, and Mrs. Barry made a galaxy of "stars" almost unsurpassed at any period of the drama; these had the monopoly, so to speak, of public favour, and there seemed to be no place for the beginner. The dramatic censor of the day gave her some mild words of encouragement, somewhat akin to damning with faint praise; assurances that later on she might hope to be an acquisition; but before that time arrived she should conquer her diffidence, learn how to tread the stage, modulate her tone of voice, study to be correct in spirit, varied in action, and give to her feelings a proper utterance, by suitable expression of voice and countenance. This was a disheartening opening for the *debutante*, who with her friends had reckoned on a brilliant success. Yet the check was wholesome, especially as the advice was taken in good part. From this time Miss Farren made every effort to correct the faults which had passed unnoticed when she was playing to provincial audiences, the result being the attainment of such a measure of success as to excite the alarm of the public favourites, who could bear no

---

[1] Colman used to tell an amusing story of Mrs. Farren having a pocket lined with tin, constructed inside her dress, in which she carried her own and her daughter's luncheon; the tin prevented the gravy from escaping.

rival to approach their throne. Her first success that can be counted as general was in Colman's play "Separate Maintenance." The part of the heroine was to have been played by Mrs. Abingdon, but Sheridan, who did not wish his great attraction to be discounted at a summer theatre, offered her her own terms to refuse the engagement, which she did. There was nothing left to Colman but to give the part to Miss Farren, which he did reluctantly. She, however, scored such a success as to be quite on the same platform as Mrs. Abingdon, in proof of which an allusion was added to the prologue on the second or third night of the performance,—

"A Younger Princess hoists the Empress' flag."

The advent of the "younger princess" had no doubt something to say to the calmness with which Sheridan viewed the retirement of Mrs. Abingdon.[1] When this event happened, Miss Farren stepped quite naturally into the popular favourite's parts, which she played to admiration.

Her fine ladies have never been surpassed and rarely equalled by any actress. "In distinction of manner and refinement she excelled Mrs. Abingdon, who," says Horace Walpole, "could never go beyond Lady Teazle, which is a second-rate character, and," he adds, "that rank of women are always aping women of fashion without arriving at the style . . .": whereas he ascribes Miss Farren's superiority in elegance and the true manners of society to the fact that she had associated with the best style of men (and he might have added women) in England; so that her fine lady was not a brummagem imitation, but the real thing, with the true ring in those elegant levities which belong to such characters as Lady Teazle, Lady Towneley, and Lady Betty Modish.[2] These,

---

[1] Mrs. Abingdon did not retire until 1782, and Miss Farren became the leading actress of Drury Lane.

[2] The latest revival of the "School for Scandal" by the Daly Company was an example of this want of grasp of the true key. All that representation could do was done; the minor details of furnishing the piece with old-fashioned bureau-chairs, dressing the characters with wigs, sacques, and patches were in perfect taste, and an excellent reproduction of a hundred and fifty years ago. This only brought out in stronger contrast the want of vitality in the Sneerwell, Backbite, Mrs.

when reproduced by the dramatists of the day, required much finesse in the acting. "No actress," says Colman, "has ever performed so perfectly the character of Lady Towneley as did Miss Farren; her levity was never wanting, and her mirth had no approach to *rudeness.*" This last word touches the real note, and it is here that the actresses of our day oftentimes misinterpret such characters as Lady Teazle, the Country girl, and Miss Hardcastle. They present vulgar hoydens, without any trace of the sly humour, elegant trifling, and real refinement which distinguished the women of the last century, and which should be delicately conveyed to the audience to make the part a real success.

It was here that Miss Farren excelled, and the delusion was so perfect that the spectators began to imagine that the actress was really the character she was only portraying; this was not quite the case with Lady Teazle, which differs very essentially from Lady Towneley. In the latter there is no disparity between husband and wife, and the vulgarity which, in the village girl, should all along be apparent through the slight veil of assumed fine-ladyism, can never be present in the lady of quality who, born to fortune and station, is secure of her place in society, and can take certain liberties with the world of fashion. If these conditions are remembered, the disputes between the married pair are simply delightful; the presentation, however, requires rare gifts, especially in the actress. It is doubtful if there is, at this moment, any one on our stage, unless, perhaps, Miss Terry (and *she* lacks certain qualities), who could essay the part with even a moderate chance of representing with success the combination of archness, repartee, spirit, feeling, and refinement which Miss Farren gave to her representation, and in which she has never been equalled. Her elegance of appearance was much in her favour, as was also her refined manner of answering her lord's reproaches. The scene is worth quoting :—

LORD TOWNELEY : Going out so soon after dinner, Madam?
LADY TOWNELEY : Lard, my lard, what can I possibly do at home?
LORD T. : What does my sister, Lady Grace, do at home?

Candour, and Lady Teazle, the one brilliant exception being Sir Peter. Here we had the real note struck, and what a difference it made !

LADY T.: Why, that is to me amazing. Have you ever any pleasure at home?

LORD T.: It might be in your power, Madam, to make home a little more comfortable to me.

LADY T.: Comfortable! and so, my good lord, you would really have a woman of my rank and spirit stay at home to comfort her husband? Lord, what notions of life some men have!

LORD T.: Don't you think, Madam, some ladies' notions are full as extravagant?

LADY T.: Yes, my lord, when the tame doves live coop'd within the pen of your precepts. I do think them prodigious indeed.

LORD T.: And when they fly wild about this town, Madam, pray what must the world think of them?

LADY T.: Oh, the world is not so ill-bred as to quarrel with any woman for liking it.

LORD T.: Nor am I, Madam, a husband so well bred as to bear my wife's being so fond of it; in short, the life you lead, Madam,—

LADY T.: Is to me the pleasantest in the world.

LORD T.: Madam, it is time to ask you one serious question.

LADY T.: Don't let it be long in coming then—for I am in haste.

LORD T.: Madam, when I am serious I expect a serious answer.

LADY T.: Before I know the question?

LORD T.: Psha—. Have I power, Madam, to make you serious by entreaty?

LADY T.: Well, then, you have.

LORD T.: Now then, recollect your thoughts, and tell me seriously why you married me?

LADY T.: Why then, my lord, to give you at once a proof of my sincerity and obedience—I think I married to take off that restraint that lay upon my pleasures while I was a single woman.

LORD T.: How, Madam, is any woman under less restraint after marriage than before it?

LADY T.: Oh, my lord, my lord, they are quite different creatures! Wives have infinite liberties in life that would be terrible in an unmarried woman to take. A married woman may have men at her toilet; invite them to dinner, call them by their Christian names, and in her *Gaieté du Cœur* toast a pretty fellow.

Miss Farren's acting of Lady Towneley raised her at once to a high position. Tate Wilkinson compared her to Peg Wollington, but considered her manner more polished. He made a scale of comparison, which was then much in vogue, between the dead and the living actress—which ran in this wise:—

Mrs. Woffington tall.	So is Miss Farren.
Mrs. Woffington beautiful.	So is Miss Farren.
Mrs. Woffington elegant.	So is Miss Farren.
Mrs. Woffington well bred (?).	So is Miss Farren.
Mrs. Woffington had a harsh, broken, discordant voice.	Miss Farren's voice is bewitching.
Mrs. Woffington could be rude and vulgar.	Miss Farren . . never.

"So undoubtedly," he adds, "Miss Farren seizes the wreath of fame with security, as she adds to her perfections in the scale of merit, virtue, modesty, reverence to a parent, and every other endearing quality; therefore, let me twirl my cap and cry, long live 'the Farren.'"

Despite Tate Wilkinson's eulogistic twirling of his cap, it may fairly be doubted that Miss Farren was possessed of even a tenth portion of the cleverness with which Peg Woffington was gifted. She lacked many of the qualities which distinguished her predecessor; she had little variety, and had none of the sympathetic gifts which are absolutely necessary for a great actress. She could not go one inch beyond light comedy parts, whereas Woffington could move her audience to tears as well as provoke them to laughter. Her versatility, likewise, was wonderful, and she could play men's parts with the same facility as women's. Miss Farren essayed but once what is called, in stage language, a breeches part;[1] it would have been more to her credit had she never done so, as one could then assume her maiden modesty stood in the way of exhibiting her person in masculine attire. The truth, however, has fairly to be told that her figure looked so exceedingly unshapely,[2] and she made altogether such an awkward appearance, that she never repeated the experiment. One of her admirers said she was a straight line from head to foot, and that her legs were like a sugar loaf.

On other points all must agree with Wilkinson that she was far superior to Mrs. Woffington. Her propriety of conduct has never been doubted; it was rare, in the time in which she lived, to find one in her profession, exposed to so many temptations, who had any claim to virtue, or who would be admitted into society — not only admitted, but received on a footing of intimate friendship, by ladies of unblemished propriety as well as of the highest position. The Duchess of Leinster, Lady Ailesbury, Mrs. Damer, Lady Cecilia Johnstone and Lady Dorothy Thompson, were amongst her friends.

---

[1] This was as Nancy Lovell in Colman's play, "The Suicide."

[2] Her figure was tall but not sufficiently muscular; with a little more embonpoint it would have been one of the finest in the theatre.

It has been urged against Miss Farren, that "being alive to
the advantages she might gain from such society, she was
careful never to do anything that might forfeit the esteem of
the crowd of fashionables who caressed her." If this were true,
it would not detract from her merit, although it might lower
the high standard upon which her virtue was founded. There
can be little doubt her disposition was cold, if not calculating;
she was never known to give way to any gusts of passion, and
all through her career is not credited with any "green-room
attachment" for man or woman; except a short spasm of
sentiment for John Palmer, the actor, which not being re-
ciprocated, speedily died a natural death.

It was this coldness which interfered with her playing any
tender or touching part with success. "Her sentiment," says an
intelligent critic, "was never successful, because it was over-
strained, unreal, and in contrast to her fine lady parts, artificial.
There was no pathos in her grief, nothing spontaneous in her
love." This was the only false note in her acting, it rendered
the penitential scene of Lady Towneley ineffective, her sentiment being so evidently artificial. The young actress herself
was aware of her deficiency, and her taste led her to prefer
light comedy, but either her managers or the public forced her
to play romantic heroines.

Towards the end of 1777 an event happened which influenced the young actress's future, and changed her position
very considerably. It would be idle to speculate whether,
without the incentive of a coronet in the future, Miss Farren's
life would have been so entirely *sans reproche* as it was; she
no doubt had everything to gain by an exercise of proper
restraint, and it is due to her to say she realized this fact very
thoroughly, and never lost sight of the end she had in view.
That her dreams of future greatness depended for fulfilment
upon the length of life accorded to another woman, would
seem to some minds unpleasantly calculative. But it does
not appear to have shocked her ideas of decorum, or those
of that dragon of propriety, her watchful mother, that the
encouragement she gave to the attentions of a married man
were hardly in accordance with the Farren *standard*. Lord

MISS FARREN, COUNTESS OF DERBY.

[To face page 296.

Derby, it is true, was not living happily with his wife, but it is worthy of notice that there was no talk of a separation until after his admiration for Miss Farren had become the passion of his life. It has been said that this attachment began after Lord Derby's separation from Lady Derby, which separation was due to her levity of conduct; an examination of those silent witnesses "dates" disproves this statement. It was in 1777 that Miss Farren first met her noble lover; the occasion some amateur theatricals given by the Duke of Richmond at Whitehall Place. The play was the "Heiress" written by General Burgoyne,[1] who only three years previously had composed the Masques in honour of Lord Stanley's marriage with Lady Betty Hamilton.[2]

Since then Lord Stanley had succeeded to his grandfather's title and estate. He and his beautiful young wife were living apparently happily together; he had just begun the em-

---

[1] General Burgoyne's "Lord of the Manor" went through ten editions, and is to be found in Villemain's "Hors d'œuvres des Theatres étrangers." Horace Walpole says :—" Burgoyne's battles and speeches will be forgotten, but his delicious comedy of the ' Heiress ' still continues to delight the stage."

[2] The "Heiress" was produced at the Haymarket, where it had a run of thirty nights, this being considered unusually long. It was pronounced by the judges to be the best comedy that had appeared since "The School for Scandal." It has not, however, held the stage as that delightful comedy has done, and hardly repays reading; its success was no doubt greatly due to the admirable performance of Miss Farren. Lord Berwick used to say, "Ah, that game of chess! that game of chess! I shall never see anything like it again." Horace Walpole was loud in praises of both the play and the actress; writing to Lady Ossory, he says, "General Burgoyne has written the best modern comedy for the same reason that Mrs. Oldfield played genteel comedy so well, because she not only followed but set the fashion. Who should act genteel comedy perfectly but people that have sense? Actors and actresses can only guess the tone of high life, and cannot be inspired by it. . . Why," he adds, "are there so few genteel comedies? But because most comedies are written by men not in that sphere. Etheridge, Congreve, Vanbrugh and Cibber wrote genteel comedy because they lived in the best company: so too with Miss Farren, who is as excellent as Mrs. Oldfield, and for the same reason." By this last sentence is meant that Miss Farren knew well all the ways and customs of the great ladies she imitated.

It does not seem quite certain whether Miss Farren acted the heroine, or merely directed the performance; having offered her help to oblige the Duchess of Leinster, sister to the Duke of Richmond.

s

bellishment of his magnificent house in Grosvenor Square, and was lavishing large sums of money upon the apartments set apart for the Countess. All seemed *couleur de rose;* the world had, at all events, heard no hint of domestic incompatibility.

I think, therefore, that one may fairly—without throwing any slur on Miss Farren's good name—date the change that came over the spirit of Lord Derby's dream to the amateur performance at Richmond House. His lordship was passionately fond of the stage, and his own pretensions to be an actor were fairly good. He played with a certain gravity and steadiness. The caste included the ladies of the family, with Mrs. Damer and Lord Henry FitzGerald, who was a light comedy actor. Charles Fox was stage manager, and Miss Farren directed the performance, having probably offered to do so, as she was under great obligations to the Duchess of Leinster, a daugher of the Duke of Richmond. The result of this green-room intimacy was to give the fascinating actress two lovers, Charles Fox and Lord Derby. At first Fox seemed to be first favourite. Miss Farren was either not aware of the impression she had made upon her noble admirer, or she was not able to resist the fascination which Fox is said to have exercised over every woman. She gave such decided encourgement to his attentions, as to set wagging the tongues of the Backbites and Sneerwells of society, who now predicted the immediate surrender of the immaculate star of propriety. Their astonishment was great when Fox suddenly withdrew into the cold shade of friendship; rumour, at fault for a reason, decided that his susceptibilities had been wounded by the thickness of his divinity's legs, when she deigned to show herself in masculine attire. The truth, however, gradually oozed out. Fox had made the actress an offer of what was called in the language of the day "carte blanche," and had been haughtily and decidedly repulsed. This affair raised her immensely in the estimation of her friends, especially Lord Derby, who was speedily made acquainted with all the particulars.

Matters at this moment were at high tension between him
and his young wife. Kind friends had been sure to tell her of
her husband's devotion to the new actress, and stung by
jealousy, she foolishly retaliated by a reckless levity which
her dignified Lord resented. Lady Derby's flirtation with
the Duke of Dorset has been spoken of elsewhere; [1] that there
was anything serious in it is clearly disproved by the fact that
Lord Derby's threats that he would seek a divorce came
to no fruition from want of evidence.

This is not the place to discuss what was the maximum or
minimum of Lady Derby's fault; there has been silence for
over one hundred years on the subject; it was said at the
time that she ran away, and, being caught by her brother,
the Duke of Hamilton, was brought back like a naughty
child, and punished accordingly. The separation which took
place by mutual consent after the birth of the third child,
proved beyond a doubt that the Countess was innocent so
far as any major fault was in question, for if the Earl could
have procured a divorce, he would have gladly availed himself
of the chance, in order to make Miss Farren his wife. As it
was, he entered into a conditional engagement with the actress.

"These sort of prospective arrangements, which hang upon
the life or death of an existing impediment, would be," says
Hazlitt, "to some minds quite as abhorrent as putting the impediment out of the way." Nor can there be any doubt that
in the case which we are considering, Lady Derby's death was
anxiously looked for by the pair of lovers. It is repulsive to
consider such a condition of things, so utterly out of accord
with either morality or religion; and although casuists may
defend such indecent compacts, we feel sure that at a higher
tribunal than ours they will meet the condemnation they
deserve. In this world, however, Miss Farren's cold-blooded
calculation was successful, but not for many long years.
Ill and suffering, a wreck in beauty and shattered in mind, the
Countess held firm hold of the title and position for which
her rival craved. Our sympathy for Lady Derby lessens
somewhat when we find that she too was anxious to divorce

[1] See memoir of Duchess of Argyll.

her husband, in order, it was said, to marry the Duke of
Dorset. Miss Farren was, however, far too astute to give
even a loophole to her enemies; it was asserted that she
never saw her lover alone even for the space of a minute.
Such extreme caution showed a want of confidence not
flattering to the Earl; it was, however, no part of the actress's
game to marry the man without being able to enjoy to the
full the benefits his position would afford her, and she was
therefore careful never to lower her guard, so that when the
moment of triumph did come, society should give her the
reward she deserved. One cannot help a feeling of malicious
pleasure in knowing that this reward was so long delayed;
years rolled on, and Miss Farren had to be content with playing
stage ladies of rank, her popularity in this line being ever
on the increase. Hazlitt, who rather sneers at her ladylike
airs and graces, acknowledges she had the most elegant
manipulation of her fan, and an indescribable turn of the head,
which went well with her tripping tongue. The refined and
difficile Walpole considered her the first of all actresses, but
makes an exception for her Beatrice, which he thought she did
not play well. This is strange; Beatrice being one of those
arch yet vivacious parts, mingled with a certain elegance, which
should have suited an actress of her style and figure. How
charmingly it has been played in our own day by one
who somewhat resembles Miss Farren, although it may be that
there are broader touches in Miss Terry's style than in that of
her predecessor, who was remarkable for the exquisite finish
of her acting. This last quality is not so much needed in
Shakspeare's heroines, who are more flesh and blood than
ideal women; and for this reason Miss Farren affectioned them
less than other actresses of her day. In 1779, Miss Farren
paid a short visit to Dublin, and played a round of her
favourite characters at Smock Alley Theatre. No particulars
of her visit are handed down either by Genest or Victor. This
silence on the part of two such garrulous writers would lead us
to the presumption that the actress had not made a success in
the Irish capital, which in those days had a reputation for
theatrical criticism beyond that enjoyed by either London or

Edinburgh. If she did not please her critics, she must have drawn large audiences, for her receipts were over 800*l*. On her return to London, she once more settled down to steady work. She was hardly a night absent from Drury Lane, playing a round of characters truly surprising: *Berinthia*, in the "Trip to Scarborough"; *Belinda*, in "All in the Army"; *Angelica*, in "Love for Love"; *Elvira*, in "The Spanish Friar"; *Hermione*, in "The Winter's Tale"; *Olivia*, in "Twelfth Night"; *Portia*, etc. It is not astonishing that some of this varied *repertoire* should not have suited her; one of her critics complains of an error into which her great popularity induced her to fall, and which she is entreated to correct. "She is too playful, too free in the management of her countenance, and understands too soon, and more than is consistent with the character she is playing. It is exceedingly painful," goes on this candid critic, "to the rational part of the audience, to see a young lady who is to take the head of an honourable house insinuate that she understands more than is becoming; she will be certain of giving more satisfaction by softening the colouring than by making it more glaring." She was likewise accused of certain tricks which were not approved of; "the nod of recognition and the simper of friendship should never make part of a public performance, neither should an actress fix her attention upon one box, and play to it rather than to the audience." This habit drew down upon the actress a rebuke from Lord Chesterfield who, when Colman's play "Lady Newberry" was much the fashion, came to see it. Chesterfield had just published one of his famous letters to his son, Philip Dormer, in which he had insisted strongly on the graces of manner, deportment, etc. In one of the scenes Lady Newberry says she has a receipt for making a fine gentleman. "A fine gentleman by receipt? Why, how is that?" asks one of the characters. "I will tell you in three words, the graces, the graces, the graces!" When the play was over, Lord Chesterfield came round to the green room and angrily told Miss Farren that when she had said "the graces," she had looked towards him, and so had turned the attention of the house on him.

Miss Farren was now in the perfection of her charms; her figure was above the middle height, graceful, and suited to the disposition of drapery, in which she was exceedingly happy, this serving to conceal the lack of plumpness which was her only defect; her eyes were blue, she had a lovely mouth and winning smile; her voice was sweet, more by cultivation than from nature, her intonation being occasionally somewhat nasal. After Mrs. Abingdon's retirement, in 1782, she at once stepped into the position of leading actress at Drury Lane, but this advance made no difference in the amount of work, or the punctuality with which she fulfilled her engagements; she seems to have steered her course through the theatrical world, which, as everyone knows, bristles with pitfalls for the unwary, with the utmost caution and dexterity. All through her career we hear of no quarrels with her managers, no bickerings with rival actresses, no stories attaching to her name. Much of this, no doubt, was due to the natural reserve of her character, and the excellent training she had received from her mother, whose own experience was beneficial to her daughter. It was she who advised the avoidance of green-room friendships, which generally share the fate of violent delights, in having violent endings. She put before the young actress the steady purpose she should have in view, and taught her to dissociate herself as far as possible from that lower element which unfortunately is the substratum of all professions, but more especially is to be found in the theatrical. Miss Farren had an aim in view, and never forgot that one day she might be called to fill a high position, and that it would be to her advantage to avoid any contact with those, the disorder of whose lives was matter of notoriety, and who thus brought the stage into contempt.[1] One must admire

[1] The only time she departed from this rule was when she spoke the appeal for the unfortunate Ann Bellamy, but this was in the cause of charity, see page 40. It is worth while to quote here an incident which took place before Miss Farren joined the Drury Lane company, and which gives an idea of the character of such women as Mrs. Baddeley and Mrs. Abingdon, as also of the manners of the day. In 1773 the managers of the Pantheon had framed strict rules for the exclusion of doubtful characters; these were much resented by the young bloods of the day, who were resolved that whoever were excluded, Sophia

her for her steadiness in refusing to hold any connection
beyond what stage requirements necessitated with such
"damaged peaches" as Mesdames Abingdon, Baddeley, or
Robinson, while to Mrs. Siddons she accorded the honour of
a close friendship; and also to the charming authoress of the
ever delightful simple story, she extended a kind and eminently useful patronage, remembering the friendship which,
in the old days of struggle now so far behind, had existed
between her father and Mr. Inchbald.

We can easily imagine with what feelings she was regarded
by those of her sister actresses whose life was cast on such
different lines. How they envied her, and turned into ridicule
her fine lady airs, and jeered at her chariot, and her footman,
and her noble admirer. The sting of it all was, that there

Baddeley should be admitted. Twenty gentlemen, headed by Mr.
Hanger and Mr. Conway, Lord Hertford's son, met together and vowed
to carry the matter through. They formed an escort round her chair as
she proceeded along Oxford Street, and by the time she was set down
in the porch of the Pantheon, her escort had increased to fifty of the
most elegant noblemen and gentlemen in town. The constables allowed
her amiable friend Mrs. Steele to pass. When, however, the fair
Sophia followed, they lowered their staves, and civilly but resolutely
refused to allow her to enter, saying their orders were not to admit any
players. This was putting the refusal in the politest form, for Mrs.
Baddeley's reputation was such that she would have been refused
entrance, had her station in society been of the most unexceptional. Her
gallant defenders were not going to let the matter end thus. Fifty
swords flew from their scabbards, the constables gave way before this
valorous onslaught; the chivalrous protectors of the offended lady then
raised their sword-points, and with flashing steel surrounding her, the
heroine of the hour passed proudly into the Rotunda. Even then the
"honest indignation" of the escort was not appeased. They refused to
sheath their swords until an apology had been offered by the management, and when this was done the two highest ladies in the room, the
Duchess of Ancaster and her Grace of Argyll, came forward to assure
the blushing actress of the satisfaction it gave them to receive such an
addition to their assembly. A messenger was immediately despatched
to Mrs. Abingdon, who was waiting in her chair hard by to hear the
result of Mrs. Baddeley's attempt to force the citadel of propriety.
Forthwith this fair but doubtful lady made her entrance, and from this
night no further effort was made to keep the Pantheon more select as
to company than was either Ranelagh or Vauxhall. One would have
supposed that the introduction of these "damaged peaches" would have
induced ladies of rank and with proper feelings of decorum to withdraw
their countenance from places of amusement where their daughters were
likely to rub shoulder to shoulder with such characters. Nothing of the
sort; the very fact added piquancy to the entertainment, and the rooms
were more crowded than before, after the Baddeley incident.

was no weak point in her armour of propriety for malice to seize upon, while the respectful devotion paid to this statue of virtue increased their hatred and envenomed their malice, which in no way injured the object of their dislike.

Her popularity as an actress, instead of diminishing, seems to have been on the increase ; the nights she played the house was always crowded. The manager, with a due regard to the coronet looming in the near future, put her forward on all public occasions, knowing that to see " Miss Farren " was a sure draw. When Drury Lane was opened in 1794, after its being rebuilt by Holland, it was Miss Farren who spoke the epilogue. In this she assured the audience that there need be no panic at any time as to fire, as there was water enough in the house to drown them all at a moment's notice. The scene then shifted and showed a real lake on the stage, with a boat which was rowed by a man, while the band played " A Jolly Young Waterman." After this realistic performance, an enormous sheet of iron [1] descended, leaving Miss Farren between it and the footlights, when she pointed out in her bewitching voice that this strong defence was meant (in case fire broke out on the stage) to ensure the safety of the spectators.

> No, we assure you generous benefactors
> Will only burn the scenery and the actors. [2]

Miss Farren had now been close on twenty years before a London audience ; her popularity was untouched. A greater triumph still was the constancy of her noble lover, who for seventeen years had served for his mistress as faithfully and far longer than Jacob had done for Rachel. Fidelity like this, seeing

---

[1] The opening for the curtain was 45 feet wide, and 38 high. It was about seven times the height of the performers. There was room in the theatre for 3000 persons all seated, but it was with difficulty the actors could be heard.

Despite this assurance, Drury Lane was again destroyed by fire in 1809. This was the third time. The original theatre was burned in 1671 ; the second, designed by Wren in 1674, new faced and decorated by Adam in 1771, was taken down in 1794, and replaced by Holland's Wilderness, as Mrs. Siddons called it, burned in 1809. The present structure was erected in 1812 from designs by Wyatt.

that it is a rare virtue, excites both wonder and respect. He was never happy but when he was with her. Every afternoon the now rather obese Earl could be seen crossing Grosvenor Square to the little bow-windowed house in Green Street, where Miss Farren had established herself (in the opinion of some, rather indecorously near). On other occasions he would accompany her home from rehearsal, puffing hard from want of breath, as he tried to keep up with her more youthful steps, she sometimes out of mischief going on very fast, to his infinite distress. In the evening he was always in his box close to the stage, listening with never wearied attention to the tones of the voice he loved, and glass in hand studying every turn of her head, every glance of her eye. Miss Wynne, whose "Diary of a Lady of Quality" is such pleasant reading, records when she went with friends to see "The School for Scandal," how they noticed, in the screen scene, Lord Derby leave his box and creep round to the stage to have a word with Miss Farren; and wicked Miss Wynne, then a mischievous young girl, wished that the screen behind which he had hid himself, would fall, and disclose to the audience Lord Derby as well as Lady Teazle.[1] Occasionally his lordship, who had elegant tastes, would break out into rhyme as a vent to his feelings. There were lines to a portrait of Miss Farren by Humphrey, with all the high-flown compliments then in use, and lines to Miss Farren on her being absent one Sunday from church, which are something better.

> " While wondering angels when they looked from high,
> Observed thy absence with a holy sigh,
> To them a bright ethereal Seraph said,
> Blame not the conduct of th' exalted Maid,
> Where'er she goes, her steps can never stray,
> Religion walks, companion of her way.
> She goes with every virtuous thought impressed,
> Heaven on her face, and heaven within her breast."

Society meanwhile looked on half amused, half interested

---

[1] All the world knows that it is due to this nobleman that the time-honoured "Derby," of which every Englishman is proud, was instituted, the race being run on Epsom Downs—which forms part of "the Oaks" property at Banstead, Surrey—in 1787. The race was won by the Earl's horse, called *Sir Peter Teazle*, a delicate compliment. Sir Peter was painted by Gilpin.

at this unusual spectacle of patient love and mutual forbear-
ance. Strangely enough, as is often the case, the world
respected what it could not imitate, and did not ridicule a
virtue which was so out of keeping with the morals of the day.
Here and there a mild jest would be hazarded; some lines
were sent to Miss Farren admonishing her not to play Darby
and Joan too early; or Horace Walpole writes to his
flame, Mary Berry, and tells her "that the east wind is as constant as my Lord Derby." In some of the scurrilous papers
a few ill-natured caricatures are to be found, with very little
point. On the whole the lovers came off easy, Miss Farren's
prudence, which seemed to increase with years, rendering it
impossible to assail her character. Her position was still
further strengthened by the support she received from her
own friends, who were warmly attached to her, and likewise
from Lord Derby's circle of relations, who, with few exceptions,
treated her with all the respect and affection that was as much
due to personal regard as to the position in the family she
would one day fill. People of the best position, and distinguished as well for their own merits, were flattered at
being asked to the little suppers given by Miss Farren after
the play. Mrs. Farren always presided, and the company
included such names as General Conway, Horace Walpole,
Kemble, Mrs. Siddons, the Ogilvies, Lady Ailesbury, Mrs.
Damer, General Burgoyne, and all the pleasantest and best
known people in London. "Ah, those charming suppers,"
Lord Berwick would say, "where we meet the best of good
company."

Through all this weary time of waiting, which grew more
weary as time went on, Miss Farren was punctual in her attendance at the theatre. Only once was there a little friction
with the public; this was in 1796, on the occasion when
Holcroft's "Force of Ridicule" was produced, in which Miss
Farren created the part of the heroine. When the usual time of
commencing had elapsed, some disapprobation was expressed,
and Mr. Palmer appeared to inform the audience that as Miss
Farren had not come, they were apprehensive she had been
taken suddenly ill, but that a message had been despatched to

her house. The messenger returning with the news Miss Farren
was too ill to leave her room, the manager announced that
Isabella was to be substituted, but that those who wished to leave
would receive their money. The pit and galleries were at once
deserted, few remaining to see Mrs. Siddons, who came from
Covent Garden, where she was witnessing the performance.
A letter appeared next day in the paper to assure the public
Miss Farren's illness was *bona fide*; nevertheless, there were
rumours that jealousy of a new actress, Miss Ducamp, and
some dispute about a satin gown, was at the bottom of the
affair. The piece came on on the 6th of December, 1796 : the
house was crowded, and when the curtain rose there were
some signs of dissatisfaction, which made the actress nervous.
Wroughton, however, made an apology for her unintentional
offence, and the play proceeded.

This incident must have shown Miss Farren that favour even
such as she had enjoyed was liable to a reverse. Fortunately
for her, she had only to seek popularity for a short time ; her day
of triumph was at hand. In the April following the production
of "The Force of Ridicule," the only impediment to her
elevation to rank and wealth ceased to exist ; the Countess of
Derby, on the 4th March,[1] 1797, passed away from a world
which had not shown itself too kind to her. The later years
of her life had been very different from that of her brilliant
rival.

For years she had suffered from a slow and painful disease,
and society had seen little of the once gay, beautiful, and
wilful young creature, who had turned the heads of half
London. Her coronet, which for so long had been Miss
Farren's ambition, now lay within her grasp. When the
news of Lady Derby's death was known, there was a
wonderful clatter of tongues, and high betting at White's ; not
that this was a particular compliment, as the members would
bet on the wagging of a sparrow's tail. However, there were

---

[1] Lady Derby died at the house of G. J. Hamilton, Gloucester Street,
Portman Square, and was buried at Bromley, Kent, on the 2nd April.
The papers of the day add " her own family paying all her debts, which
amounted to £5000."

doubts as to whether the Earl would fulfil his promise (every-one knew there was a promise), and gratify Miss Farren's ambition by making her at last his Countess. Report said his affections had grown somewhat cooler, or that time had staled her infinite variety; then, again, it was whispered young Lord Stanley had entered the field against his father, and was now Miss Farren's chaperone to and from the theatre. The malicious forgers of all these *on dits* were destined to be disappointed.

The newly-made widower showed an indecent haste in avail-ing himself of his happiness. Lady Derby died on March 4th, and the marriage took place in six weeks. It would have been sooner, only that the *youthful* bridegroom was seized with a fit of the gout, which is no respecter of lovers' vows. Previously to this, Miss Farren took leave of the stage. This was made the scene of a demonstration in favour of the popular actress, who must have felt a curious but mixed sensation of triumph, regret and nervousness, as she came on the stage for the last time. It was on the 8th of April; the house was crowded from floor to ceiling. The play was "The School for Scandal," and the cast was as follows :—

Sir Peter Teazle .	.	.	Mr. King.
Charles Surface .	.	.	Mr. Wroughton.
Joseph Surface .	.	.	Mr. Palmer.
Careless .	.	.	Mr. C. Kemble.
Crabtree .	.	.	Mr. Suett.
Mrs. Candour .	.	.	Miss Pope.
Lady Teazle .	.	.	Miss Farren.

Miss Farren was (her detractors said *pretended* to be) much moved ; as the play went on her emotion was painfully exhibited, it was with the utmost difficulty she got through her part. When she came to the last scene, her emotion overpowered her. This was evident in the concluding words of Lady Teazle's last speech.

" Let me also request that you will make my compliments to the scandalous college of which you are president, and in-form them that Lady Teazle, licentiate, begs leave to return the diploma they granted her, as she leaves off practice, and kills characters no longer." Here she stopped, looked at the audience, and burst into tears. King then led her forward, and Wroughton spoke the following lines,—

> But ah, this night adieu the joyous mien,
> When Mirth's loved favourite quits the mimic scene ;
> Startled Thalia would the assent refuse,
> But Truth and Virtue sued and won the Muse.
> Awed by sensations it could ill express—
> Though mute the tongue, the bosom feels not less—
> Her speech your kind indulgence oft has known
> Be to her silence now that kindness shown,
> Ne'er from her mind th' endeared record will part,
> But live, the proudest feeling of her grateful heart.

She was then led away amidst a scene of much excitement. In the green-room another ovation awaited her ; it was crowded with admirers, friends of high and low degree ; every-one was in tears. Dejeune the singer sobbed convulsively, the heroine was fainting ; she had to be almost carried to her coach.

Whether all this emotion was sincere even on her side, may fairly be doubted ; it was a sort of theatrical display, very well arranged and carried out. On the evening of her wedding day Mrs. Siddons paid her the compliment of reciting some verses in praise of her many virtues. This was the closing scene so far as her dramatic career was in question—the curtain had now to rise on a totally different stage.

The marriage had to be delayed a fortnight on account of the fit of the gout with which the elderly bridegroom had been seized in rather a *mal à propos* fashion. The happy event, however, took place on May 1st, by special license, in his lordship's house, Grosvenor Square, at 9 o'clock in the morning ; after which the newly married pair set out for " The Oaks," where they spent the honeymoon—a short one, for to the surprise of their friends they returned to town in two days !

As may be supposed, their being so soon satisfied with the delightful *tête-à-tête* they had been so long pining for, caused some merriment ; it must, however, be remembered that they were no longer in the flower of youth, the bridegroom being forty-six and the bride forty ; they were too sensible to indulge in silly transports, and being secure by long experience of their mutual affection, settled down into a quiet Darby and

Joan life. The new Countess was moreover devoted to her mother, who from the time of the marriage lived with the married pair, accompanying them to their country seat, and having her own apartments in Grosvenor Square. Her maternal pride must have found infinite satisfaction from the manner in which her daughter was received in the high circles into which she was now introduced; not as an intruder, but as one of the intimate society of what was then an exclusive nobility. The Queen distinguished her by different marks of favour; she made one of the procession at the Princess Royal's marriage, and when she was first presented she was especially singled out for the most flattering attentions. It was said that on this occasion she assured the Queen that the most blissful moment of her life was "appearing before Her Majesty *in a new character.*" This speech, which was probably made for her, was *ben trovato.*

Lady Derby, however, could not escape the shafts of malice which indeed are always in attendance on great success, it being the unsuccessful and feeble persons who escape the jealous detractor. Soon after her marriage an ill-natured pamphlet appeared, written by an anonymous scribbler who took the name of Petronius Arbiter. It is full of inuendoes as to Miss Farren's origin, and accusations of meanness—which had a slender, if any, foundation—ingratitude towards those who befriended her in her early days of struggle, and of her turning from her door Younger, who had been the first to help her to fortune. This question of gratitude is always a difficult one; on the one hand there is the impossibility of satisfying the claims which in many cases are exaggerated; and there is likewise the bridge which lies between the past and the present, and which those we have left behind in the journey of life cannot hope to cross. "Arbiter's" pamphlet seems to have been written by such a one. It was answered by a very full denial of these accusations, and soon fell into the limbo of neglect to which such anonymous slanders should be consigned.

In the "Illustrious Irishwomen" series a story is told of the meeting between Miss Farren and one of her early friends, which has a dramatic flavour. On one of her visits to their Majesties at Windsor, Lady Derby's carriage broke down; it was Christmas time, and the snow fell heavily, and lay inches deep on the ground. The prospect was growing unpleasant, as it was getting late, and there seemed no mode of extrication, when fortunately another carriage appeared on the scene. Seated in this was an elderly gentleman, also on his way to the Castle, and he at once offered his assistance in conveying the countess. This gentleman turned out to be Chief Justice Boroughs, who, like herself, had taken the tide of fortune at its flood, and was now in the enjoyment of fortune, position, and the friendship of the King. As the pair drove along through the dark, the curtains of the past must have rolled back, and presented to the memory of both the Christmas morning at Salisbury, and their first meeting at the prison window.

There is little more to be said concerning this charming woman, whose story will ever excite interest. She lived to over seventy years of age, dying so far on in this century as 1829. In her later years she grew fond of the rather uninteresting habit, much in fashion with our grandmothers, of snuff-taking. Her features coarsened, and her appearance lost the delicacy which had been her charm in youth, and which she had preserved in her maturity. Of three children born of this marriage only one daughter lived. She married in 1821 the Earl of Wilton. Lord Derby survived his wife five years, dying in 1834 at the ripe age of eighty-two.

The well-known picture by Lawrence gives us some idea of those charms which fascinated those who lived in the Countess's day: it has the airy grace and arch expression which her contemporaries dwell upon with so much admiration. Small trifles indicate character, and a close observer will note the cautious manner in which the cloak is gathered round her slender shoulders, which caution was, as we know, a salient feature of her character. The half-length which was painted for Mrs. Farren is, to my thinking, more attractive than this better known picture.

[For list of portraits, see Appendix.]

APPENDIX.

PETER GUNNING.

(See page 30.)

PETER GUNNING, son of the Vicar of Hoo, and brother to Richard Gunning. A famous preacher: elected Fellow of Clare Hall, Cambridge, in 1633; an ardent Royalist: published a formal protestation against the rebels; preached against them at Tunbridge and other places; was imprisoned and deprived of his fellowship. He retired to Oxford, where he was appointed Chaplain to the New College; was tutor to Lord Hatton and Sir Francis Compton, and chaplain to Sir Robert Shirley; he conducted the services at Exeter Chapel, after the true Anglican manner, under the very nose of Cromwell, who secretly connived at this malpractice. Evelyn mentions going to Exeter Chapel to hear Gunning preach. On this occasion (1657) he was in the act of administering the sacrament, when the chapel was surrounded and all the communicants surprised. When the Restoration came, Peter received his reward. 1660 he was created D.D., presented to a prebend in Canterbury Cathedral, instituted to the rectory of Cottesmore in Rutlandshire, elected Master of Clare Hall, Cambridge, and made Regius Professor of Divinity at Cambridge: 1669 he was promoted to the Bishopric of Chichester, and 1674-5 translated to Ely, where he died 1684. He was a man of most decided convictions; took a prominent part in the Savoy Conference, where he was pitted against Baxter. Baxter, in his account of the Conference, speaks of Gunning's passionate addresses. He says Gunning was the forwardest and best speaker on the Church side, a man of greater study and industry than any of them, well read in the Fathers and Councils, and he adds: " I hear of very temperate life as to all carnal excesses whatever." Burnet speaks of the whole affair contemptuously; he accuses Gunning of a desire to reconcile the Church of England and Rome by restoring crosses and surplices. Peter Barwick, on the other hand, calls the Bishop " the hammer of the Schismatics "; while Denis Grenville, Dean of Durham, regarded Gunning as the first spiritual father, and records how, on November 9th, 1679, he had the contentment of receiving the sacrament at the hands of good Bishop Gunning, to whom the evening before he had unburdened his conscience. Pepys, in his Diary, mentions over and over again the excellent sermons of Gunning; and many writers bear testimony to his excellent life, character, and liberality alike to the poor and to scholars. He wrote a multitude of works, all on Church matters. A list

T

of these will be found in the *Dictionary of National Biography*, Volume XXIII., from which this short notice of Bishop Gunning has been abridged.

Sir Robert Gunning, of Herton, Northlands, was the great-grandson in direct succession from Richard Gunning, through John Gunning. Richard's eldest son. Sir Robert was highly distinguished, being Minister Plenipotentiary to the Court of Denmark 1765, to Berlin 1771, St. Petersburg 1770; created a baronet 1778; member for Wigan 1796. (See Foster's Peerage and Baronetage.)

PETER GUNNING, BISHOP OF ELY.

Owner.	Painter.	Description.	Engraver.
Sutherland Gallery.	—	Half-length, cap, long hair, peaked beard, wide bands, black robe. Underneath is written, "The Bishop of Ely."	T. Beckett for the first plate; for the second, J. Smith is substituted for Beckett.

JOHN GUNNING,[1] OF CASTLE COOTE.

Owner.	Painter.	Description.	Engraver.
—	Liotard.	A miniature. Underneath the likeness four verses in Latin, six circles, doves on each side, and eight verses, etc.	Houston. Very rare, only two known.

The portraits of Lady Coventry, like those of the Duchess of Hamilton and Argyll, are numerous. Every artist of any note being anxious to transfer the lovely faces of the two sisters to their canvas, makes it a matter of some difficulty to present a complete list. The following is taken from the best sources of information.

MARIA, COUNTESS OF COVENTRY.

Owner.	Painter.	Description.	Engraver.
Unknown.	Wilson, 1751.	As the fair Hibernian. Standing with her hair dressed with pearls, feathers, etc.; hands holding a wreath of flowers.	This is very rare, only one engraving known, on the back of which is written, "Miss Gunning, before she left Ireland," and " by Mr. Galston. This was *scraped* by Wilson, the painter, and given by him to Mr. Bindley, who gave it to me." There is an etching likewise of the same by Wilson.

[1] Reproduced on page 35 from the original in the Iveagh Collection, National Gallery, Dublin.

Owner.	Painter.	Description.	Engraver.
—	Griffin, 1751.	Fair Hibernian. Standing, her hair dressed with pearls, feathers and a veil, round her neck a jewel hung by a triple ribbon.	Paul Patton. Very similar to Wilson's, only reversed, and underneath there are these lines:— By famed Apelles drawn, the Cyprian Queen Of perfect beauty has the standard been; The brightest nymphs from every part of Greece Did all contribute to adorn the piece: But happier for our age that gives to view In this one fair Hibernian all he drew.
—	Wilson, 1751.	With her right hand to face.	Wilson.
—	Liotard, 1751.	A short half-length with a muslin veil, and ring on little finger.	Sayer.
—	Liotard, 1752.	Another nearly similar, with an embroidered dress and veil fantastically arranged, a black ribbon on wrist.	Houston. This is well known to collectors as a mezzotint. Houston also incorporated it in the triple oval in which the three Gunnings appear in one frame.
—	Liotard, 1751.	Short embroidered robe, made in a Turkish fashion, scarf round her waist, rose in her bosom.	MacArdell.
Museum at Amsterdam.	Liotard.	Another of the same with the addition of a harp, and styled Hibernia.	—
—	Unknown.	The two sisters as the Hibernian sisters. The elder is on the left with a dog in her lap, the younger on the right with a fan in her hand, the background a garden wall with Cupids.	Okey . . . with those lines at foot:— Hibernia long with shame beheld Her favourite toasts by ours excelled Resolv'd t' outvie Britannia's Fair By her own beauties, sent A Pair.
Lately bought for the National Gallery, Dublin.	Francis Cotes, R.A., 1751.	1. Half length (oval) with slashed sleeves, lace cape. Hair in curls . . . very girlish.	MacArdell. This was published by Sayer, 1751, as a watch paper.[1]
Duke of Argyll. Knock in Mull.	Cotes.	2. Half length. Hair in curls with a few pearls. Scarf floating.	Ford.
—	Cotes.	3. Standing with a hat on her head, her hand on a figure of Cupid.	Ford.

[1] Reproduced on page 51, by the kind permission of Hon. Gerald Ponsonby.

Owner.	Painter.	Description.	Engraver.
—	Unknown, but probably Cotes.	With a lace cape close to throat, pearls in her hair.	MacArdell, worked over by Spooner.
Earl of Coventry.	Hogarth. Now at Crome, Lord Coventry's seat, near Worcester.	Small whole length of Lord and Lady Coventry standing in a garden, on the right is the Earl pointing to a building in the background, on the left Lady Coventry in a white dress and flat hat leans on the pediment of a vase, between them a dog. Lent by Lord Coventry to the Guelph Exhibition.	Never engraved.
Earl of Coventry.	Gavin Hamilton, R.A. This picture is at Croome, set in a panel, the companion panel having a full length of the Duchess of Argyll; both are fine pictures.	Whole length, standing on terrace.[1]	MacArdell. Only two of these are known.
Duke of Hamilton.	Gavin Hamilton, R.A.	Standing head to left, hand on the figure of Cupid.	MacArdell. Only five known.
Gilbert Coventry, Esq.	Maurice Quintin de la Tour.	Half-length; blue dress, feather or ribbon in her hair. Exhibited Grafton Gallery, 1894.	—
The Marquis of Lorne. This picture belonged to Mrs. Lyon, daughter to Lady Charlotte Bury. It was sold by Mr. Graves, of Pall Mall, to Lord Lorne.	Sir Joshua Reynolds, 1759.	Half-length; scarf over shoulders; a companion to the Duchess of Argyll, painted at the same time. Lady Coventry's face bears traces of ill-health; she was then dying.	—
Duke of Argyll. Inverary Castle.	Catherine Read, 1771.	Hair falling over shoulders, robe of ermine, pearls across the bosom. This was painted many	Finlayson. (The original is in Pastelle.)

[1] By the kind permission of Lord Coventry this picture is reproduced on page 56.

Owner.	Painter.	Description.	Engraver.
—	Holland, 1757.	years after Lady Coventry's death as a companion to the portrait of the Duchess of Argyll, to whom it is dedicated. It is rather a formal composition. This etching is very rare, although it is a grotesque representation of beauty. On the back is written the name of "Mr. Gulston" (well known in his day as a virtuoso and collector), with the words, "Given to me by Mr. Bindley."	—

A portrait of Lady Coventry was published by Bowles, of Cornhill, but the name of the artist is not known. Her portrait by Cotes (No. 1) was copied in enamel, likewise that of the Duchess of Argyll, and is in the possession of Lord Beauchamp. There is also one in the Schreiber collection, South Kensington Museum; also a miniature by Gavin Hamilton is worthy of mention.

ELIZABETH GUNNING, AFTERWARDS DUCHESS OF HAMILTON AND ARGYLL.

Owner.	Painter.	Description.	Engraver.
—	1751.	With Lady Coventry as the Hibernian Sisters.	Okey.
—	Unknown. 1751.	A very early one, with pearls in her hair and a wand or crook in her hand. The expression is altogether different from the later portraits.	—
The Duke of Argyll. The picture is at Knock in Mull.	Cotes. 1752.	Half-length, in oval frame looking to front, hair plain, with curls, bodice with ribbons, ermine robe. Pearls fastening dress on shoulder. Scraped underneath, "The late Miss Gunning."	MacArdell.
—	Cotes.	With a small hat on the side of her head.	Sayer. Reproduced as a watch paper.

Owner.	Painter.	Description.	Engraver.
—	Cotes.	Another almost similar.	Houston.
—	Cotes.	Another similar, without pearls, and the dress edged with fur.	Houston.
—	Cotes.	Another of the same.	Millar.
—	Cotes.	Another similar to No. 3.	Purcell.
—	Cotes.	Another similar to No. 1. This plate is identical with MacArdell's, the position being reversed.	Brockshaw. Houston composed a plate which presented three ovals of the sisters in one frame. Lady Coventry after Liotard is to the left. The Duchess of Hamilton after Cotes, No. 1, in the centre. Miss Kitty Cunning also after Cotes to the right. Above the portraits are the words "Utruisque generis opere Johannes Gunning, A.M." Underneath each portrait are lines of poor doggerel in praise of the sister Graces. At the foot of plate a poem "Gratitude," inscribed to the Earl of Harrington by John Gunning, two letters etc. There are only two of this plate.
Earl of Coventry. The picture is at Croome, as a companion to the picture of Lady Coventry by Gavin Hamilton.	G. A. Hamilton.	Standing on terrace with her hand on the head of a greyhound. Companion to the picture at Croome of Lady Coventry by Hamilton.[1]	Faber. Another engraving of same mentioned by Bromly.
Lady Northwick.	Sir Joshua Reynolds.	Whole length. This picture was exhibited in the large room, Strand, 1760. It was in Lord Gwydyr's collection, and was sold to Lord Northwick in 1829. She wears a magnificent costume.	Spicer.

[1] Reproduced as *Frontispiece* from original engraving in the Iveagh collection, National Gallery, Dublin.

Owner.	Painter.	Description.	Engraver.
The Duke of St. Albans.	Allan Ramsay, 1763.	In a blue dress—a hard, unpleasant portrait exhibited Grafton Gallery, 1894.	—
The Duke of Argyll. It is at Inverary.	Catherine Read.	As Duchess of Argyll; in a high cap, ribbon tied under her chin.	Finlayson.
—	C. Read.	Another, similar, only smaller.	Laurie. The original picture is in Pastello.
The Duke of Argyll.	Angelica Kauffmann. This picture was consumed in a fire which took place at Inverary.	Representing the Duchess with an infant on her knee, holding a dove. Her little boy, afterwards sixth Duke of Argyll, stands beside her.	—
Sir Tollemache Sinclair.	—	Miniature. Exhibited Grafton Gallery, 1894.	—
Limesden Propert, Esq.	—	Miniature. Exhibited at Grafton Gallery, 1894.	Plimer.

CATHERINE GUNNING.

(*Afterwards Mrs. Travis.*)

Owner.	Painter.	Description.	Engraver.
Unknown.	Cotes.[1]	Portrait, with hair plain, girlishly dressed, ribbons on bodice.	Houston.
Hamilton Palace Collection.	Unknown.	Another portrait.	Unknown. This engraving is in the possession of Arthur Kimber, Esq., Roland Gardens.

LADY ELIZABETH HAMILTON, AFTERWARDS COUNTESS OF DERBY.

(*Daughter to 6th Duke of Hamilton.*)

Owner.	Painter.	Description.	Engraver.
The Duke of Argyll. Sold in 1883 to W. King, a dealer.	Sir Joshua Reynolds.	As a child, 1758.	—
The Earl of Derby.	Zucchi.	Dancing a Minuet, 1774.	—
The Earl of Derby.	Angelica Kauffmann.	As Countess of Derby, with the 12th Earl and their infant son. The Earl is in a Spanish costume, Lady Derby in a blue dress.	—

[1] Reproduced on page 98.

Owner.	Painter.	Description.	Engraver.
The Earl of Derby.	Sir Joshua Reynolds.	Placing a wreath on a term of Hymen. Macaw on perch. Exhibited at the Royal Academy, 1777. This picture has disappeared. It is not in the Knowsley collection, and it is supposed that it was destroyed by the Earl in a fit of jealous fury.[1]	Dickinson and Watson.
Sold in 1869 by G. F. Seymour to Anthony for £77.	Romney.	In a simple dress of white; hair coiled on top of her head; wooded landscape in background. Chaloner Smith says, "It is interesting to compare the styles of the two great painters in this picture of the same lady; one in a blaze of colour, surrounded by all accessories; the other pure and simple, with no object to draw attention to her beauty." Curiously enough this lovely picture is likewise exiled from Knowsley.	Dean, 1780.

LADY AUGUSTA CLAVERING.

(Daughter to John, 5th Duke of Argyll.)

Owner.	Painter.	Description.	Engraver.
Duke of Argyll, Inverary.	Opie.	Classical.	Not engraved.
—	Angelica Kauffman.	H. L. in profile.	—
H. H. Almack, Esq., Suffolk.	John Hedges Benwell.	As a "St. James's Beauty." Exhibited at the Grafton Gallery, 1794. This picture is the subject of a controversy as to its "colloquial nickname." Mr. Almack, the owner of the picture, has the	Bartolozzi.

[1] Reproduced on page 90, from the original engraving in the possession of Messrs. Colnaghi, Pall Mall.

Owner.	Painter.	Description.	Engraver.
		family tradition handed down to him by his father, who received the portrait from Lady Charlotte Bury, sister to Lady Augusta Clavering. On the other hand, Mr. Tuer (an excellent authority) maintains that the original of the "St. James' Beauty" was one of the five beautiful Miss Boroughs, her sister being the model of the "St. Giles' Beauty." Conflicting evidence is hard to sift : neither is the matter of much importance. The picture is undoubtedly like the Bartolozzi engraving.[1]	

DOROTHEA MONROE.

Owner.	Painter.	Description.	Engraver.
Given by the late Marquis of Ely to the National Gallery, Dublin.	Angelica Kauffmann.	Large family group of the Earl and Countess of Ely, with their niece Dolly seated at the harpsichord, and Angelica Kauffmann standing.	Never engraved.
National Portrait Gallery. Bought at Lord Ely's sale, 1888.	Angelica Kauffmann.[2]	Half-length[1] of Dorothea Monroe. Blue shawl across shoulders. A very stiff portrait.	Not engraved.
Unknown. Sold at Lord Ely's sale, 1888.	—	Another half-length.	—

THE MISS MONTGOMERYS.

Owner.	Painter.	Description.	Engraver.
Given by the Earl of Blessington to the National Gallery, London.	Sir Joshua Reynolds.[3]	The three Graces— Anne Lady Townshend, Elizabeth Lady Mountjoy, Barbara Mrs. Beresford.	Consens.

[1] Reproduced by the kind permission of the owner, Mr. Almack, of Long Melford, Suffolk.

[2] Reproduced on page 143 from a drawing made by the late Henry Doyle, director of the National Gallery, Dublin.

[3] Sir Joshua, writing to Luke Gardiner, says :—

"SIR,—I intended long ago to have returned thanks for the agreeable employ-

Owner.	Painter.	Description.	Engraver.
Captain G. L. Holford. This picture belonged to Sir C. Lamb, and was sold in 1860 to a dealer, William King.	Romney.	Anne, Marchioness of Townshend, in a dress of old gold coloured Brocade, her hair powdered and crimped, two long curls, the eyes of a dark grey; a sweet matronly expression. Exhibited at the Grafton Gallery, 1894.[1]	—
Duke of Leeds.[1]	—	A miniature of Anne, Marchioness of Townshend. Exhibited at the Grafton Gallery, 1894.	—
The Marquis of Townshend.	Sir Joshua Reynolds.	Anne, Marchioness of Townshend, in a white dress, leaning on a pillar. A fine picture.	—
Earl of Home.	Angelica Kauffmann.	Portrait.	—
—	—	Elizabeth Montgomery, Lady Mountjoy, in the character of Lady Macbeth.	Walker's Hibernian Magazine.
—	Gainsborough.	Barbara, Hon. Mrs. Beresford.	Jones.

ment in which you have engaged me, and likewise for the very obliging manner in which the favour is conferred; but unfortunately after the beads were finished I was enticed down to Petworth, and from there to Oxford, from whence I am but just returned, so that this is the only quiet moment I have had for this month past. Though it has been a little delayed by these holidays, it will not on the whole fare worse for it, as I am returned with a very keen appetite for work. The picture is the great object of my mind at present. You have already been informed, I have no doubt, of the subject we have chosen—the adorning a term of Hymen with festoons of flowers. This affords sufficient employment to the figures, and gives an opportunity of introducing a variety of graceful historical attitudes. I have every inducement to exert myself on this occasion, both from the confidence you have placed in me, and from the subjects you have presented to me, which are such as I am never likely to meet with again so long as I live, and I flatter myself that however inferior the picture may be to what I wish it, or what it ought to be, it will be the last picture I ever painted."

In spite of Sir Joshua's endeavours to place on canvas a record of these Irish beauties, he was considered to have failed in expressing the peculiar character of the beauty of the sisters.

[1] In 1882 a replica of this picture was exhibited at the Old Masters' Exhibition, Royal Academy. Owner, Sir Graham Montgomery.

MRS. WOFFINGTON.

Owner.	Painter.	Description.	Engraver.
The Marquis of Lansdowne, Bowood.	Hogarth.	Waagen says of this picture that " it has a singular liveliness of conception, great warmth and transparency of colouring, although somewhat empty in the forms."	—
Garrick Club.	Hogarth.	On a couch. This picture came from Charles Mathew's collection.	—
—	Mercier.	Portrait.	—
—	Wilson.	—	—
Sir Charles Tennant.	Hogarth.	This was originally in Mr. Addington's collection, but was sold at Messrs. Christie's in 1886, and exhibited by Sir Charles Tennant at the R.A., 1888.	—
National Portrait Gallery.	Arthur Pond.	Half-length. This remarkable picture represents her in the last stage of illness and decay, in profile: lying in bed towards the left, wearing a lace cap, and resting her head on a pillow. Her eyes have a peculiar expression. Her face is pale, save where the rouge makes a brilliant spot. Her lips are livid. The quilt is white satin. The crimson curtains of the bed are the background. This picture, which belonged to Sir Theodore Martin, was given by him to the Portrait Gallery. It must have been the last picture painted by Pond, as he died 1758.	—
—	Arthur Pond.	A portrait painted in 1746, when she was barely twenty. It is quite unlike her later portraits, and wears an innocent expression. The lips curve in a remarkable manner.	Brooke.

Owner.	Painter.	Description.	Engraver.
This was in the possession of the late Earl of Charlemont.	A. Pond.	A later portrait, with lace cap and tucker, white satin bodice.	MacArdell.
—	A. Pond.	Same in a lace cap, side face.	Freeman.
—	A. Pond.	Same, holding a dog on her lap.	—
—	A. Pond.	Same, with a wreath of flowers. These portraits were painted by Pond for Provost Andrews. At his death they were sold by auction.	Millar.
—	Eccard.	Full face. Hair upon shoulders. Holds a large volume.	Faber.
Sir Henry Bellingham, Bart., Dunany, co. Louth, Ireland.	—	The same, only reversed. This portrait came into the family through the marriage of Miss Cholmondeley with Sir William Bellingham, Bart. There is a portrait of Miss Cholmondeley by Cotes at Bellingham Castle.	Marchand.
European Magazine.	—	With a veil, and holding a wand in her hand.	—
—	Hayley.	As Mrs. Ford.	Ford.
—	Blecker.	As Phœbe.	Miller.
—	—	Watch paper as Mrs. Ford.	Sayer.

ELIZABETH LA TOUCHE, AFTERWARDS COUNTESS OF LANESBOROUGH.

	Howe.	Elizabeth la Touche, Countess of Lanesborough.	Bartolozzi.
—			

ANN LUTTRELL, AFTERWARDS DUCHESS OF CUMBERLAND.

The Queen, Windsor Castle.	Gainsborough.	Three full-length figures, the Duke and Duchess walking, Lady Elizabeth Luttrell seated on a garden chair in the background. The Duchess wears evening dress, but has thrown a light scarf over her shoulders. She likewise has a flat garden hat on her head, tied under her chin with a narrow velvet ribbon. She	V. Green.

Owner.	Painter.	Description.	Engraver.
		leans on the Duke's arm, her face is turned to the spectator; the Duke, a dapper little man in a green coat, is looking at her with admiration. She is considerably taller than he is. Lady Elizabeth on her garden seat has rather the air of the wicked Otrude in Lohengrin, her face wears a malevolent expression. She looks years older than the Duchess. This picture was exhibited at the Royal Academy, 1777. This year exhibited at the Old Masters' Exhibition.	
Lady Wilmot Horton.	Sir Joshua Reynolds.	Whole length. Standing dressed in a court robe trimmed with ermine ; handsome jewels. A queenly figure. Exhibited with a portrait of the Duke at R.A., 1773.	Watson. There is a mezzotint of the Duchess published by Bryer to which a curious story is said to attach. In 1766 Sir Joshua painted the portrait of Lady Arundel, wife to the 8th Lord Arundel of Wardour. When it was engraved the plate was not satisfactory and only one impression was taken. The head was then taken out and that of the Duchess of Cumberland substituted. Bromley, who tells the story, adds, this engraving is rare and unique. The best authorities on this subject are of opinion that the substitution never could have taken place, for the reason that it would have been impossible to have concealed the joining. It is likewise curious that this rare and unique engraving is not known to collectors.
The Queen, Buckingham Palace.	Gainsborough.	Whole length. Head by Gainsborough, figure by Cosway.	—

Owner.	Painter.	Description.	Engraver.
Sir Simeon Stuart, of Chittle, representative of the Carhampton Peerage.	Gainsborough.	Half-length. This picture conveys better than any other the fascination which was the Duchess's charm. She is simply dressed, the bodice is low, the neck lovely, but the arms too long.	—
Lord Wenlock.	Gainsborough.	Half-length, similar to above.	—
—	Cosway.	Full-length, holding a wreath of flowers. Painted in 1784.	Sherwin.
—	Romney.	Half-length. In any of the published lists of Romney's paintings the name of the Duchess of Cumberland does not appear. In a recent life of the artist by Mrs. Gamlin this portrait is mentioned. The fact that it was painted in 1786, the year that the Duchess visited Naples, would lead to the supposition that it was suggested by Lady Hamilton, as a help to Romney, who had never received any royal patronage.	—

ELIZA FARREN, AFTERWARDS COUNTESS OF DERBY.

(*As Miss Farren.*)

—	Zoffany.	1. Hermione in "The Winter's Tale."	Fisher.
—	Zoffany.	2. In a print with King.	Fisher.
	—	3. Beatrice in "Much Ado About Nothing."	Walker's Hibernian Magazine.
Lord Ronald Gower.	J. Downham.	4. Large oval.	—
—	Humphrey.	5. Miniature.	—
Earl of Wilton.	Sir Thomas Lawrence.	6. Whole length, walking on a terrace with muff and tippet. 1792.	Bartolozzi.
Painted for Mrs. Farren, mother of the actress. Now in the possession of Wentworth Beaumont, Esq.	Sir Thomas Lawrence.	7. Half-length, very beautiful.	Bartolozzi.

Owner.	Painter.	Description.	Engraver.
Earl of Derby.	After Lawrence.	8. Whole length. Copy [1] of No. 6. 1803.	Bartolozzi.
S. Lumsden Propert.	Nixon.	9. Miniature.	—
Earl of Wharncliffe.	Cosway.	10. Miniature.	—

HONOURABLE MRS. BERESFORD.

Barré Beresford.	Romney.	Portrait.	Jones.

[1] A replica of this picture belonged to Mr. Grant, and was sold at Christie's, June 27, 1863, to Mr. Smith's commission agent, for 79 guineas.

AUTHORITIES CONSULTED.

Autobiography of Mrs. Delauey.
Autobiography of Ann Bellamy.
Barnard's " Retrospections of the Stage."
Barratariana.
Ballads of the day.
Bowden's " Life of Mrs. Inchbold."
Chambers' Journal for 1846.
Criticisms by William Hazlett.
Cabinets of George III.
Dublin, description of the City.
Dublin, Memoirs of.
Dublin Magazine.
Dublin City.
Dublin in an Uproar.
Dublin Monthly.
Fitzgerald's " Kings and Queens.'
Fitzgerald's " Royal Dukes."
Fitzgerald's " Life of Garrick."
Fitzgerald's " Life of George IV."
Fitzpatrick's " Before the Union."
Fitzpatrick's " Sham Squire."
Fitzpatrick's " Secret Service of Pat."
Fitzgerald Molloy's " Life of Peg Woffington."
Gilbert's " History of Dublin."
Genest's " History of the Stage."
Grattan's Life and Times.
Gunning Documents, by George Gunning.
Gronow's Reminiscences.
Gunning's Pamphlets and Poems.
Gunning Novels.
Hitchcock's " History of the Stage."
Hibernian Cresses.
Horace Walpole's Letters.
Irish Builder.
Illustrious Irishwomen, by Owen Blackburne.
Kilkenny Theatricals.
Lemarchant's " Life of George III."
Leland's " History of Ireland."
Lecky's " History of Ireland."
Maxwell's " History of the Irish Rebellion."
Macaulay's " History of England."
Miscellanea Nova, by Samuel Whyte.
Memoirs of George III.   Doran.
Memoirs of George III.   Horace Walpole.
Monthly Mirror.
National Biography, Dictionary of.

Ottway's " Sketches."
Petronius Arbiter.
Phelan's " History of the Church."
Sheridan's Life.
Swift's Pamphlets.
Tate Wilkinson's Memoirs.
The Theatre, by Samuel Whyte.
Testimony of Truth, old pamphlet.
Victor's " History of the Irish Stage."
Wraxall's Memoirs.
Walker's *Hibernian Magazine.*
Walpole's Letters, etc.
White's Club, by the Honourable A. Bourke.
Also old Pamphlets, Ballads, and Letters.

Articles from *Harper's, Scribner's,* and *Dublin University Magazines, Colburn's Magazine,* Hamilton MS., and information from private sources.

INDEX.

LONDON :
PRINTED BY GILBERT AND RIVINGTON, LTD.,
ST. JOHN'S HOUSE, CLERKENWELL, E.C.